Land Use
and
The Constitution

Principles for Planning Practice

Land Use and The Constitution
Principles for Planning Practice

Brian W. Blaesser
Clyde W. Forrest
Douglas W. Kmiec
Daniel R. Mandelker
Alan C. Weinstein
Norman Williams, Jr.

Edited
by

Brian W. Blaesser
and
Alan C. Weinstein

An AICP Handbook

PLANNERS PRESS
AMERICAN PLANNING ASSOCIATION
Chicago, Illinois   Washington, D.C.

This book is published in cooperation with the American Institute of Certified Planners, an institute of the American Planning Association.

Copyright 1989 by the American Planning Association,
1313 E. 60th St., Chicago, IL 60637
ISBN 0-918286-58-1
Library of Congress Catalog Card Number 88-72355

This book is dedicated
to the men and women
of the planning profession.

Contents

Foreword

De Tocqueville's saw that "scarcely any political question arises in the United States which is not resolved sooner or later into a judicial question" could easily be amended by substituting the words "land use" for the word "political." Land use planning that ignores the lessons of constitutional cases and principles would be a little bit like driving a trailer truck down a freeway blindfolded: disaster awaits.

Thus, how welcome a guide for the planning profession that avoids the Scylla of ignorance and the Charybdis of overly refined, legalistic theorization! The book is neither vapid nor turgid.

One cannot forget the other old saw that "he who is his own lawyer has a fool for a client." Localized land use planning problems cannot be solved with just this book. But in today's complicated confrontational world, land use planners must deal with, and hence talk to, lawyers; the APA's planning guide, practical tool that it is intended to be, should enable the planner to make his or her legal dialogues meaningful, as well as his or her own thinking constructive.

James L. Oakes
Chief Judge
United States Court of Appeals
for the Second Circuit
March 29, 1989

Acknowledgements

As editors, our first expression of appreciation must go to our fellow authors, without whose commitment and receptiveness to constructive criticism this book would not have been possible. We also owe a special thanks to Israel Stollman, Executive Director of the American Planning Association, for the confidence he expressed in this project from its inception and his willingness to have APA fund the symposium and scoping group meetings that provided the substantive foundation for this book. We also thank Dean Dorsey D. Ellis and Dean John N. Drobak of the Washington University School of Law for graciously hosting the symposium held in St. Louis in December, 1987.

Those individuals who attended the symposium and contributed their thoughts and criticism to the text of the book and in the roundtable discussion of each constitutional principle are described on the pages that follow. The willingness of these individuals to convene in St. Louis on relatively short notice and to work together during and following the symposium to make this book a reality was remarkable, demonstrating a serious desire for this type of collaborative work to assist planners in their practice. Others who were unable to attend the symposium but who nevertheless provided written and oral comments that have been valuable in preparing this book are David Brower, Stuart Deutsch, Dean Macris, Dwight Merriam, and Paul Sedway. The U.S. Supreme Court case summaries were prepared with the assistance of Diane Peters of the Washington University School of Law; Sally Erickson of the University of Maine Law School; Robin Graine of the Illinois Institute of Technology Chicago-Kent College of Law; Douglas Hayes of the University of Notre Dame Law School; and Paul Baum, Howard Kingsley, and Larry Kushnick of the Touro College Jacob D. Fuchsberg Law Center. We owe a very special thanks to Sanda Benesh, whose many excellent illustrations enliven the text throughout. We were also greatly assisted by Melora Furman, who refined the matrices in the book and provided constructive comments on its text and format from a practicing planner's perspective. We are indebted to Kathy Tisza for her patience, good humor, and technical expertise in typing the many drafts and complicated formats of the manuscript. Last, we are grateful to Sylvia Lewis, Director of Publications at the American Planning Association, for her creativity, flexibility and, most importantly, her patience in working with us in the preparation and design of the book for publication, and to Frank So, Deputy Executive Director, for his supportive role.

Because this book reflects the work of the many persons mentioned who contributed along the way, the editing process was a logistical task of significant proportions. Nevertheless, as it was our task to manage that process, any errors and omissions that may be found in the pages that follow are our responsibility alone.

Brian W. Blaesser
Alan C. Weinstein

Authors

Brian W. Blaesser is a partner in the Chicago-based law firm of Siemon, Larsen & Purdy. He specializes in land use, real estate, and litigation, and serves as counsel to both public sector and private sector clients throughout the United States. He also holds a Masters in City Planning (M.C.P.) and is the chair of the Planning and Law division of the American Planning Association. He is the author of numerous publications on land use planning and implementation techniques, litigation, and housing.

Clyde W. Forrest, an attorney and planner, is a professor in the Department of Urban and Regional Planning at the University of Illinois, where he teaches land use, environmental and planning law, and local and community planning. He is the author of various publications on land use and planning.

Douglas W. Kmiec is a professor of law at the University of Notre Dame and the author of a treatise on land use law, the *Zoning and Planning Deskbook,* and numerous law review articles. While on leave from the University of Notre Dame, he served as the head of the Office of Legal Counsel of the U.S. Department of Justice, which provides constitutional and legal advice to the President, the Attorney General, and the executive branch of the federal government.

Daniel R. Mandelker is the Howard A. Stamper Professor of Law at Washington University in St. Louis. Prof. Mandelker teaches property law and land use and is the author of numerous books and articles on environmental and land use law, including the recently published *Federal Land Use Law* (with Jules Gerard and Thomas Sullivan).

Alan C. Weinstein is an associate professor of law at the Touro College Jacob D. Fuchsberg Law Center in Huntington, New York, where he teaches property, land use, environmental law, dispute resolution, and state and local governmental law. He specializes in issues concerning land use and the First Amendment and has authored or coauthored numerous publications in the field. Mr. Weinstein is the chair-elect of the Planning and Law division of the American Planning Association.

Norman Williams, Jr. is a professor of law at both the Environmental Law Center of Vermont Law School and the University of Arizona Law School. He is the author of *American Land Planning Law,* a six volume treatise on land use law, as well as numerous law review articles.

Symposium Participants

Richard F. Babcock is a retired partner in the Chicago law firm of Ross & Hardies and continues to write and teach as a visiting professor at law schools around the country. He is the author of numerous publications on land use, including *The Zoning Game,* and, most recently, coauthor (with Charles Siemon) of *The Zoning Game Revisited.* He specializes in land use and housing law for both public sector and private sector clients. He is a former president of the American Planning Association and from 1965 to 1975 was chair of the Advisory Committee of the American Law Institute Project on a Model Land Development Code.

Gus Bauman, chairman of the Maryland–National Capital Park and Planning Commission, was formerly a partner in the Washington, D.C., office of the law firm of Beveridge & Diamond. He was previously litigation counsel for the National Association of Home Builders and is the author of various articles on land use and housing.

Estelle B. Berman served as a member of the Cincinnati Planning Commission from 1973 to 1988 and was the first chair woman in the commission's 59-year history. She was also a member of the Cincinnati Zoning Board of Appeals. Ms. Berman presently serves on the board of trustees of the Cincinnati Hillside Trust and is a frequent participant in planning commissioner workshops around the country.

H. Bissell (Ted) Carey, III is a partner in the Hartford, Connecticut, law firm of Robinson & Cole. He specializes in trial work in the fields of land use and constitutional law and is a frequent lecturer on state and federal constitutional issues in land use regulation.

Orlando E. Delogu is a professor of law at the University of Maine Law School, where he teaches property, land use, water law, environmental law, administrative law, and state and local government law. He is the author of numerous publications in these fields.

Jules B. Gerard is a professor of law at Washington University in St. Louis. He is a coauthor, with Daniel Mandelker and Thomas Sullivan, of the recently published *Federal Land Use Law* and has written many other articles in professional and popular periodicals dealing with constitutional law.

Gary Hack is a professor of planning in the Department of Urban Studies and Planning at the Massachusetts Institute of Technology, where he teaches urban design. He is also a principal in the planning consulting firm of Carr, Lynch Associates.

William Lamont, Jr. is director of planning and development for the city and county of Denver. He has practiced planning as both a municipal city planner and as a private consultant for over 20 years and is the author of several articles on planning.

Larry Livingston, Jr. is a principal in the California planning firm of Livingston & Associates and is also an attorney. He has worked as a consultant on urban and regional planning with states, counties, and cities throughout the United States and served as assistant planning director of the city of Oakland from 1949 to 1953. In 1987 he received the American Planning Association's National Distinguished Leadership Award.

Stuart Meck is assistant city manager and planning director for Oxford, Ohio, and is the president-elect of the American Planning Association. He has served on the staffs of the Miami Valley Regional Planning Commission in Dayton, Ohio, and the Memphis and Shelby County Planning Commission in Memphis, Tennessee. Mr. Meck has taught planning at Ohio State University, Miami University, and the University of Dayton. He has written numerous articles on planning.

Joy A. Mee is assistant planning director for the city of Phoenix, with responsibility for general, neighborhood, and historic preservation and transportation planning and research. She also works with various citizen commissions and committees and holds a Master of Urban Planning degree.

Sy J. Schulman, a planner and engineer, is president and director of the Westchester County Association, Inc., a membership organization of business, industrial, and related civic and governmental interests. He is a former commissioner of planning for Westchester County and was the first general manager of the New York State Park Commission for New York City. Mr. Schulman has been an adjunct professor in graduate courses in both city planning and transportation planning and zoning and has published many articles on these subjects.

Charles L. Siemon is a partner in the Chicago-based law firm of Siemon, Larsen & Purdy. He specializes in comprehensive plan and land use implementation mechanisms and represents both public agencies and private clients throughout the United States. He is the author of numerous publications on land use and is a coauthor of several books, including, most recently, the *Zoning Game Revisited* (with Richard Babcock).

Israel Stollman is executive director of the American Planning Association and executive secretary of the American Institute of Certified Planners. He was formerly planning director in Youngstown, Ohio, and chairman of the Department of City and Regional Planning at Ohio State University.

Ann L. Strong is a professor of planning in the Department of City and Regional Planning of the University of Pennsylvania, where she teaches land use, environmental law, and historic preservation law. She has served as a consultant to various public and private organizations and is the author of numerous books and articles on land use planning, including *Land Banking: European Realty, American Prospect*.

Edward J. Sullivan is a partner in the law firm of Mitchell, Lang & Smith in Portland, Oregon, where he specializes in land use and administrative law. He previously served as county counsel for Washington County, Oregon, where he was a major participant in the county's appeal of the decision in *Fasano v. Board of County Commissioners*. He has taught graduate and undergraduate courses on land use law and is the author of many publications on land use, administrative law, and constitutional law.

A. Dan Tarlock is a professor of law at the Illinois Institute of Technology Chicago-Kent College of Law and is codirector of the law school's Program in Environmental and Energy Law. He is the author of numerous publications on land use and environmental law and is the coauthor of the casebook, *Environmental Law and Policy*. He is also coeditor, with Stuart Deutsch, of the APA Planning & Law division newsletter.

Richard E. Tustian has been the planning director of Montgomery County, Maryland, for the past 20 years. He is the author of numerous plans, programs, and studies in the fields of land use, urban design, transportation, common natural resources, economic development, demographics, capital programing, fiscal policy, and intergovernmental coordination in community relations.

George A. Williams, Jr. has been assistant director of city planning for the city and county of San Francisco for the past 15 years. He is in charge of comprehensive planning and program development and has been responsible for formulation of most of the planning policies for the city. He is the primary author of the new downtown plan for San Francisco and of the office-housing linkage program.

PART

I

Introduction

SECTION 1:
PURPOSE

This handbook for planners was conceived by planners and lawyers in the summer of 1987 in the wake of the U.S. Supreme Court's important land use decisions in *Keystone, First English*, and *Nollan* which, incidentally, coincided with our country's bicentennial celebration of the U.S. Constitution. The book's purpose is to provide professional and citizen planners with a practical, usable guide to federal constitutional principles for land use planning practice. In short, it is a response to Justice Brennan's exhortation in *San Diego Gas and Electric Co. v. City of San Diego*, 450 U.S. 621, 655 n.26 (1981), (Brennan, J., dissenting) that planners as well as policemen should "know the Constitution." Some planners may not agree with Brennan's equation of the extent of policemen's and planners' responsibilities in the constitutional arena. However, there is no doubt that the Supreme Court's recent decisions have motivated planners to know the constitutional limits of the regulatory programs that they propound—to avoid what one planner described as "the feeling of walking backwards toward a cliff."

Why the focus on federal constitutional principles? After all, landowners' property interests are defined by state law, and the vast majority of land use court decisions concern questions of state law decided by state courts. There are four principal reasons. First, the supremacy clause, Article VI of the Constitution, states that there are certain minimum constitutional requirements that the states must observe. That clause, in effect, places a floor of constitutional limitations below which local governments may not go in their imposition of land use controls.

1

Second, land use decisions by local governments can raise federal constitutional questions based on the Fifth Amendment's just compensation (takings) clause made applicable to the states through the Fourteenth Amendment, and based on the due process and equal protection clauses of the Fourteenth Amendment itself. These federal constitutional provisions drawn from the Bill of Rights and the supremacy clause together establish the floor of federally protected rights. The constitutions of the individual states and court decisions interpreting them can always *expand* on individual rights. But the Constitution establishes the minimum floor of protection against the exercise of governmental power. It is that floor which this book endeavors to define in practical terms for planners (see illustration).

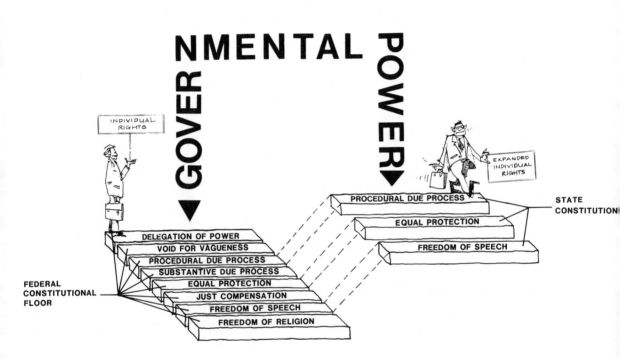

Third, consistent with the supremacy clause, the U.S. Supreme Court has now determined that if it can be proven that certain land use regulations effect a taking of property, then just compensation in the form of monetary damages is due to the property owner as a matter of law under the Fifth Amendment regardless of what the state law says. It is this newly enunciated principle that perhaps gives Justice Brennan's exhortation the most urgency.

Finally, the Supreme Court has said that the Civil Rights Act of 1871 [42 U.S.C. §1983] applies to the actions of local governments. This law does not give property owners any additional rights, but it does, by statute, give them an independent source of remedies, including injunctive relief, damages, and attorneys' fees. As applied to local governments this law potentially gives property owners the right to damages on proof of any deprivation of their rights under the Constitution, not just the taking clause.

For these reasons, planners are well served to have a book which dimensions the edges of each of the boards making up the floor of federal constitutional principles that apply to land use planning practice. At the same time, the book does not ignore state law, because it is important for planners to know that there are areas in which the state courts have established doctrines that either parallel the federal constitutional doctrines or largely supplant federal courts' pronouncements in a particular area. Indeed, throughout the book, particularly in the transcribed dialogue of the planners and lawyers who participated in a symposium in St. Louis to discuss the draft manuscript of the book, readers will note some marked differences in emphasis and interpretation among the symposium participants concerning federal and state legal principles. This is not surprising. It reflects the larger tension between the federal government and the states that was recognized by the original drafters of the U.S. Constitution and ultimately in the adoption of the Bill of Rights.

SECTION 2:
FOCUS

The book owes much of its substantive focus and organization to the planners and lawyers who participated in a symposium sponsored by the American Planning Association through its Planning and Law Division and hosted by the Law School of Washington University in St. Louis in December 1987. The purpose of the symposium was to bring together recognized practitioners and academicians in the fields of planning and law to evaluate and discuss draft statements prepared by the authors that summarized constitutional principles of relevance to planning practice. Those who participated in the symposium were: Richard Babcock, Gus Bauman, Estelle Berman, Brian Blaesser, Ted Carey, Orlando Delogu, Clyde Forrest, Jules Gerard, Gary Hack, Douglas Kmiec, William Lamont, Larry Livingston, Daniel Mandelker, Stuart Meck, Joy Mee, Sy Schulman, Charles Siemon, Israel Stollman, Ann Strong, Edward Sullivan, Dan Tarlock, Richard Tustian, Alan Weinstein, George Williams, and Norman Williams.

Despite the divergent views represented within the group, the participants were asked to approach their task with a commitment to collaborate as planners and lawyers to define key constitutional principles and to discuss their application to planning practice in a manner that would provide practical guidance to practitioners. The outcome of that cooperative effort is this book.

The presentation and explanation of the constitutional principles in the book are similar in format to what lawyers will recognize as a "Restatement of the Law." Each statement of constitutional principle reflects a general consensus among the symposium participants. However, in order to grasp fully the substantive contours of each statement, planners are strongly advised to read the points of dissent and differences of interpretation expressed by individuals in the symposium dialogue that accompanies each statement of constitutional principle.

This book is not a substitute for the advice of legal counsel when planning and land use issues of potential constitutional import arise. Rather, planners should use this book to strengthen their understanding of the meaning of constitutional principles and of their relevance to the decisions they must make and to build a more common vocabulary of terms and concepts for use in dialogue with their legal counsel.

Finally, this book is designed to enable planners to approach the subject of constitutional principles from a planner's perspective, namely, in terms of fact situations involving important problem areas that planners must address. In analyzing these problems, it is useful to keep in mind that there are always potentially four actors, or parties, who may have a legal status or interest in the outcome of a land use controversy. First, a controversy frequently arises because a *developer* or *landowner* wishes to do something on a parcel of land that requires either a change in, or a different interpretation of, the applicable land use regulations. The *local government*, which must respond to the developer's request, is the second party with a legal interest in the outcome. The type of land use case that may arise will depend on whether or not the local government approves the developer's request. If the local government denies the developer's request, the developer may bring a legal action challenging the reasonableness of the decision, thus creating a developer's case. If the local government approves the developer's request, there may be an objection and ultimately legal action against the local government brought by neighboring property owners. The *neighbors* constitute the third party in interest. Finally, there are often other *interest groups*, whether in the private or the public sector, that may seek to intervene in the land use controversy and align themselves with either the developer or the local government. In a case brought by neighbors challenging the local government's decision—a neighbors' case—it should be remembered that the real defendant in the case is the developer. The actual alignment of the local government's interest in a land use controversy, therefore, depends on whether the case is a developer's case or a neighbors' case.

Which constitutional principles are relevant to specific land use controversies will depend on whether the dispute is essentially a developer's case or a neighbors' case and what type of decision the local government makes. For example, in a rezoning case in which the local government has granted the developer's requested zoning over the protests of neighbors, a taking claim will not arise because the developer is, in fact, satisfied with the zoning classification obtained. Nor can a procedural due process issue usually be raised by the objecting neighbors. This is because in those states in which the courts regard zoning amendment decisions as legislative, such decisions, as a matter of constitutional law, are not subject to the requirements of procedural due process.

Also, because of either the particular doctrines applied by state courts, and some federal courts, or the patterns of their decisions, there are states in which the outcomes of land use litigation frequently are more favorable either to the developer or to the local government. Hence, certain states are generally viewed as developers' states, while others are known as states whose judicial attitudes favor local government. An understanding of these basic distinctions is helpful in sorting through the facts and legal issues involved in land use disputes.

SECTION 3:
ORGANIZATION AND SPECIAL FEATURES OF BOOK

In Part II, each statement of constitutional principle is organized with the following format:

◆   Principle
       Comment(s)
          Illustration(s)
            Symposium Discussion.

The diamond (◆) symbol is used throughout Part II to indicate the beginning and the end (◆ . . . ◇) of each key statement of constitutional principle. The principle should be read first, before the comments, illustrations, and symposium discussion that address the statement of constitutional principle in greater depth.

In Part III, 12 planner problem-solving areas are presented in which the constitutional principles explained in Part II are applied to specific fact situations. These were prepared by symposium participants organized into planner-lawyer teams. They were then edited. Part IV sets forth a constitutional analysis tree designed to assist planners in asking constitutional questions relevant to the types of problem-solving areas presented in Part III. Part V of the book contains brief summaries of the principal cases of relevance to land use planning practice which have been decided by the U.S. Supreme Court. These summaries are written in a format designed to highlight the essential information and assist planners in understanding the legal principles discussed in Part II.

In addition to a table of contents and a subject index, the book contains three matrices, followed in each case by a topical index to the symposium discussion. The first matrix, found at the beginning of Part III, relates the 12 planner problem-solving areas to the constitutional principles. The second matrix, found at the beginning of Part V, relates the key Supreme Court decisions to the constitutional principles in order to assist planners in quickly selecting cases in Part V that are relevant to a particular issue they wish to address. The third matrix, which follows the second, identifies the key Supreme Court decisions that are relevant to the 12 planner problem solving areas. Together, these matrices and the other special features of this book are designed to give planners different channels or points of access to the sections that are most pertinent to problems they face in their planning practice. However, in using these special points of access, planners are cautioned not to overlook the comment and symposium discussion sections which clarify or limit each of the eight statements of constitutional principles. The special user features are no substitute for reading the book as a whole.

In portions of the text, but particularly in Parts II and III, cross references to sections at which constitutional principles are discussed, or key Supreme Court cases are summarized, are indicated in brackets: [ ]. The bracketed information refers first to the *Part* of the book (e.g., I, II, III, IV or V) and then to the *Section* within the part (e.g., 1, 2). For certain references, the *Subsection* (e.g., §2.02) is also indicated. Thus a cross reference to a constitutional principle such as procedural due process would be indicated as: [II-3]. A reference to one of the Supreme Court cases summarized in Part V, such as *Agins v. City of Tiburon*, would be indicated as [V-2.01].

SECTION 4:
OVERVIEW OF LEGAL TERMS
IN RELATION TO
CONSTITUTIONAL PRINCIPLES

The constitutional principles are presented and discussed in the following order:
- Principle 1: Delegation of Power
- Principle 2: Void for Vagueness
- Principle 3: Procedural Due Process
- Principle 4: Substantive Due Process
- Principle 5: Equal Protection
- Principle 6: Just Compensation (the taking clause)
- Principle 7: Freedom of Speech
- Principle 8: Freedom of Religion

To the extent possible, these constitutional principles are organized and explained so as to reflect a sequence and interrelationship that will be useful to planners. In doing so, it is necessary to use certain legal terms, which, once understood, will greatly assist planners in understanding and discussing the constitutional principles and their application to typical land use planning problems. What follows is a brief overview of those legal terms as they relate to the constitutional principles presented in Part II.

4.01 Legal Terms Generally

[1] police power; [2] property interest; [3] entitlement; [4] vested right; [5] estoppel; [6] expectancy interest; [7] nuisance; [8] downzoning; [9] upzoning; [10] as applied challenge; [11] facial challenge.

Police power is a shorthand term for the legislative or policy-making power that resides in each state to establish laws and ordinances to preserve public order and tranquility and to promote the public health, safety, and morals and other aspects of the general welfare. The zoning of property derives from the state's police power. Generally, each state has delegated the power to zone property and exercise other land use controls to the local governments (counties, cities, villages, and towns) within their jurisdictions by means of specific zoning enabling legislation. Local governments may also have additional authority to regulate land use deriving from a more general delegation of the police power.

The application of zoning and other land use controls by local governments affects land, also known as real property, or more accurately, affects **property interests**. The term property interest, when referring to real property or land, is not synonymous with *title* to property, since legal title to real property is only one form of property interest. A property interest is merely a person's right to have the benefits of the particular type of interest the person holds in the property. For example, a person who holds legal title to a parcel of real property has the right to use the property, to exclude others from using it, and to sell the property for value. By contrast, a person whose property interest is the grant of an *easement* of access to certain property does not actually own the land across which the easement lies, but merely has the right to use the land described within the easement area for access to the property. Depending on the nature of the grant of the easement, the person who is given the easement may or may not have the right to exclude others from using the easement for the same purpose for which it was given. A permit is another form of property interest.

If an individual actually has a right to a particular property interest, that right is often referred to as an **entitlement**. In the land use context, a landowner is frequently said to have an entitlement to a property interest if his or her right has accrued or vested. A **vested right** to a property interest is a right which the law recognizes as having accrued to an individual by virtue of certain circumstances and that as a matter of constitutional law cannot be arbitrarily taken away from that individual. The theory of vested rights has particular application in cases where government makes zoning changes which affect development projects in progress. In such cases, a developer may argue that it has acquired a vested right in the prior zoning. The developer may also use the theory of **estoppel** and argue that the government is estopped, or precluded by its own acts, from making the zoning change that affects the developer's property. Unlike the theory of vested rights, estoppel is based on the concept of equity or fairness. It requires proof that the landowner or developer made substantial expenditure in good faith reliance on some act of omission of the government. As a practical matter, the facts needed to prove a vested right or estoppel in a zoning case are identical, and the courts frequently use the terms *vested rights* and *estoppel* interchangeably.

If a right to a property interest is merely hoped for or not yet vested, it is frequently referred to as an **expectancy interest**. For example, a landowner can usually demonstrate an entitlement to a building permit on compliance with all the application requirements, because the administrative official authorized to approve building permits usually has no discretion to grant or deny a building permit if all the requirements for issuance are met. However, where the administrative official or body is delegated the authority with standards to exercise discretion in deciding whether or not to give a certain type of approval such as a variance, a landowner is said merely to have an expectancy interest in the variance.

The term **nuisance** refers to the use of one's property in a manner that seriously interferes with another's use or enjoyment of his or her property (a private nuisance) or is injurious to the community at large (a public nuisance). Unlike trespass to land, nuisance does not require a physical invasion of others' property. In a private nuisance case, the land use that is claimed to be a nuisance is usually adjacent or close to the plaintiff's property and the plaintiff seeks to prohibit the use by injunction and obtain damages for injury suffered. Zoning was originally based on concepts of nuisance and consisted of a comprehensive scheme for separating incompatible land uses into mapped zones or districts. Because of the adoption of zoning in most communities, private nuisance actions are used less frequently by landowners to resolve land use disputes. However, a land use permitted by a zoning ordinance may still be operated in such a way as to constitute a nuisance.

In the exercise of zoning under the police power, a local government may decide to change the zoning classification of certain property or reduce the permitted density. For example, a zoning classification may be changed from commercial to residential or from industrial to residential, or the density may be reduced from 30 units per acre to 10. This change in the zoning classification to a less intensive use or a lower density is referred to as **downzoning**. The reverse action is frequently referred to as **upzoning**. These terms can be misleading. In some parts of the country, they are sometimes used to mean the opposite from the definitions just given. Furthermore, a developer's view that the rezoning of a parcel of property constitutes a downzoning may be directly at odds with the perspective of the neighbors.

Regardless of what terminology is used, a property owner whose property is rezoned against his or her will, or a neighborhood which objects to a rezoning, may decide to bring suit in state or federal court claiming that way the zoning ordinance was applied to particular property was unconstitutional. In this type of legal challenge, termed an **as applied challenge**, the landowner or neighbor does not attack the constitutionality of the zoning ordinance itself; rather, they argue that while the ordinance may be constitutional in general terms, its application to the property under the specific facts of the case is unconstitutional. However, if the person suing believes that the zoning provisions themselves are inherently unconstitutional, that is, that the language of those provisions violates certain constitutional limitations, then that person may decide to challenge those zoning provisions in their entirety without reference to any specific case in which they have been applied. This type of legal challenge is referred to as a **facial challenge**. A challenge to a regulation on its face is also sometimes described as a challenge to the regulation per se.

4.02 Legal Terms: Procedural Due Process

[1] due process; [2] separation of powers; [3] legislative decision-making; [4] ex parte contacts; [5] findings of fact; [6] administrative decision-making; [7] quasi-judicial decision-making; [8] adjudicative.

The term **due process** or, more accurately, due process of law, refers to the constitutional protections given to persons to ensure that laws are not unreasonable, arbitrary, or capricious. When such laws affect individuals' lives, liberty, and property, due process requires that they have sufficient notice and opportunity to be heard in an orderly proceeding suited to the nature of the matter at issue, whether a court of law or a zoning board of appeals. In a word, due process means fairness.

There are three terms which have particular application in the context of procedural due process—separation of powers, legislative decision-making, and quasi-judicial decision-making. The term **separation of powers** refers to the notion originally expressed by the Supreme Court in the late Nineteenth century that each branch of government must be limited to the powers appropriate to its functions. Through subsequent decisions, the term has come to encompass the concept that each branch is also dependent on the others to exercise their respective functions and that at least two branches of government must cooperate before governmental choices affecting individual rights can be put into effect.

Legislative power is the power of the legislative branch to make laws, that is, to establish public policy. The making of legislative decisions is generally not subject to the requirements of the due process clause. This means that **legislative decision-making** is relatively informal. Members of the legislative body are not prevented from communicating with individuals outside the legislative chamber before making a decision. Such **ex parte contacts** outside of the hearing on a particular matter are permissible in legislative decision-making, and participants at a legislative hearing cannot challenge the information obtained through such contacts. In addition, in making legislative decisions, the legislative body, whether it is a state legislature, a county board of commissioners, or a city council, is not required to recite the facts it considered in reaching its decision. Such a requirement that a decision-making body make written **findings of fact** and demonstrate in writing that its decision is supported by those facts is a procedural requirement that the due process clause imposes on **administrative decision-making**.

Administrative decision-making concerns actions or decisions to carry out policies or purposes previously declared by the legislative body. At the federal level, by virtue of the doctrine of separation of powers, such decisions are viewed as falling within the governmental powers assigned to the executive branch and its departments. At the local level, where the separation of powers doctrine does not apply in the same fashion, such administrative decision-making is usually performed by boards or commissions established by the legislative body. These bodies are subject to procedural due process requirements which include holding formal hearings on matters for decision, avoiding *ex parte* contacts outside of hearings, providing the opportunity for cross examination on the evidence presented, and preparing written findings of fact and conclusions. Because administrative bodies must review and draw conclusions from facts presented with respect to a specific parcel of property under procedural requirements that are similar to those followed in a court of law, their actions are sometimes referred to as **quasi-judicial** or **adjudicative**, that is, judicial-type or adjudicating actions performed by individuals who are not judges. In some jurisdictions, notably Oregon, the courts have held that a decision by a local legislative body concerning the zoning of an individual parcel is a quasi-judicial rather than a legislative decision.

✳4.03 Legal Terms: Substantive Due Process

[1] presumption of constitutionality; [2] fairly debatable rule; [3] arbitrary and capricious.

In addition to imposing procedural requirements on land use decision-making, the due process clause also imposes substantive requirements; for example, the requirement that land use controls further legitimate governmental purposes. When a land use regulation is challenged in court as not advancing a legitimate governmental purpose, the court usually will start its analysis of the regulation with a legal presumption, namely that the regulation in question is constitutional. This **presumption of constitutionality** means that the person challenging the regulation, or regulatory decision, has the burden—a heavy one—of presenting evidence sufficient to overcome the presumption in favor of the constitutionality of the regulation.

This presumption cannot be overcome if the evidence presented regarding the legitimate purpose of the regulation merely raises questions about which people could reasonably differ. This judicial rule is known as the **fairly debatable rule** or the reasonably debatable rule. When the evidence presented does not raise questions about which people could reasonably differ and indicates instead that the government's action was arbitrary, the court may invalidate the regulation on the ground that it is **arbitrary and capricious**, meaning that the regulation has no substantial relation to the public health, safety, morals, or general welfare.

✳4.04 Legal Terms: Equal Protection

[1] equal protection; [2] suspect classification; [3] strict scrutiny.

Because land use regulation involves the classification of land uses through the drawing of zone lines and the imposition of use standards, such classifications can raise questions of **equal protection**. Equal protection is a shorthand way of referring to equal protection of the laws which, in general constitutional terms, refers to the right of all persons under like circumstances to enjoy equal protection and security in their life, their liberty, and their property and to bear no greater burdens than are imposed on others under like circumstances. Equal protection in the land use context means that there must be a legitimate governmental purpose for the classifications and use restrictions that are applied to properties; properties which are similarly situated must be treated similarly, unless there is a rational justification for their disparate treatment. In sum, equal protection means equal treatment.

Where a land use classification impinges on such constitutional rights as freedom of speech, freedom of association and privacy, and freedom from discrimination on the basis of race—all considered fundamental rights guaranteed under the First and Fourteenth Amendments to the Constitution—a court will term such classification a **suspect classification**. A suspect classification triggers a more rigorous form of judicial review called **strict scrutiny**, meaning that the court requires a precise showing by the proponents of the regulation that it is justified by a compelling governmental interest.

4.05 Legal Terms: Just Compensation (Taking Clause)

[1] taking; [2] eminent domain; [3] regulatory taking; [4] just compensation; [5] inverse condemnation; [6] development exaction; [7] nexus; [6] average reciprocity of advantage.

Government appropriation of private land, either directly pursuant to a statute, or indirectly, through the restrictive effect of its regulations, is termed a **taking** of property. A taking of property by local government may occur directly through **eminent domain**, which is the power of government to condemn or take property for public use, an attribute of sovereignty. Or, it may occur indirectly through regulation. The latter is termed a **regulatory taking**. The Fifth Amendment limits the government's power by requiring that government pay **just compensation** when it takes private property under the eminent domain power or by regulation. The term *just compensation* means that the owner is entitled to the fair market value of the property which was taken. The owner is entitled to the value of the property to the owner—not the worth to the government—at the time of taking. Where government regulation has taken private property and the government has not exercised any formal eminent domain proceedings, a landowner may seek to recover the value of property taken by instituting a legal action known in most states as an action for **inverse condemnation**.

One form of regulation which raises taking issues is the **development exaction**. A development exaction is a contribution requirement in the form of land or money which government imposes on new development as a condition for development approval, usually in order to accommodate the need for capital facilities and services created by the new development.

In order to determine the constitutionality of a development exaction, a court will address various questions, including whether there is a sufficient demonstrated relationship or **nexus** between the burden imposed on the development and the need which the development is said to have created.

In determining whether a regulatory taking has occurred, the court will examine some, but not necessarily all, of the factors discussed in Part II, Section 6. Usually, however, the court will at least examine the degree of decline in property value in order to determine if the economic loss imposed by the regulation amounts to a taking. There are various economic loss theories. In a landmark opinion in *Pennsylvania Coal Company v. Mahon*, 260 U.S. 393 (1922), Justice Holmes labeled one of these theories **average reciprocity of advantage**. This phrase refers to the proposition that a land use restriction that burdens all land within a district may also benefit that land by virtue of the fact that all of the land is equally restricted. Thus a regulation which prohibits certain uses in a residential area has the reciprocal benefit of preventing all property subject to the regulation from being harmed by those uses. Where a court determines that this circumstance exists, it may conclude that there is no taking because the benefits conferred equal the burdens imposed.

4.06 Legal Terms: Freedom of Speech and Religion

[1] overbreadth doctrine; [2] vagueness; [3] prior restraint.
Because freedom of speech and freedom of religion are fundamental rights guaranteed by the First Amendment, a principal area of inquiry when courts review regulations which may impinge on those rights, is whether the regulation sweeps so broadly that it encompasses subject matter or behavior that is constitutionally protected. That is the meaning of the **overbreadth doctrine**. This doctrine, while important in the application of other constitutional principles, has particular application to regulations challenged on first amendment grounds. In applying the overbreadth doctrine, a court examines the extent to which regulatory terms are vague. The term **vagueness** has particular legal significance; it is a concept, based on procedural due process concerns about adequate notice, which requires courts to invalidate a regulation that is so unclear or

ambiguous that a person of normal intelligence will not be able to comprehend what the regulation forbids or permits.

One other possible effect of regulation which the Supreme Court has held to be particularly offensive to the free speech protections afforded by the First Amendment is **prior restraint**. In essence it means the preventing or forbidding of speech unless there is prior approval by a government official. Licensing requirements, when made part of land use regulatory schemes that apply to expressive activities, can potentially create prior restraints. The concept of vagueness and prior restraint are interrelated. Where a regulation is so unclear or ambiguous that a person does not know whether a particular type of expression is permitted, there is a strong likelihood that unregulated expression will be deterred, which effectively causes a voluntary prior restraint.

PART

II

Constitutional Principles

SECTION 1:
PRINCIPLE 1:
DELEGATION OF POWER

◆ 1.01 Introduction

Delegation of power in the context of planning, zoning, and other land use controls has two meanings: (1) the delegation of power to zone from the state to local government and (2) the delegation of power from a legislative body to an administrative body at the local level. ◊

◆ 1.02 Delegation of State's Police Power to Local Government

In order for a local government to zone and impose other land use controls, there must be a delegation of the state's police power to the local government. This principle—that local governments do not have inherent powers but are limited to those granted by a state constitution or legislature—is called *Dillon's rule*. Because of this rule, a local government can only exercise zoning power after there has been a delegation of the power to zone by the state. The appropriate subject matters for coverage by the local zoning ordinance, the procedures to be followed, and other aspects of the land use control scheme must be defined by the state. ◊

Comment

The U.S. Department of Commerce in 1926 (under then Secretary of

16

Commerce Herbert Hoover) recommended a standard state zoning enabling act as a guide for the delegation of state power. Within a short time
many states had adopted a version of this act. It authorizes municipal zoning for a particular set of purposes, following set procedures and techniques. Many states have now superseded the act with more modern
versions.

◆ 1.03 Delegation of Power from a Local Legislative Body to an Administrative Body

Local legislative bodies may not delegate their legislative or policy making
power to administrative agencies. However, legislatures may delegate substantial discretion to such agencies, so long as this delegation is accompanied by clear-cut policy guidelines to control the exercise of the delegated
authority, particularly when the regulation potentially affects fundamental rights such as those protected by the First Amendment. ◊

Comment

The rule against delegation of legislative power is one of the principal constitutional doctrines involved in planning law. The rule played a major role
in federal judicial review in the 1930s, but less so in subsequent decades,
and rarely in federal land use cases. However, the nondelegation doctrine
has continued to play a significant role in state land use cases. Active judicial review by the state courts to address planning and environmental law
issues in the 1970s has led to increased interest in the delegation of power
issue. The type of administrative judgment most likely to raise questions in
the land use context involves one in which the standards set forth as policy
guidelines are either very broad or nonexistent.

The rule against delegation of legislative power closely relates to the
vagueness doctrine defined in Section 2. Most of the earlier decisions in
various fields of law concerning delegation of legislative power tended to
approve very broad and rather vague standards, without much critical
judgment, while cautioning that such broad standards could give rise to a
delegation problem. However, in recent years the state courts have begun
to insist that if an administrative agency is given broad responsibility to
address a problem, the legislature must first establish standards and
guidelines which express the essential policies that are to be implemented.

The delegation problem, therefore, concerns how specific the standards
established for the administrative agency need to be in order to guide con-

crete decisions. The argument in favor of broad standards has often been phrased in terms of the impossibility of defining more specific ones. This argument, however, does not withstand scrutiny. Certainly the extent to which specific standards can be devised varies widely among different subject matters. However, in most instances relatively specific standards can be defined. Planners who draft land use regulations should be careful to articulate specifically the basic policies that must be followed by administrative agencies. Although the recent cases on the delegation question are few in number, more delegation cases may be anticipated.

Another delegation issue concerns the ability of the legislative body itself to act as an administrative body. In most states the city council is authorized to act as an administrative body for certain purposes, such as granting special uses or approving planned unit developments. However, there is a difference among the states regarding the need for predefined standards in such cases. The courts in some states hold that the legislature is acting in a quasi-legislative manner which requires no preestablished standards. In other states, however, the courts hold that the legislature must establish for itself the same standards that any administrative agency would be required to follow.

Delegation of power problems also arise where a zoning ordinance authorizes private parties to be formally involved in the zoning process. Generally, an ordinance may not require neighbor consent for a zoning amendment, a variance or such other special permission. However, the U.S. Supreme Court has held that consent provisions are valid if they provide for the waiver of a zoning restriction. Such consent provisions, however, cannot impose a new zoning restriction on a property owner.

Caselaw

City of Eastlake v. Forest City Enterprises, Inc., 426 U.S. 668 (1976) [V-2.06]
Panama Refining Co. v. Ryan, 293 U.S. 388 (1935)
Schechter Poultry Co. v. U.S., 295 U.S. 495 (1935)
Washington ex rel. Seattle Title Trust Co. v. Roberge, 278 U.S. 116 (1928)
Thomas Cusack Co. v. City of Chicago, 242 U.S. 526 (1917)
Eubank v. City of Richmond, 226 U.S. 137 (1912)
Maher v. City of New Orleans, 516 F.2d 1051 (5th Cir. 1975), *cert. denied,* 426 U.S. 905 (1976)
Shannon v. City of Forsyth, 666 P.2d 750 (Mont. 1983)

Morristown Road Associates v. Mayor and Common Council and Planning Board of Borough of Bernardsville, 394 A.2d 157 (N.J. Super. Ct. Law Div. 1978)
South of Second Associates v. Georgetown, 580 P.2d 807 (Col. 1978)
Penn Central Transportation Co. v. New York City, 366 N.E.2d 1271 (N.Y. 1977), *affirmed*, 438 U.S. 104 (1978) [V-2.34]
Figarsky v. Historic District Commission of Norwich, 368 A.2d 163 (Conn. 1976)
Town of Deering ex rel. Bittenbender v. Tibbetts, 202 A.2d 232 (N.H. 1964)
City of Santa Fe v. Gamble-Skogmo, Inc., 389 P. 2d 13 (N.M. 1964)
Hayes v. Smith, 167 A.2d 546 (R.I. 1961)
State ex rel. Saveland Park Holding Corp. v. Wieland, 69 N.W.2d 217 (Wis. 1955), *cert. denied*, 350 U.S. 841 (1955)
Concordia Collegiate Institute v. Miller, 93 N.E. 2d 632 (N.Y. 1950)
City of New Orleans v. Pergament, 5 So. 2d 129 (La. 1941)

Delegation of Power Illustration No. 1

A town which has been predominantly developed in the distinctive architectural style of a particular past historic period adopts an historic district ordinance, requiring approval by a special commission for all new buildings and for all changes to the exterior of existing buildings within the district. Under the ordinance, the commission is required to consider the effect of a proposed development on the general historical and/or architectural character of the structure or area and, more specifically, to consider the architectural style, textures, and materials in relation to other structures in the area.

The ordinance raises the problem of delegation. Opponents of the ordinance could argue that the standards are not specific enough to provide any real guidance to the commission, so that decisions may be based on no more than whim and caprice. To date, courts in a majority of jurisdictions have upheld such general standards. However, in more recent decisions, the courts have shown considerable reluctance to do so.

Could the town argue that the observable character of the area provides sufficiently specific standards? Do these have to be set forth in the ordinance? If the area is characterized by a distinctive historical style, a court would probably decide that the observable characteristics of the style can provide the necessary standards. However, it would be better practice to set forth these standards in the ordinance.

Would it make any difference if the ordinance was adopted by a traditional, small New England town? Traditional New England towns, while not as distinctive as New Orleans (the Vieux Carre) or Santa Fe, New Mexico, have special characteristics which the courts have recognized in upholding requirements for architectural conformity in such towns.

What if the ordinance applied to a half-built-up suburban subdivision with a great variety of familiar and conventional architectural styles? In such a case, there would be more serious delegation problems if the regulation did not contain specific standards. However, courts have upheld anti-look-alike (or anti-look-different) requirements under such circumstances. Whether these precedents will survive the present period of more active judicial review in the federal and state levels is not yet clear.

What if the criteria in the town's ordinance required that proposed structures harmonize with the terrain and nearby buildings that have a visual relationship to the proposal, and more specifically to colors, facade, and roof materials, to avoid a displeasing clash of design? Such specific references would be sufficient to protect an ordinance from attack on delegation grounds.

Delegation of Power Illustration No. 2

A suburban town with a long-established local college places the college in a restrictive residential zone, which requires the college to obtain the written consent of a stated percentage of adjoining landowners for any new college building.

Most courts would find the consent requirement invalid, since it represents a delegation of governmental power (1) to private parties and (2) without controlling standards. However, some courts would uphold similar requirements if the neighborhood's role was advisory only.

Delegation of Power Illustration No. 3

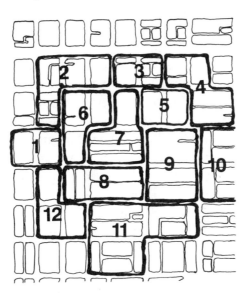

A large city, under strong public guidance, wishes to encourage imaginative redevelopment of a large area (several hundred acres) currently devoted to an obsolete, semi-industrial use. A new zoning district applied to the area divides the area into 12 subareas. The city council approves a specific series of planning standards for each subarea which are set forth in the zoning ordinance. These standards address general principles concerning the location and orientation of buildings, open space, view corridors, circulation and parking, and preferred land uses. However, the precise location of buildings is left to a detailed site plan application prepared by the developer, which must be approved by the planning board on the merits and for its conformity to the standards prescribed for the particular subarea. The only appeal provided is to the local district court.

If the planning standards for each subarea are specific enough to guide actual decisions, that is, if they go beyond generalities such as adequate parking must be provided, such a scheme would not be subject to attack on delegation grounds—particularly because the city council, by amendment to the zoning text, has established most of the rules to guide the planning board in evaluating specific proposals. It would be preferable if each subarea were designated as a separate zoning district in order to avoid a possible problem under the uniformity rule, which requires that regulations within each zoning district must be uniform as to all uses within the district. It would also be preferable if the planning board had limited discretion to change the permitted uses.

1.04 Symposium Discussion

N.Williams: Under the delegation doctrine, a legislative body may not turn over purely legislative power to an administrative agency. When a legislative body delegates significant jurisdiction to an administrative agency, there have to be policy guidelines to guide the agency in exercising the jurisdiction that it has been given. The question is how specific the policy guidelines have to be. It seems clear to me that the delegation of power doctrine is coming back and that more courts are worrying about this. There have been some major federal cases quite recently, including the one on the Gramm-Rudman-Hollings Act, *Bowsher v. Synar*, 478 U.S. 714, 106 S.Ct. 3181 (1986), which makes this a bigger deal than it has been in the past.

Perhaps the most striking thing in planning law in the last 15 years has been the shift away from the period of judicial laissez faire when practically anything would survive judicial scrutiny. Then, all you needed to show was that the regulatory decision was fairly debatable. That is no longer true. Starting about 1970 there was a shift in judicial attitude on issues such as exclusionary zoning, variances, and the comprehensive plan document. Now the local government better not depend on the presumption of validity. It had better have a good explanation of what it's trying to accomplish.

It is my impression that the courts are increasingly interested in more specific standards. For example, there is the decision in Maryland, *West Montgomery County Citizens Assoc. v. Maryland–National Capital Park and Planning Commission*, 522 A.2d 1328 (Md. 1987), declaring invalid the TDR scheme, in part because of a funny quirk in Maryland law where planning takes the back seat and the zoning machinery must be used for everything, and in part because of a lack of sufficient standards governing when transfer should occur and where the receiving area should be. Another equally important case comes out of Florida, *Askew v. Cross Key Waterways*, 372 So. 2d 913 (Fla. 1978), where, in the course of the state's critical area legislation, there was a limitation that only 5 percent of the area of Florida could be declared critical areas. Well, obviously a lot more than 5 percent of Florida could be declared a critical area. Therefore, the court held that the real decision came not just on telling what a critical area might be, but choosing which areas were critical and which were not.

That, however, was left to administrative discretion, which the court held invalid.

Federal and State Delegation of
Power Principles Distinguished

Delogu: I think it is important to keep in mind that the delegation principles that have been fashioned at the federal level are quite separate and distinct from delegation principles at the state level. The delegation doctrine at the state level has been alive and well, for the most part, over the past 30 or 40 years. I want to emphasize Norman Williams's observation that an increasing number of state courts are suggesting that there needs to be a shift from the use of subjective development criteria to more objective development criteria. For example, in Maine such terms as adequate parking, reasonable setbacks, no adverse impact, suitable soils, all are going out the door because they are too ill-defined and the Maine courts are requiring more precision in the standards for these concerns. Without more precision, those terms can mean whatever the planning board, or the zoning board of appeals, wants them to mean.

Federal Impetus to Delegation Principles

I think this trend will continue because I think the whole delegation principle is going to get more rather than less impetus through the decisions of the U.S. Supreme Court. Justice Rehnquist will be with us for some time to come, and he now has ample support in the Court for a revived delegation theory on the federal level; it always has had considerably more support at the state level. It will also gain impetus because courts in more jurisdictions are growing impatient with the perception that the police power is being used in an exclusionary manner. As that perception gains momentum, the movement to more objective criteria, more objective standards, will gain further support.

Forrest: I agree with those comments. But I want to point out that there is also a movement to more delegation of administrative discretion from the legislative body. I like the idea of delegation because it supports the basic organizational principle that policy is properly legislative, and that the administration and implementation of planning policies is becoming more and more technical. Quicker action and more precision is being demanded by objective standards, yet there is still a considerable need for discretion. Precise plans or planned discretion will be a continuing problem of how you put more predictability and accountability into the delegation of discretion to administrative bodies.

Intermediate Document to Improve Delegation

There was an article some years ago in the *Illinois Law Review*, entitled "Every Use a Special Use," and that kind of encapsulates the problem. It's like the old kids' game of playing doctor, "you show me yours and I'll show you mine," or "let's make a deal." I don't believe that such an approach can withstand a serious legal challenge. When there are multiple parties at interest, the city and the developer, perhaps, a neighborhood, and then an active environmental group, or a good government organization, you get a serious challenge.

We need to control the special use approach because it tends to put pressure on the plan, which is supposedly adopted as a standard to guide discretion. But we all know how vaguely worded some planning documents are, such that you can accept nearly any proposal under a provision of the plan and reject it under another provision. Yet, we still want to maintain some flexibility at the project planning level. I suppose we need another document, a document between the plan with its general comprehensive policies, and the ordinance. Most communities don't have that intermediate document, where standards of development are more objectively stated. If we don't specify and become more objective, the responsibility of government is fragmented and it's hard for citizens to require any accountability of their administrative bodies.

Livingston: Clyde Forrest touched briefly on how planners ought to avoid these problems. He suggested some kind of intermediate document between the comprehensive plan and the zoning ordinance. Well, such an intermediate document exists under California statutes. It's called the specific plan, an example of which, even though it is not so labeled, is the San Francisco Downtown Plan. It seems to me that a specific plan which contains both very specific standards—standards which are readily transferable into ordinances—and in some cases even ordinances themselves can be included in the specific plan. Another option is to include specific standards in the comprehensive plan itself, which, in appropriate instances, is a direction I particularly favor.

Lamont: I would agree on the first point that you could have subarea or neighborhood plans. Neighborhood plans for a long time have been ignored as an integral part of comprehensive plans. You can literally use a neighborhood plan or a specific plan such as a downtown plan to take the comprehensive plan down to the next level of detail. But I don't think the comprehensive plan per se, particularly in a larger community, can get to a sufficient level of detail and have any value. Policy plans in the 1970s were a real effort in trying to do that and we ended up with policy plans that were too nebulous. I would support, from a planning standpoint, going to the subarea or using a neighborhood plan, to get to the level of detail that Ed and others have talked about. Then you can get specific.

Hack: I have felt for sometime that cities ought to have a code of development standards which really were the collection of the standards that they apply. A few communities have adopted a statement of development standards that might be the kind of intermediate documents that Clyde Forrest suggested.

Architectural Control Committees

Babcock: I agree with Norman Williams's and Orlando Delogu's analysis, that there has been an increasing judicial demand for clear delegation standards. But what about the ubiquitous architectural control committees set up by local governments with no clear legislative authority and who are just told: "You make a judgment, and decide if you like it or don't like it." The case law, as far as I know, is still pretty much sustaining those ordinances. Where is the trouble coming from?

Blaesser: It comes from the person who is turned down by the architectural review committee.

N.Williams: He challenges the jurisdiction. While we haven't gotten much of this yet, we're just plain lucky. A lot of towns seem to have the notion that everything has to be looked at architecturally, meaning that one set of architects and maybe a bunch of laymen go and criticize another architect's work. I think in the historic district situation the standards are inherent in the traditional architectural style. That's why an awful lot has slid through with very little trouble. But towns that think they can set themselves up as architectural judges on all new development are asking for adverse opinions.

Babcock: I'm talking about the post WWII development in a suburb. The standard for these architectural review ordinances usually say that new development should be "substantially similar to" or "not substantially different from" what's already there. It's important to point out that this is a ubiquitous condition and it has not yet been challenged.

Delogu: We are seeing some challenges. *Wakelin v. Town of Yarmouth*, 523 A.2d 575 (Me. 1987), a case that just came down in Maine, threw out the very phrase that you're alluding to. The court said it didn't provide the developer sufficient constitutional protection. If you look at a broad range of challenges based on improper delegation and inadequate standards, I think that the more subjective ones are caving in and that by and large there's a broad retreat in this area.

A Dissenting View

Sullivan: I disagree slightly with what I've heard from Norman Williams. I think it's important for us to make a clearer distinction between delegation of power under federal law and under state law. It is important to understand the particular state constitutional system of your jurisdiction in order to determine whether or not it grants authority for, or places limits on, the delegation of legislative power. There certainly are cases in which significant delegations have been upheld, such as *Ramapo*, *Petaluma, Stoyanoff* and *Jordan*, the exactions cases. [*Golden v. Planning Board of the Town of Ramapo*, 285 N.E.2d 291 (N.Y. 1972), *appeal dismissed*, 409 U.S. 1003 (1972); *Construction Ind. Assn. of Sonoma County v. City of Petaluma*, 522 F.2d 897 (9th Cir. 1975) *cert. denied*, 424 U.S. 934 (1976); *State ex rel. Stoyanoff v. Berkeley*, 458 S.W.2d 305 (Mo. 1970); *Jordan v. Village of Menomonee Falls*, 137 N.W.2d 442 (Wis. 1965)]. So there's a great deal of delegation that has been traditionally upheld. We'll always have these cases. We may have more and I welcome that. However, I think that less than reviving the delegation theory, courts are simply manifesting their well-founded distrust of local governments, which, using the "legislative" label, try to insulate themselves from judicial review.

I think that we do ourselves a disservice if we try to see planning law as a body of law independent of administrative law. It seems to me that we ought to be talking about traditional administrative law principles such as rulemaking and consistent adjudication. If we let the courts do our work for us and create a principled body of planning law which deals with the delegation of authority, I don't find that necessarily unconstitutional. But I do think there's an obligation incumbent on local governments to flesh out what those very broad statutory terms mean, and to develop a body of administrative law that is consistent in terms of precedent with the court cases.

Dick Babcock, in a law review article back in 1959, "The Unhappy State of Zoning Administration in Illinois," 26 U. Chi. L. Rev. 509, 533 (1959), talked about courts using two braces of axiom, depending on where they wanted to be. If they liked what you did they talked about legislative deference and the like. If they didn't like what you did, they made up something, like spot zoning. I think it's improper for courts to do those things. I think that has to go back to the legislature; we've got to deal with these things on an administrative law basis and not through planning law as something independent of administrative law.

Standards and the Exercise of Discretion

Tarlock: In response to what Ed Sullivan said, I think it's important in the delegation doctrine to make the point that courts obviously are looking for some handle to review what an agency did. Standards can exist at two levels: (1) standards that exist before the discretion is exercised and (2) standards or reasons for the exercise of the discretion. A lot of states bought Professor Davis' argument in his treatise on administrative law that you shouldn't worry about prediscretion standards but you should worry about the reasons. I think both are part of the modern delegation packages of state law. Planners can save themselves by putting standards in the ordinance or by providing better explanations for a particular decision.

Blaesser: I would disagree if you are suggesting that the planners go ahead and do what they believe is right and afterwards, in a *post hoc* fashion, justify it by good reasons.

Tarlock: I'm not suggesting that. I'm saying that the whole delegation problem is part of a more general problem of more intensive scrutiny of these types of decisions. And the scrutiny can come either by looking at the standards under which the decision was made or the reasons offered for the decision. The lesson for planners now is that at some point in the process, a much more detailed statement of reasons is going to have to be forthcoming. But there is some discretion to decide what point that is.

*Hearing Officers and Citizen
Advisory Committees*

Forrest: A final point concerns the delegation of considerable administrative authority to hearing officers. I would like to encourage it because in many of the communities where they have been used there are more specific standards to guide their exercise of discretion. Their decisions may be subject to appeal to the elected officials, but many of the decisions are being made by hearing officers with greater efficiency, more professionalism, and in a way that might tend to neutralize some of the political implications of long standing plan commissions and zoning boards in *some* cities where these bodies develop a life of their own and go off in their own directions.

Mee: I have a comment and a question. First, I think specific plans are being used much more by many jurisdictions. In fact, we have an ordinance pending right now to explain the content, adoption process, and use of specific plans. Second, we also have a document which explains how to use and interpret the comprehensive plan. This document was developed by the city council subcommittee, then adopted by the entire county, so it is a legislative act.

My question concerns the fact that there is increased use of different types of hearing officers not only because of the burden of cases, but also because the policies that those hearing officers must follow are clearly established in statutes and by ordinance and their decisions are all appealable and in fact must be ratified by legislative bodies. The quasi-judicial decisions of hearing officers are appealable to a board of adjustment and ultimately to a court. We also have an abundance of citizen committees which are advisory to the legislative body. They have no power of their own. They are given a specific charge, told what they are to do and when they are to report back. Do you see a delegation of authority problem either with these hearing officer processes or with these advisory committees?

Referendum

Tarlock: I think the citizen advisory committees do pose a potential problem, because if you're going to deal with delegation of power, you also have to bring in the referendum problem which cuts against specific standards. There is one group of cases which says throw it into the public arena, and another group which says you have to take it out of the public arena and adjudicate it carefully. There has always been this lurking question of tension between popular sovereignty and reasonable decision. I think the more the citizen groups you have the more you raise the question—especially if it's a quasi-judicial administrative body—that you are delegating the power to make the decision to some improper body or group.

Forrest: Joy, does your council adopt a document, state how the plan is to be interpreted and then they go on and interpret the plan itself? Or is it somebody else's responsibility to interpret the plan?

Mee: The plan itself says that the council is the final interpreter of the plan; however, when any zoning case is filed, for example, it is reviewed by the staff to see if a general plan amendment is needed. If we determine that an amendment is needed before the zoning can be improved, we notify the parties and that decision can be appealed to council. This means that if it is determined that an amendment is needed, that amendment must be processed before the rezoning process can proceed. The council can't amend the plan without formal hearings.

Forrest: The council doesn't interpret it, you interpret it for them as an administrative officer?

Mee: If we are challenged it ultimately goes to the council to resolve.

Schulman: It goes ultimately to the legislative body?

Mee: Yes.

Schulman: Then there's no delegation.

Forrest: That is what I was driving at. If the plan is a policymaking device, what you're doing as an administrative officer is interpreting and you can only, in my opinion, interpret it pretty much exactly as it says. And if it is vague, then you can't invent language that's not there. The council can't interpret it either. It has to change it through formal precedures for a plan amendment.

Tustian: I think this is very important for planners. I have neighborhood plans, intermediate documents, hearing examiners—all of the kinds of things we're talking about. We're doing them, and we're not challenged on it. But I'm confused about what lawyers believe are the principles that are at work here. My way of sorting it out is to say that the comprehensive plan is like a constitution which we refer back to, and then to say that every detailed decision all the way down the line is potentially subject to review against this constitution. There's an entire chain of decisions from the broad policy to the detailed implementation. The question is how do you slice that chain apart, and say the legislature must decide this, but this can be delegated to somebody else. It all seems related to the question of who reviews the decision, and how far back up it goes to be ratified.

Delogu: The short answer to Dick Tustian's question is when the legislative body is purporting to deal with an application before it, it is an administrative body at that point in time. It is not a legislative body. It is disposing of a specific application, presumably pursuant to criteria which it or its delegatee previously established, and it may not depart from that. It may not conveniently, slip off its administrative hat in the middle of the disposition of the application and relegislate because they see something they don't happen to like.

No Separation of Powers Doctrine
at State and Local Level

Mandelker: The separation of powers doctrine under federal law does not apply at the state and local level. The U.S. Supreme Court made that clear in *Dreyer v. Illinois*, 187 U.S. 71 (1902). That's why the local legislative body can exercise administrative functions. Unfortunately, as the planners have been telling us, there has been a proliferation of various regulatory techniques which are not always authorized by the enabling legislation. As a result, the municipalities have had to deal with these techniques in their ordinances and the courts have been a little confused about how to handle them. But they're beginning to insist that municipalities provide standards for these new kinds of review powers, such as site plan review.

Impact of the Free Speech Clause

There's one other point I've been wanting to make that feeds into this and that has to do with uses protected by the free speech clause of the First Amendment. If it's a use protected by the free speech clause, such as an adult business or a sign, the courts insist on very clear and explicit review standards. The courts will not allow discretionary review unless it is very carefully channeled by very precise standards. Otherwise, if you subject the approval of any of these protected uses such as a sign or an adult business to discretionary review, you have what the court calls a prior restraint on free speech. There are now cases holding that traditional types of standards, such as adverse impact and the like, are not acceptable under the free speech clause and are a prior restraint because they are too broad. I cannot help but believe that these very restrictive free speech case standards will permeate the whole field eventually.

Lamont: I would like to renew an issue that Dan Mandelker touched on when he talked about the standards and about delegation, and specifically site plan review, architectural review and things of that nature. I think that to a great extent an emphasis is developing on delegating the approval of actual uses. Increasingly, planners are simply making more and more categories of uses into special uses and then applying a conditional review and not going to the city council for final approval. They are saying, for example, you can put the use in as a special use as long as you don't change the character of the house and the traffic and so on. Special uses then do not go to the city council. So it's a delegation in that sense from council to the planning boards, because they're saying if the special use meets certain criteria, and frequently they're fairly vague, they can be approved by the board. When dealing in uses these criteria are vague because you can't measure them.

Technical Expertise versus Standards

Meck: I'd like to respond to that. The question has been raised, how can this book be more useful to planners in drafting ordinances to deal with the delegation of legislative power and the ambiguity of standards? My feeling is that if you were drafting an ordinance and you weren't really sure what your objective was—couldn't define it or couldn't define what traffic congestion or what adequate storm drainage are—you should instead substitute an evaluation technique for the standard. For example, with site plan review and planned development, there is always the problem of storm water drainage. Our city council always handles it by approving the site plan subject to the review and approval of the city engineer. But, what does that mean? It means the city engineer basically has all the powers of the city council. I think the way to correctly draft an ordinance is to set forth the techniques that the city engineer would use to analyze the storm water system of a new development, describe the analytical framework, and give some objectives that the analytical framework is supposed to address.

Proper Place for Specific Standards

Delogu: I'd hate for us to give planners the impression that the courts are going to be fooled by statements in interim documents or in neighborhood plans. I would put more of whatever precision we could fashion into ordinances and not into what really should be larger policy statements.

Tustian: Orlando, you are saying on the whole, everything ought to move toward more specific standards. Maybe that has to be the direction. I'm in a situation where we have some very specific standards, but we're also administering site plan review with a significant degree of discretion. The legal process deals with dimensions in time, a sequential process. The planning process deals with dimensions in space, which are structural and finite and concrete, and we're dealing with how to change those spatial things over time. You can set down specific criteria for time processes that endure. The U.S. Constitution sets down certain things that are procedural and they haven't been changed very much. But the physical environment is changing all the time and is supposed to be responsive to social pressures for such change—new building types, group homes, etc. And so to force the planning profession in the direction of requiring preset spatial criteria is to hamstring the ability of our society to marginally change the house it lives in. A rigid insistence upon preset quantitative criteria will prevent the holistic judgment that has to be made to blend all of these things together. I'm talking about an extreme, I recognize, but I'm arguing that we should keep the window open sufficiently to allow for change and discretion and rely more on procedural due process. For example, with site plan approval and with storm water standards, it's better to say that the planning board should make the final decision rather than leave it to a single expert. The city engineer needs to bring the storm water decision to the board, where it can be considered together with other competing functional demands as part of a comprehensive review.

In my county, these kinds of decisions are made by a five-member collegial planning board, not a single staff hearing examiner. A board can be given more discretion in its decision-making because, with a collegial body, there is necessarily a more open process than with an individual, and you get multiple perspectives.

Hack: I want to reinforce Dick Tustian's point. There is a bit of an illusion here, which is that you can actually put these standards into some reasonably compact code. Take just one subject, storm water standards, which

Stu Meck mentioned. If you try to actually codify judgments that are vague on the adequacy of the storm system, it will require a textbook worth of stuff. Because you're in different spatial conditions, different land forms, it really is not a case of writing two or three pages of standards. It is a complicated subject and behind those standards are an immense number of judgments that have been made. You are then talking about ordinances which are burdened with enormous levels of technical detail.

I wonder whether there isn't another way of cutting it which is to have many more of these matters be finally disposed of by city councils. That is, that the site plan review go back to the council or legislative body for final disposition so that you're not in the situation where you have to hold everything on the adequacy of the standards that have gone with the delegation.

Schulman: The way storm water is normally handled is that there would be language in the ordinance that says, in effect, that any subdivision (or development) shall result in no more storm water runoff than existed prior to the development. The matter is then typically turned over to the applicant's professional engineer, subject to review by the city's engineer. I don't see any problem with the standard. You adopt the more specific standards by reference, and you allow the detailed application to be handled as a matter of best practice by another profession, by the engineers.

Tustian: Is the responsibility of setting standards delegated to another professional body?

Limits on Delegating Authority to Set Standards

Mandelker: It's unconstitutional to delegate standard setting to another body unless the agency that makes the delegation retains the discretion to approve or reject the standards on a case-by-case basis. So you're right back where you started.

Standards and Techniques Distinguished

Livingston: There has been some confusion between standards and techniques. The standard can be stated in Sy Schulman's ordinance. The technique for attaining that standard does not have to be spelled out in the ordinance or in the intermediate document or in the plan itself. The technique for attaining the standard can be in some best management practices manual, or in some engineering textbook, or wherever it is appropriate.

But I'm a little confused. I thought Norman Williams started this off by saying planners have got to be specific about standards in some kind of document. I agree that you must make things predictable to the applicant. Then later, I think I heard Dan Tarlock saying, "Well in some cases, maybe you don't have to prescribe the standards, but be sure you cover up your tracks by making clear, unmistakable findings." Is that what I'm hearing?

Schulman: That's a different kind of a standard because the required result is clearly explicated and quite different from Dick Tustian's comment about the kind of architectural result you may want. That's highly judgmental. This more technical material does not involve much of a range of judgment, in my opinion. I would be delighted to dispose of the concept of delegation as related to local land use controls and focus on procedural due process and the vagueness doctrine.

Inherent Limitations of the Subject Matter

Blaesser: The message here is that depending on the subject matter, you may be able to articulate very explicit standards, while in other cases your standards may have to be less clear but you can compensate with procedures that provide for good findings of fact and other procedural safeguards against abuse of discretion. Still, planners should err on the side of devising better standards where possible.

Siemon: Sy Schulman said it all. It's fundamental fairness, you do the best you can to be as fair as you can.

Spelling Out the Standards Where Possible

Livingston: Do I understand that insofar as possible, we ought to spell out the standards?

Everyone: Yes.

SECTION 2:
PRINCIPLE 2:
VOID FOR VAGUENESS

◆ **2.01   Vagueness Doctrine Defined**

The void for vagueness doctrine is derived from the due process clause of the Fourteenth Amendment; specifically, the procedural due process requirement of notice. The doctrine concerns the lack of clarity or certainty in the language of a regulation. A regulation can be attacked on its face as a violation of the due process clause under the void for vagueness doctrine. ◊

Caselaw

Gary-Wheaton Bank v. Village of Lombard, 404 N.E.2d 1115 (Ill. 1980)
Grant County v. Bohne, 577 P.2d 138 (Wash. 1978)
O'Connell v. City of Brockton Board of Appeals, 181 N.E. 2d 800 (Ma. 1962)

◆ 2.02 Overbreadth Doctrine Distinguished

The overbreadth doctrine focuses on the extent to which the language of a regulation sweeps too broadly and, therefore, encompasses subject matters or behaviors that are constitutionally protected, or which need not be affected in order to carry out the goals of regulation. ◊

Caselaw

Members of the City Council of the City of Los Angeles v. Taxpayers for Vincent, 466 U.S. 789 (1984) [V-2.25]
Broadrick v. Oklahoma, 413 U.S. 601 (1973)

◆ 2.03 Standard

In drafting regulations, planners should be concerned with two problems which the vagueness doctrine addresses: (1) whether the regulation is so vague that it does not give an individual of ordinary intelligence sufficient notice of what the law is that the individual has a reasonable opportunity to comply with the law; (2) whether the regulation lacks sufficiently explicit standards for its application by an administrative body and thereby impermissibly delegates to that body the freedom to decide basic policy matters on an *ad hoc* and subjective basis. ◊

Comment

The void for vagueness doctrine has been used by both the federal courts and the state courts as a buffer of added protection against the threat to individual freedoms posed by arbitrary and discriminatory legislative action. The doctrine is directed at language in statutes, ordinances, and other regulations that contain terms of judgment and degree that provide the opportunity for arbitrary or discriminatory action by administrative bodies and officials. The fact that the record of the decision of an administrative body in a specific case indicates that it did not act arbitrarily under an ordinance with constitutionally vague standards is irrelevant. It is the opportunity for arbitrary action, not the arbitrary act itself, that makes an ordinance vulnerable to attack on vagueness grounds. However, where standards in a statute or ordinance are based upon a familiar mode of practice in matters heard by the administrative body and common meanings of terms can be ascertained, such standards will not be viewed as impermissibly vague. In reviewing statutory or ordinance language challenged on vagueness grounds, a court is not limited to interpretation of the language in isolation but may ascertain its meaning by reference to similar regulations, other judicial determinations, and to the dictionary.

Caselaw

Grayned v. City of Rockford, 408 U.S. 104 (1972)
Lanzetta v. State of New Jersey, 306 U.S. 451 (1939)
Connally v. General Construction Co., 269 U.S. 385 (1926)
Gary-Wheaton Bank v. Village of Lombard, 404 N.E.2d 1115 (Ill. 1980)
Grant County v. Bohne, 577 P.2d 138 (Wash. 1978)
O'Connell v. City of Brockton Board of Appeals, 181 N.E.2d 800 (Ma. 1962)
People ex rel. Drobnick v. City of Waukegan, 116 N.E.2d 365 (Ill. 1953)

Void for Vagueness Illustration No. 1

A developer wants to build an asphalt plant in a "Limited Industrial District" of a village. The zoning ordinance regulations for that district permit "industrial-type uses, such as but not limited to manufacturing and industrial activities, laboratories and research firms, printing establishments, and railroad freight yards." The special use provisions for the district permit "similar and compatible uses to those allowed as 'permitted uses' in the Limited Industrial District." The district regulations also contain a section on prohibited uses that prohibits "all uses not expressly authorized as permitted or special uses, including but not limited to residential uses, drive-in restaurants, and salvage yards." Because the asphalt plant is not specifically named as a permitted, special, or prohibited use, the developer applies for special use approval. Her application is denied.

A court would find the foregoing ordinance provisions unconstitutionally vague because they do not contain any standards or criteria upon which the village can determine whether a proposed use that is not specifically listed is permitted, prohibited, or special. Because the phrase "but not limited to" is used without any accompanying criteria, an ordinary person exercising ordinary common sense would have to guess as to whether an asphalt plant is a permitted, special, or prohibited use. If approval is sought under the special use section of the district regulations, the incomplete list of permitted uses and the lack of criteria for determining what might be included as a permitted use make it impossible to determine whether the asphalt plant is a use that is "similar and compatible" to those already allowed as a permitted use.

Void for Vagueness Illustration No. 2

The provisions of a county zoning ordinance permit a county planning commission to limit development of island property by denying site plan review approval upon findings that:

1. The safety and convenience of the public is not provided for;
2. The applicant has not provided safe access or minimized traffic congestion; and
3. The proposed development would impose an excessive burden on public facilities such as schools, parks, and sewers.

Developers challenge the ordinance on the grounds that the phrases "convenience of the public," "safety," and "excessive burden" are unconstitutionally vague and do not adequately limit the discretion of the commission in making its findings. Although such terms of judgment and degree are the target of the void for vagueness doctrine, federal courts and most state courts would probably uphold such standards on the grounds that the terms used in these standards have commonly understood meanings within the law of zoning and are capable of definition by the administrative body in its capacity as factfinder.

Void for Vagueness Illustration No. 3

A city adopts a planned development ordinance that authorizes the city commission to approve a planned development under a list of specific criteria. In addition, the ordinance provides that fact findings by the commission "may include but are not limited to . . ." the listed criteria. A court would nullify this permissive phraseology on the ground that the language allows the commission to disregard the listed criteria and instead base a decision upon criteria that are not listed or that may not be criteria at all. The fact that in a specific case the city commission could argue that it had, in fact, considered the listed criteria only and that there had therefore been no arbitrary action would not remedy the constitutional defect of the ordinance. It is the opportunity for arbitrary action, not the fact itself, that renders an ordinance void for vagueness.

2.04 Symposium Discussion

Vagueness Distinguished

Blaesser: Delegation of power is concerned with the source of policy-making; while vagueness is derived from the due process clause and concerns the adequacy of standards that control individual decisions. In the land use context, the vagueness doctrine means that zoning and other types of ordinances must be clear and precise, particularly as to their provisions for enforcement. If a property owner is going to be penalized for failure to comply with the terms of an ordinance then due process requires that he or she have clear notice of what may or may not be done under the ordinance.

Delegation and Vagueness Intertwined

Delogu: I think that statement has a theoretical correctness which can't be denied on one hand, but as a practical matter the two doctrines become intertwined because the courts deal with them in an intertwined way. Take, for example, the language that I culled from one case: "The legislative body cannot delegate to the board a discretion which is not limited by legislative standards." When the developer sues he is suing, in effect, on a due process theory, arguing that the regulation is too vague. The board can do whatever it wants. The court in disposing of the case agrees with the developer and says, yes, those standards were too vague, they did allow boundless discretion. The court, accepting the due process argument, characterizes the failure of the legislature to fashion appropriate standards in their delegation as a failure of or an inappropriate delegation. And so the court talks about it in delegation terms and not due process terms, and there you have the two doctrines intertwined.

Siemon: The difference is that if you have a delegation problem, you can't cure it with process. And if legislative power is delegated to an administrative body you cannot use due process to solve that. But there are some subject matters that you cannot subject to specific standards, and I believe the courts have said that where those subject matters are not amenable to such definite standards, local governments may compensate for that with process. And that is where vagueness is extremely important in my judgment because vagueness is a rule of fundamental fairness and the objective is, as Dan Mandelker said, for the court to be able to look over the local government's shoulders. Findings of fact is one way that you can provide the court with a vehicle for looking over a local government's shoulders in the area where there has to be that fettered discretion. That's why the distinction is important.

SECTION 3:
PRINCIPLE 3:
PROCEDURAL DUE PROCESS

◆ **3.01 The Due Process Clause of the Fourteenth Amendment**

The Fourteenth Amendment to the U.S. Constitution prohibits any government action that deprives "any person of . . . liberty or property, without due process of law." This clause imposes both substantive and procedural requirements. ◊

Comment

The Fourteenth Amendment plays a unique, dual role in contemporary planning law. It serves as a pass-though for applying First Amendment freedom of speech and religion and Fifth Amendment taking limitations to the states and their political subdivisions. It also serves as an independent source of individual rights that are protected from governmental actions. More specifically, federal courts apply the Fourteenth Amendment to constitutional problems raised by the actions and decisions of local governments in land use cases. This amendment is also applied by the state courts, and many state constitutions have equivalent due process clauses. Although the language of the federal and the state constitutional clauses is the same, the federal courts and the state courts differ in their application of the due process clause to land use cases.

The constitutional limitations or standards which the due process clause of the Fourteenth Amendment imposes on land use regulation overlap. They also overlap with the constitutional limitations imposed by the taking clause. The substantive element of constitutional due process requires a legitimate governmental purpose as a justification for land use regulation. Governmental purposes also provide the basis for the classifications in land use regulation that are reviewed under the equal protection clause of the Fourteenth Amendment. The U.S. Supreme Court and some state courts consider the governmental purposes advanced by land use regulation when they consider whether the regulation is a taking of property.

Caselaw

Chicago, B. & Q.R.R. v. Chicago, 166 U.S. 226 (1897)

General Due Process Clause Illustration

A municipality adopts an historic district ordinance for an area of the city that has historic buildings. It does not adopt an historic district for another area of the city which also has historic buildings. The ordinance provides that the owner of an historic building in the newly established district may not demolish it without a permit from the historic preservation commission.

The historic district ordinance raises a substantive due process problem because a court must determine whether historic preservation is a legitimate governmental interest. The ordinance raises a procedural due process problem if the procedures provided for the consideration of demolition permits are inadequate. The ordinance also raises a problem under the taking clause of the Constitution, which is applied to the states through the Fourteenth Amendment, because the restriction on the demolition of historic buildings may, in certain cases, deprive a landowner of all use of his property.

◆ 3.02 Procedural Due Process Defined; Scope of Application

1. The due process clause requires minimal standards of fairness in administrative and quasi-judicial decision-making in land use regulation. These procedural requirements of the due process clause do not apply to legislative decision-making.
2. In administrative or quasi-judicial decision-making, a governmental body applies an established land use policy to a land use controversy involving a specific parcel of property. In legislative decision-making, a governmental body adopts a land use policy that is applicable to future land use controversies that may arise concerning properties which are made subject to the policy.
3. *Federal.* Procedural due process requirements apply only to an entitlement to a property interest, not to an expectancy. A landowner has an entitlement:
   a. if he has a vested right in a particular use of his land; or
   b. if his land use is permitted at the time he makes an application for a permit or requests development approval, and the land use

agency does not have the discretion to deny the permit or request for approval.

4. *States.* Procedural due process requirements apply to administrative decision-making by land use agencies, such as the zoning board of adjustment. In some states these requirements also apply to decision-making by the local governing body if the applicable state law characterizes this type of decision-making process by the local governing body as quasi-judicial. ◊

Comment

Procedural due process in the land use context is required only for administrative or quasi-judicial decision-making. It does not apply to legislative decision-making. It may apply to decision-making by a local governing body, such as the denial of special permit, if a court holds that this type of decision-making process is administrative. In states such as Oregon, procedural due process requirements may also apply to certain legislative acts because the courts have held that they are quasi-judicial. Examples are rezonings and decisions on special use permits when the zoning ordinance provides standards for these decisions.

There is no fully accepted definition of the distinction between legislative and administrative decision-making. The courts usually base this distinction on whether the decision adopts a policy for general, future application or whether it applies an established policy to a specific request for a change in land use. The number of landowners affected by the decision is also important. Courts tend to hold that a decision is administrative or quasi-judicial if one or only a limited number of landowners is affected.

Caselaw

Rogin v. Bensalem Township, 616 F.2d 680 (3d Cir. 1980), *cert. denied,* 450 U.S. 1029 (1981)
Fasano v. Board of County Comm'rs of Washington County, 507 P. 2d 23 (Or. 1973)

Comment

Federal. Even if a land use decision is administrative, procedural due process requirements do not apply if a landowner has only an expectancy interest and not a property entitlement. A landowner has a property entitlement if his or her land use is vested under a land use ordinance or if a zoning body is required to issue a permit or give approval at the time a landowner applies for it and cannot exercise discretion in its decision on the permit or approval.

States.   How a state court characterizes a land use decision determines whether procedural due process requirements apply. Most state courts apply procedural due process requirements to administrative decision-making under land use ordinances, such as variance and special use permit decisions. State courts do not always base their procedural due process requirements on the state Constitution. For example, they may require findings of fact in administrative proceedings in order to facilitate judicial review of the administrative decision.

Caselaw

Yale Auto Parts, Inc. v. Johnson, 758 F.2d 54 (2d Cir. 1985)
Topanga Ass'n for a Scenic Community v. Los Angeles County, 522 P.2d 12 (Cal. 1974)

Procedural Due Process Illustration No. 1

A landowner applies for a variance under a zoning ordinance. The board of appeals holds a hearing but denies the applicant the right of cross-examination. The landowner brings suit, claiming a procedural due process violation.

A federal court would hold that due process requirements do not apply, even if variance procedures are administrative. The landowner has only an expectancy interest in the variance because the board exercises discretion in the review of variance applications, and the landowner is not entitled to a variance as a matter of right. A state court would hold that procedural due process requirements are violated if it characterized the variance decision-making process as a quasi-judicial administrative process.

♦ **3.03 Judicial Standards for Determining Procedural Due Process Violations**

   1. *Elements of Procedural Due Process.*   When courts apply procedural due process requirements to land use cases, they consider the extent to which the following elements were present in the administrative or quasi-judicial decision-making process:
   a. an unbiased decision;
   b. adequate notice of the hearing;

> **c.** a hearing in which witnesses are sworn and in which there is an opportunity to introduce evidence and an opportunity for cross-examination; and
>
> **d.** a decision based on the record supported by reasons and findings of fact.

However, the extent to which all of these elements must be present will differ, depending upon whether the case is brought in federal court or in state court.

> **2.** *Federal.* The federal courts apply a balancing test to administrative decision-making to determine whether an administrative decision violates procedural due process. In addition to the above-listed elements, they consider:
>
> **a.** the private interest affected by the official action;
>
> **b.** the risk of an erroneous deprivation of such an interest through the procedures used and the probable value of additional or substitute procedural safeguards; and
>
> **c.** the government's interest, including the function involved and the fiscal and administrative burdens that the additional or substitute procedures require.
>
> **3.** *States.* The state courts selectively apply some or all of the procedural due process requirements listed in Section 3.03(1) to land use decision-making, which they characterize as administrative or quasi-judicial. They have not adopted a balancing test. ◊

Comment

In the federal courts, a land use decision does not necessarily violate procedural due process even if the court characterizes it as administrative. The federal courts apply a flexible balancing test adopted by the Supreme Court to determine whether procedural due process is violated. In applying this test in land use cases, the federal courts have considered procedural due process violations such as a lack of notice or lack of meaningful participation in hearings. They have not found procedural due process violations in most of these cases, and have held that participants in land use proceedings received adequate notice and were not entitled to cross-examine opposing witnesses. However, the federal courts have held that decision-makers in land use proceedings must be unbiased.

The state courts have not adopted a balancing test that determines when procedural due process requirements apply to land use decision-making. Procedural due process requirements in the state courts vary. State courts require adequate notice of land use hearings. They may require the cross-examination of witnesses in land use hearings. Many state courts require findings of fact for variances and similar land use decisions. Procedural due process requirements in some states are governed by the state administrative procedure act if this act applies to local land use decisions.

Caselaw

Mathews v. Eldridge, 424 U.S. 319 (1976)
Fasano v. Board of County Comm'rs of Washington County, 507 P.2d 23 (Or. 1973)

Procedural Due Process Illustration No. 2

A zoning ordinance authorizes a special permit for a child care center in residential zoning districts if the center meets specific requirements such as minimum lot size, adequate parking, and adequate access. The zoning board of adjustment authorized to grant the special permit includes two members who own competing child care centers. It denies the special permit for the child care center and does not make findings of fact. This decision is administrative.

A federal court would find a procedural due process violation. It would hold that the board was biased because it included business rivals of the applicant and that the record was inadequate because it did not include findings of fact. A state court would find a procedural due process violation for the same reasons.

Procedural Due Process Illustration No. 3

A developer applies for a zoning amendment to rezone 500 acres of vacant land in a medium-size city from single-family to multifamily use to allow construction of a major planned development project. The comprehensive plan designates this tract for multifamily use, and the level of services proposed for the tract in the plan also assumes multifamily development. The city council grants the amendment but does not state reasons for its decision. Neighbors have brought suit, claiming that the failure to state reasons is a procedural due process violation.

Both a federal court and a state court first would have to decide whether the rezoning was legislative or quasi-judicial. The court could decide that the rezoning was quasi-judicial because it implements the land use policies in the comprehensive plan. The court could also decide that the rezoning was legislative because it rezoned an extensive area of the city and because the planned development will have a substantial impact on municipal services. Some state courts hold that all zoning actions by the governing body are legislative.

A court would not find a procedural due process violation if it held that the rezoning process is legislative because legislative bodies do not have to state reasons for their decisions. However, a court would find a due process violation if it held that the rezoning process is quasi-judicial because quasi-judicial bodies must state reasons for their decisions.

Procedural Due Process Illustration No. 4

A zoning board of adjustment holds a hearing on a special permit for a group home for the mentally retarded. During the hearing it becomes apparent that additional studies are necessary on the impact of the home on the adjacent residential neighborhood. The board closes the hearing and requests additional studies from the applicant and the city. These studies are received by the board one month later. The board does not hold a new hearing but allows the applicant and the city to comment on the new studies. It then denies the permit.

A federal court, and most state courts, would hold that the board's decision violated procedural due process. The additional studies were not part of the hearing record, and cross-examination of the experts who prepared the studies was not possible because a new hearing was not convened.

3.04 Symposium Discussion

Mandelker: To the extent that developers have won procedural due process cases in the federal courts it has been primarily on the basis of claims alleging bias in the decision-making process. Apart from these cases, the federal courts have usually dismissed most procedural due process claims. But lately, developers' lawyers have begun to craft more effective pleadings, claiming various kinds of conspiracies and arbitrary actions, and they're defeating government motions to dismiss. So I view this as a growing area.

The state courts base procedural due process protections on very different concepts that do not reflect the U.S. Supreme Court's interpretation of procedural due process limitations. Most states characterize the rezoning process by the governing body as legislative and do not apply procedural due process limitations except for bias or conflict of interest limitations in some states. At the same time, the state courts increasingly require procedural due process in administrative decision making, such as the decision-making process for variances and conditional uses. But these requirements may not be based on the state constitution. Even when the courts impose a finding of fact requirement, for example, they base it on the need to achieve principled decision-making and to permit effective judicial review. It's kind of a common law of procedural due process. The zoning statutes contain minimal notice requirements, so the notice problem is usually a statutory rather than a constitutional issue.

Carey: I fully agree with Dan Mandelker regarding procedural due process in the state courts. In most situations it's entirely dependent on state statute and state law. It also bears repeating that in applying procedural due process you cannot even determine what test you're going to use until you know the type of interest that is involved.

Planners' Ho Hum Attitude

I also have another comment which concerns the generally ho hum attitude of planners toward procedural due process. To be sure, affording procedural due process costs money. But lack of process costs even more money. My view is that virtually anything that's questionable should be accorded procedural due process steps. I think it is a small price to pay for a very large insurance policy. I believe that's the root of planners' ho hum attitude because I think that most planners believe that as well. If there's a question, let's give it procedural due process protections.

It all gets back to essentially what the Fourteenth Amendment says. That amendment doesn't say that you cannot deprive people of their liberty and property interests; it says you cannot do it without due process. You may end up violating other federal constitutional amendments, but you will survive the Fourteenth.

Schulman: I can think of instances over the years where procedural due process has arisen in professional practice. For example, there is the situation where a matter is the subject of a public hearing, and because of the testimony that the legislative body received, it decides that it ought to adopt an ordinance that's significantly different from the ordinance which was the subject of the public hearing. The question is "Does that require a rehearing?" That's a serious technical problem. Most city attorneys will say, "Let's have another hearing."

Mandelker: It's like Procedural Due Process Illustration No. 4 above, where they find new evidence after the hearing.

Stollman: They want to adopt something not advertised.

Schulman: That's a serious problem at times. Politicians hate to go back.

Cross-Examination

Mee: As for the list of procedural due process elements, I would also generally say ho hum with the exception of this idea of cross-examination. The standard procedure that I see being followed is the applicant presents, the staff or whoever is representing the community makes a presentation, and the public gets to comment. A period of rebuttal follows and then the legislative body can ask questions back and forth. This idea of cross-examination by the applicant and everyone who speaks is something I have not seen followed. And I think if that is going to apply we need to know when and where.

Mandelker: It certainly applies in the states like Oregon that treat the process as quasi-judicial. There's no question.

Mee: But this cross-examination could be very time consuming.

Blaesser: You need to understand that the procedural due process elements listed in Section 3.03 are compiled from state cases all over the country, and these elements have been distilled over time from various state cases and U.S. Supreme Court cases. No one case really lists everything. The list is all-inclusive, and therefore a particular element such as the right of cross-examination may not be required under the law of your state.

Schulman: I think there are two things that need to be clarified. One has to do with access to records that are filed. Sometimes all of the records are not available to both sides or all sides of a dispute. Second, it's not clear to me what you mean by an unbiased decision: Are you speaking of an unbiased decision or an unbiased decision maker?

Mandelker: An unbiased decision maker. It's Procedural Due Process Illustration No. 2 above.

Schulman: The notion I'm trying to get at is that most people think of bias as conflict of interest. That's what the state statutes deal with and that usually means a financial conflict of interest. But the typical situation is officials making public statements as to what their decisions are based on.

The decision-maker has got to approach the hearing like a blank sheet of paper. He doesn't have to leave all of his values at home, but certainly he shouldn't talk about his values regarding the case until after the decision has been made.

Availability of Staff Report Before Hearing

Livingston: As for Sy Schulman's question of the record being available for examination, in most instances there is a staff report to the planning commission and/or to the legislative body on the case at hand. Don't the applicant and other interested parties have a right to examine that part of the record in advance of the hearing?

Carey: What constitutional provision would require that disclosure?

Mandelker: It seems to me that if the decision is quasi-judicial, it is necessary to base it on the record and to provide an opportunity to cross examine. If the record is not made available to me at all, but the decision-maker uses that record, that violates procedural due process.

Carey: I thought you were saying two or three days before the hearing.

Siemon: I don't think there is any constitutional provision that requires that disclosure. If it's made a part of the record, the applicant's given it. If it isn't made part of the record, and they rely on it outside of the hearing, then you may have a problem.

Mandelker: I agree with you on that. But if a staff study is not made available within a reasonable time before the hearing, that limits my right of cross-examination. Let's assume I appear before the hearing board and I say Mr. Chairman, I just saw the staff report one hour ago, I move for a continuance and he rules no, then that limits my right of cross-examination.

Carey: I agree with you but I think we're back into the area where, as a practical matter, cross-examination has been a constitutional requirement only in those states where you're essentially following courtroom procedures. Even those states that apply the term quasi-judicial to their proceedings haven't adopted a cross-examination requirement. That's why it's important to emphasize to planners that the procedural due process elements listed in Section 3.03 are possible elements but not necessarily adopted elements in all cases.

Livingston: There are cases in California and some other states where there is no cross-examination or quasi-judicial type of procedure in which the courts have held that interested parties are entitled to see the staff report in advance of the hearing.

Blaesser: I think that's pretty fundamental. Ted; it's not just cross-examination, it's the ability to know all the information that may be relevant to the decision as you come into a hearing, whether you're a citizen opposed to the proposal or whether you are the applicant.

Carey: I'm just disputing whether such a requirement falls within the gamut of the Constitution. There may be all sorts of state rules or state constitutional provisions that would require that.

Blaesser: I would agree. But it's equally important to stress that procedural due process, at least in state jurisdictions, may require that the report, which the planning staff may not always like to make available in advance of the hearing, must be made available.

How Specific a Statement of Purpose?

Schulman: Another question is whether, in the adoption of an ordinance of whatever sort, there should be a clearer statement of legislative purpose and intent. The municipal attorney is usually dead against that. He doesn't want to reveal intent, he wants to let the results speak for themselves; and I can't tell you how many times I've been told by municipal attorneys, "Let's not put that on the record because, if we get into court, we don't want to have too clear a record because then they'll be able to attack us." I think that this partakes of procedural due process when a legislative body tries as best it can to reveal why it came to a certain conclusion. Municipal attorneys don't like doing that. Planners, in my opinion, like to say why you say yes or no and say it publicly. Isn't that a procedural due process issue?

Blaesser: Unless the legislative body is acting in an administrative capacity it doesn't have to provide a statement of reasons.

Legislative versus Administrative Procedures

G.Williams: I think it is important to explain the difference between a legislative procedure and an administrative procedure, so planners get a sense of the different types of notice requirements and the differences in other requirements.

Mandelker: The distinction is that a legislative decision is the making of policy; the administrative decision is the application of policy. The state courts disagree on whether or not a rezoning of an individual tract falls in one category or the other, with only a minority of the states saying that it's an application of policy.

Notice

Babcock: You also need to draw out the difference in notice requirements if it is legislative versus administrative. You said if it's administrative, you have to give adequate notice of the hearing and you probably really mean individually mailed notices.

Berman: What about the time factor?

Mandelker: That time factor would apply in a quasi-judicial proceeding. I use the word adequate notice to mean adequate personal notice.

SECTION 4:
PRINCIPLE 4:
SUBSTANTIVE DUE PROCESS

◆ 4.01 Substantive Due Process Defined; Scope of Application

Under the substantive component of the due process clause, a land use regulation must advance a legitimate governmental purpose. ◊

Comment

The substantive component of the due process clause tests the governmental purposes implemented by land use regulations, such as zoning ordinances. Legitimate governmental purposes are frequently described in state zoning legislation in terms of the protection or furtherance of the public health, safety, morals, and general welfare.

Substantive Due Process Illustration No. 1

A local government adopts an ordinance requiring design review of all new development. This ordinance raises a substantive due process question because a court must determine whether the aesthetic purposes advanced by design review are legitimate.

◆ **4.02 Judicial Standards for Determining Substantive Due Process Violations**

1. The courts apply a presumption of constitutionality when they consider substantive due process challenges to land use regulations. The presumption of constitutionality means that a court will accept the legitimacy of a governmental purpose if it is reasonably debatable.

2. *Federal.* The federal courts almost always apply the presumption in substantive due process cases and rarely hold that a land use regulation violates substantive due process.

3. *States.* The state courts are more likely to find a substantive due process objection to a land use regulation than are the federal courts. They do not apply the presumption of constitutionality if they believe that the land use regulation affects a fundamental constitutional interest such as freedom of association or privacy, which is vulnerable to adverse regulation in the land use control process. In such cases, the local government must carry the burden of justifying the regulation. ◊

Comment

When a court applies the presumption of constitutionality, a local government does not have the burden of proof to justify the governmental purposes advanced by a land use regulation. It is enough if the regulatory purpose is reasonably debatable. A different rule will apply when a court reviews the legitimacy of a governmental purpose under the taking clause.

The U. S. Supreme Court has approved virtually all governmental purposes implemented by land use regulations. These purposes include land use zoning, open space zoning, historic landmark preservation, and regulation for aesthetic purposes.

The state courts generally apply substantive due process requirements more rigorously than the federal courts. Although the courts in most states also approve most regulatory land use purposes, the courts in a minority of states will not approve aesthetic purposes in zoning unless they advance other governmental purposes, such as the protection of property values.

The state courts may reverse the presumption in land use cases when a fundamental constitutional interest is affected. An example is a zoning ordinance that restricts the location of group homes. In these cases, the local government has the burden of justifying the land use regulation and showing that a less restrictive regulatory alternative is not available. Such cases may also raise an equal protection problem.

Caselaw

Village of Euclid, Ohio v. Ambler Realty Co., 272 U.S. 365 (1926) [V-2.49]

Substantive Due Process Illustration No. 2

A city adopts a moratorium on new development to prevent environmental damage in an area of the city where it has never provided sewer and water facilities. In a suit challenging the moratorium, evidence is introduced showing that the city does not have plans to provide necessary sewer and water facilities in the area covered by the moratorium and that the moratorium was adopted in response to community pressures to halt all city growth in that area. A court would hold that the moratorium violates substantive due process because it does not advance legitimate governmental interests.

Substantive Due Process Illustration No. 3

A suburban city adopts a zoning restriction that requires ten-acre lots in all of its undeveloped areas. The city justifies this restriction by claiming that large lots are necessary to limit growth in this area, even though adequate public facilities are available to serve new development at much more intensive densities. The suburban city is located on the fringe of a rapidly growing metropolitan area.

A federal court would probably apply the presumption of constitutionality and uphold the ten-acre lot restriction. A state court may find that the restriction violates substantive due process. It could hold that the restriction is not justified because adequate public facilities are available for development at much greater densities. It could also hold that the restriction is exclusionary because it bars development that would provide affordable housing for lower-income groups.

Substantive Due Process Illustration No. 4

A city adopts an appearance code for single-family dwellings. The code requires "the use of external wall treatment similar to that used on existing single-family dwellings in the adjacent area." Both a federal and a state court would probably hold that the code advances legitimate aesthetic purposes because it requires new dwellings to conform with existing dwellings in the area. A court could hold that the code does not advance legitimate aesthetic purposes if it concluded that the type of external wall treatment used is not relevant to aesthetic values.

4.03 Symposium Discussion

Mandelker: There are two points that need to be made about the substantive due process clause. First, although I believe Judge Posner of the U.S. Court of Appeals for the Seventh Circuit was correct when he described substantive due process as a "diluted constitutional clause," that view is really correct only when a facial attack is made on a land use regulation. Serious substantive due process problems may arise when a land use regulation is attacked as applied. For example, most states accept aesthetics as a legitimate zoning purpose, but in some cases a due process problem arises because an aesthetic regulation is not justified as applied. An example is a refusal to approve a home designed in a modern architectural style in an area where many homes of this type already exist.

The second issue concerns exclusionary zoning. This category includes not only zoning ordinances that exclude lower income housing but also ordinances that exclude or restrict mobile homes or group homes of various kinds. Indeed, Substantive Due Process Illustration No. 4 presents this particular problem in a very nice way because it is clear that the appearance code would exclude mobile homes in areas of the community where homes are built of traditional materials. The problem is that state courts have treated exclusionary zoning as an equal protection problem under the state constitution or, as in New York, as a question of statutory interpretation. Pennsylvania, more than the other states, has applied substantive due process analysis in exclusionary zoning cases. In the group home and mobile home cases, the tendency is to construe the ordinance to allow the use rather than get into the constitutional issues.

Importance of the Comprehensive Plan

Siemon: I see increased judicial deference to the comprehensive plan as a substantive due process consideration. Where there is no plan, I believe the courts are looking more strictly. For example, there is a recent Third District Court of Appeals opinion in the state of Florida, *Machado v. Musgrove*, 519 So.2d 629 (Fla. App. 3 Dist. 1987), in which the court said that when we test a regulation for substantive validity, we're applying due process. And where it is alleged to be inconsistent with a plan, the burden shifts to the government to prove that the deviation from the plan is, in fact, substantively competent. I see the courts becoming increasingly impatient with local government regulations. For example, I regard *Nollan* as a case in which the regulation couldn't pass the straight face test. To argue, as the dissent did, that the beach access easement requirement could be justified under the presumptive validity standards really begs the question. I think the Court signaled its impatience with that form of argument. Therefore, it's important to get the message across to planners that the presumption of validity traditionally accorded land use regulations as legislative acts is not an invitation to ignore the straight face test.

Carey: I agree with Dan Mandelker only to the extent that the substantive due process clause, at least in my mind, is no longer a real stand-alone threat if only because it's been integrated into Fifth Amendment takings analysis by the U.S. Supreme Court's opinions in the *First English* and the *Nollan* cases. My specific comment is that substantive due process involves more than just property interests; it includes liberty interests such as the right to privacy which, in turn, is subject to substantive due process limitations. As to liberty interests, the substantive due process tests are more exacting. Land use ordinances can certainly impact on liberty interests just as well as property interests.

N.Williams: I think the Supreme Court has created massive confusion on the substantive due process issue. One block of justices, led by Justice Stevens, argues that all these taking questions should be dealt with as due process matters. Another group, which includes Justices Rehnquist and Scalia, wants to apply a different set of tests, presumably more restrictive, against the municipalities in favor of property owners.

There also seems to be a very large difference between the test used by the state courts on the combined taking and due process issues and the test used by the Supreme Court, particularly in the recent cases. What the Supreme Court has done in recent years is to vastly increase the stakes in land use litigation and destroy predictability.

State Courts

A few other observations. State courts frequently do not articulate any constitutional theory in deciding land use cases. They simply decide the case and you read the case and sort of sense that they've used an equal protection or substantive due process rationale for their decision. They do not, as the Supreme Court of the United States often does, frame the case in any precise way for us. They rarely talk about substantive due process.

They have their own equivalent rule, which is that if something is "arbitrary and capricious" it's invalid. I think there are, in fact, many more substantive due process cases when we understand that.

A Dissenting View

Sullivan: I want to suggest that we Americans try to raise everything to a constitutional issue and that substantive due process is the prime bad example of that. We try to run off and get a court's view of what's reasonable under the circumstances. I think that's a mistake. I think the now discredited *Lochner* era of cases survives to some extent in planning law. And it survives especially at the state level where state courts use their own conception of reasonableness rather than leaving these issues to the political process, with the notion that if things get too bad the political process will take care of it.

My vision of planning law is one in which there's a transition from constitutional law to administrative law, so that we get back into the traditional notions of rule-making and adjudication, without trying to build these grand edifices of constitutional law. I might suggest also for constitutional analysis purposes, that we look to one of the judges of the Oregon Supreme Court, Hans Linde, who suggests in his article, "Without Due Process," 49 OR.L. Rev. 125 (1970), that analysis should move up the ladder from construing the language of the ordinance to determining conformity with enabling legislation, then to state constitutional provisions and then, and only then, to federal constitutional law. I think trying to litigate in the federal courts, especially with a substantive due process approach, is akin to a crap shoot. We need a much more principled way at looking at planning law in this country than that.

Siemon: I think we have to keep in focus whether we're describing what is or what should be. While I can agree with Ed Sullivan that if we drop the fiction that zoning, particularly rezoning, is a legislative act and get it into the mold he has in his state of Oregon, we'd all be in a better world. But quite frankly it's my view that we died in that attempt despite a lot of bold efforts in the 1960s and early 1970s to get there. So, I think we're stuck with the fiction of a legislative act and it is in that context that I think we've got to have recourse to judicial review, or we'll have no hope in the system. There will be no rules to follow, and while each state has its own substantive rules, I firmly believe that the general federal Constitutional principles of substantive due process continue to control. *Euclid v. Ambler* is repeatedly cited in arguments before local courts and they listen to it and follow it. But I also think much of what Ed said is really right. It depends on whether we are talking about what should be or what really is.

Legitimate Governmental Purposes

Schulman: I want to discuss the idea of legitimate governmental purposes. I think some people think that there's a bedrock of legitimate governmental purposes. But most practitioners think of legitimate governmental purposes as implying a range of reasonableness; that there's a range within which government can do what it wishes and the presumption of validity will sustain it. What bothers all of us are the limits of those ranges. I think that the lawyers are a little misled by thinking that the legitimacy of a regulation can be validated by the existence of a plan, as if the plan imparts bedrock proof of legitimacy of purpose. I think that we're going to have, as we should have had over the years, a fair amount of litigation on the legitimacy of plans. Just because there's a plan doesn't confer legitimacy or validity—the plan can exceed the range of reasonableness, as can the regulations. We who are practitioners, whether lawyers or planners, are looking for that range and we want to know how to dimension it.

Increased Judicial Scrutiny of Comprehensive Plans?

Livingston: I agree with what Sy Schulman just said. Particularly after *Nollan* the courts are going to look increasingly at the plan itself and examine even more than in the past what constitutes an acceptable comprehensive plan. We have to be prepared for that.

Weinstein: Larry, I'm not sure I accept what you've said entirely. It seems to me that what *Nollan* is saying is not that they're looking so closely at the plan as they're really looking at the implementation of the plan—the way the planning principle of public access to beaches was applied in the context of that particular development and the kind of exaction that was being demanded there.

Livingston: What you said about *Nollan* is absolutely correct, of course. But the underlying and broader implication to me is that even though the Supreme Court in that case was dealing with *implementation* of the California Coastal Plan and not the plan itself, there's a lot of language in the opinion that suggests to me that the courts will look critically at comprehensive plans themselves, which I personally welcome.

Siemon: One of the things that I see in *Nollan* and in a number of other cases is an increasing distinction in the Court's mind between those things that are well-conceived and well thought-out and logical and what we otherwise term *post hoc* rationalizations. I see the Court looking at the plan not as a biblical document but as a first threshold. In other words, has there been a well-conceived, thought-out process of which this regulatory activity is a part? Or, does the local government take the person's land and then come up with all these good reasons after the fact? In *Nollan* the California Coastal Commission did not have a coherent plan for protecting the views of the ocean from public ways. Had there been, there might have been a greater judicial deference. I understand what Alan Weinstein is saying, and you're right. But it was the nexus that ultimately fell down substantively.

Strong: I think that *Keystone* and *Nollan* reinforce the view that regulation undertaken for purposes of health and safety may still be subjected to a less stringent review than regulation which advances aesthetic purposes. *Nollan* raises, but does not answer, the question of whether "protecting the public's ability to see the beach, assisting the public in overcoming the "psychological barrier" to using the beach created by a developed shorefront, and preventing congestion on the public beaches" advances a legitimate state interest. However, *Nollan* does introduce a more interventionist role for the courts in determining whether the public purpose to be advanced by regulation is sufficiently linked to the restrictions imposed on the private property. This expanded role for the judiciary could constrain regulators in their efforts to protect resources; it certainly invites more litigation.

Tarlock: Somebody ought to just say that California outdid Doonsbury. If you read too much into that case because of those facts you get terribly hung up.

Delogu: I think Sy Schulman's observation is a correct one, but the thing he wants out of his premises is, I think, unattainable in a society that is constantly changing its own sense of what is basic, what is legitimate, for a town to plan for. We would all agree that towns today cannot pass a comprehensive plan that is facially exclusionary. At the same time, if you're asking courts to define the precise point at which legitimacy ends and illegitimacy begins, in other words, to define in a rational way the edge of exclusion and the beginning of reasonable protection, given carrying capacity and other constraints that may exist in a town or locality, I think we'll never have that degree of delineation in court cases that will enable planners, with that neatness of a math problem, to direct their client group appropriately.

Blaesser: Let me try to refocus our discussion a little bit. There is a distinction between federal substantive due process and what's happening in the states. After the recent U.S. Supreme Court decisions in *First English* and *Nollan*, the question is whether substantive due process is alive and well, even in the state cases. Is the notion of substantive due process something that should guide planners as they go about their planning practice, or is it something that has now been absorbed into the Fifth Amendment as Ted Carey suggests? I don't believe that substantive due process standard, separate from the takings issue, is dead either at the federal level or at the state level, where it is known as the arbitrary and capricious standard.

Sullivan: Again, I want to raise the issue of not relying on any federal substantive due process analysis. One, it goes back to the *Lochner* era, which is dead except when the courts want to resurrect it on occasion. Second, don't confuse state constitutional provisions on due process with the federal. They have their own history, they have their own background, and to confuse the two of them and find them to be exactly the same is a mistake in approach. Third, parsimoniously we ought to go up the ladder I suggested earlier, and not run off to some sort of notion of reasonableness or fairness which changes and masks judicial value choices rather than arrives at any principled approach on how planning ought to be done. That ought to be done legislatively, not in the courts.

Linkage Between Federal and State Law

Kmiec: Ed, I think there is some linkage between state and federal law. If for no other reason, there is a supremacy clause in the U.S. Constitution. By virtue of that clause there are requirements in the federal Constitution, as construed by the Supreme Court, that the states must observe. The states and state courts can sometimes insulate themselves from being second-guessed by the federal courts by relying wholly on state provisions and their state constitutions. Nevertheless, the landowner is entitled to some protection at the federal level that was not as clear prior to *First English* or *Nollan*. That being said, I agree entirely with the notion that there is great variation among state law. I think the various state law land use treatises document the fact that substantive due process is indeed quite alive at the state level, that frequently courts engage in nothing more sophisticated than the balancing of benefits and burdens, and if they happen to hit the federal constitutional standards correctly it's purely by accident.

Delogu: I think that the concept of substantive due process has more validity within the states than the discussion has suggested. A "rose by any other name" is still substantive due process, whether the courts are talking about reasonableness, or fairness, or arbitrary and capricious, or the absence of enabling legislation or that the data will not support that degree of constraint. All of that is substantive due process, which the state court is imposing.

Schulman: That was a very helpful comment for us. It collectively clarifies what we're up to. It is Fourteenth Amendment mentality and reasoning that applies even though it's not Fourteenth Amendment language.

**SECTION 5:
PRINCIPLE 5:
EQUAL PROTECTION**

◆ **5.01 The Equal Protection Clause**

The Fourteenth Amendment to the federal Constitution provides that no state "shall deny to any person within its jurisdiction the equal protection of the laws." The Fourteenth Amendment applies to local governments within states. ◇

◆ **5.02 Equal Protection Defined; Scope of Application**

Under the equal protection clause, a local government must show that a classification in a land use regulation is justified by a legitimate governmental purpose and that the regulation is administered fairly. The judicial review standard that the courts apply under the equal protection clause varies with the nature of the interest affected by the regulation. ◇

Comment

All land use regulations classify land uses for regulatory purposes. The administration of land use ordinances also is selective. The equal protection clause requires fair classifications in the text of land use regulations and fair administration.

Equal Protection Illustration No. 1

A zoning ordinance requires special permits for mobile homes in single-family residential districts, defining *mobile homes* as homes that are manufactured as a unit and transported to their building site. The ordinance does not require a special permit for homes that are constructed on site from manufactured components. The text of the ordinance raises an equal protection problem because land use regulation is concerned with the impact of a use on its neighborhood, not how it is brought to its site.

Equal Protection Illustration No. 2

A zoning ordinance requires special permits for *manufactured homes* in single-family residential districts. The municipality has granted permits for homes built with manufactured components but has denied permits for mobile homes transported to their sites. This selective administration of the special permit requirement raises an equal protection problem for the reason stated in Equal Protection Illustration No. 1.

◆ 5.03 Judicial Standards for Determining Equal Protection Violations

1. *Federal.*   The Supreme Court has adopted three tiers of judicial review standards that federal courts apply when a claim is made that a land use regulation or its administration violates the equal protection clause:
    a. *Rational Relationship.* The federal courts apply a rational relationship standard of judicial review when economic interests in property are affected. This standard of judicial review applies in most land use cases. Under this standard of judicial review, a classification must have a rational relationship to a legitimate governmental purpose, and the land use regulation is presumed constitutional.
    b. *Strict Scrutiny.* The federal courts apply a strict scrutiny standard of judicial review when a classification affects a fundamental constitutional interest or when a classification is suspect. This standard reverses the presumption of constitutionality. Under this

standard of judicial review, the burden shifts to the local government to show that a classification advances a compelling governmental interest.

c. *Middle-tier.* The federal courts apply a middle-tier standard of judicial review when a classification affects quasi-suspect interests, such as gender or illegitimacy. This standard modifies the presumption of constitutionality. Under this standard of judicial review, a classification must have a substantial rather than a necessary relationship to an important rather than a compelling governmental interest. The federal courts have not applied this judicial review standard in land use cases.

2. *States.*   Some state courts apply the federal tiers of equal protection review. Other state courts do not apply the federal tiers, but have adopted their own standards of equal protection review. They may apply a more rigorous standard of judicial review and reverse the presumption of constitutionality if fundamental constitutional interests are affected by a land use classification or if the classification is suspect. In cases where economic interests are affected, some states apply a more rigorous standard of judicial review that is similar to federal middle tier review. ◊

Comment

Federal.   The federal courts apply the tiered standards of judicial review in all equal protection cases. The decision on which standard of judicial review to apply is critical because the standard of judicial review the court applies in a case usually determines the outcome.

Federal courts apply the deferential rational relationship standard when only economic interests in land are affected. Most land use regulations, such as zoning, fall in this category. The federal courts usually do not find a violation of the equal protection clause under this standard because they presume that the land use regulation or its administration is constitutional.

Under the strict scrutiny judicial review standard, the federal court reverses the presumption of constitutionality. The local government must show that the land use regulation advances a compelling governmental interest. The courts almost never find that the governmental interest advanced is compelling.

Because race is a suspect classification, the federal courts apply the strict scrutiny standard when a claim is made that a land use ordinance or its administration is racially discriminatory. The Supreme Court cases hold that racial discrimination need only be a partial motivating factor in a land use decision, but allow the government to rebut racial motive by showing that the decision was based on legitimate, nonracial grounds. If this is done, the strict scrutiny standard does not apply. The Court's decisions make it clear that racial discrimination is difficult to prove in land use cases. For this reason, many of the land use cases involving alleged discrimination have been brought under the federal Fair Housing Act which does not require proof of racial discriminatory intent, only discriminatory effect.

The federal courts apply strict scrutiny judicial review when the right of privacy is affected by a regulation. Because the right to an abortion is protected by the right of privacy, the courts have applied strict scrutiny judicial review to regulations prohibiting abortion clinics.

The U.S. Supreme Court has refused to apply the middle-tier standard of judicial review to the denial of a special use permit for a group home for the mentally retarded (See the *Cleburne* case, cited below). Instead, the Court applied the rational relationship standard of judicial review to invalidate the permit denial. This case indicates that the federal courts may be more willing to invalidate land use regulations and their administration under the rational relationship standard.

Caselaw

City of Cleburne, Texas v. Cleburne Living Center, 473 U.S. 432 (1985) [V-2.05]
Village of Arlington Heights v. Metropolitan Housing Dev. Corp., 429 U.S. 252 (1977) (Arlington Heights I) [V-2.47]
Metropolitan Housing Dev. Corp. v. Village of Arlington Heights, 558 F.2d 1283 (7th Cir. 1977) (Arlington Heights II), *cert. denied,* 434 U.S. 1025 (1978).

States. The state courts apply judicial review standards in equal protection cases that are similar to those applied by the federal courts, but some state courts have adopted different standards of judicial review based on their state constitutions. A state court may preclude the review of its decision in the Supreme Court if it based its equal protection standard on the state constitution. A state court is more likely to find an equal protection violation than a federal court under the rational relationship standard when a land use classification is challenged as applied to a landowner's property.

A number of state courts apply the equal protection clause more rigorously than the federal courts in cases in which a claim is made that a zoning ordinance excludes affordable housing, or that it prohibits group homes or nontraditional families or affects other interests that are vulnerable to adverse regulation in the land use control process. In these cases, the state courts reverse the presumption of constitutionality and require the government to justify the basis for the land use classification.

Most state courts hold that a zoning ordinance may not prohibit group homes or nontraditional families in single-family zoning districts. Some state courts have also invalidated zoning restrictions on mobile homes in single family districts.

Caselaw

Southern Burlington County NAACP v. Township of Mt. Laurel (Mt. Laurel II), 456 A.2d 390 (N.J. 1983)
Robinson Township v. Knoll, 302 N.W.2d 146 (Mich. 1981)
Southern Burlington County NAACP v. Mt. Laurel Township (Mt. Laurel I), 336 A.2d 713 (N.J. 1975), *appeal dismissed and cert. denied,* 423 U.S. 808 (1975)

Equal Protection Illustration No. 3

A landowner owns a tract of land in a single-family residential district. She claims the district is improperly mapped and that the municipality should have included her land in a multifamily residential district.

Most federal courts will apply the rational relationship standard and uphold this classification. A claim of this type might succeed in state court, but the landowner will usually claim that the classification is a taking of property as applied to her land rather than an as applied violation of the equal protection clause.

Equal Protection Illustration No. 4

A municipality refuses to rezone land for a multifamily, government-subsidized housing project. The project site is zoned single-family but located in an area which is zoned and developed for multifamily use. The municipality has usually granted rezonings to multifamily use in this type of area. The developer claims the refusal to rezone was racially motivated. A federal court will apply the strict scrutiny standard of judicial review if it finds that the refusal to rezone was even partly motivated by racial discrimination, because racial classifications are suspect.

The municipality claims the refusal to rezone was justified because the area surrounding the developer's tract of land is zoned and developed for single-family uses. Even if the court finds that the refusal to rezone was partially motivated by racial discrimination, it will uphold the refusal to rezone if it finds that the municipality's reason for its refusal to rezone was legitimate and nonracial. The federal courts take a less deferential view of zoning claimed to be racially discriminatory when it is challenged under the federal Fair Housing Act instead of than the equal protection clause.

Some state courts would hold this refusal to rezone invalid as exclusionary zoning because it restricts housing opportunities for lower income groups. Some state courts would also hold an entire zoning ordinance exclusionary if it did not provide adequate opportunities for lower-income housing.

Equal Protection Illustration No. 5

A landowner submits an application for a special permit for a group home for the mentally retarded in a residential district. The group home will contain medical treatment facilities. The zoning ordinance authorizes the zoning board of adjustment to grant special permits for group homes for the mentally retarded in a residential district if they are compatible with the residential area.

The board refuses to grant the permit for the group home, because visits by doctors and other medical specialists called to provide treatment would increase traffic congestion in the residential area. A federal or state court would have to decide whether this reason justified the permit denial or whether it was a pretext for a discriminatory permit decision.

5.04 Symposium Discussion

Mandelker: The three tiers of federal equal protection review are very important for planners to know. State courts do not always apply them. In addition, state courts have not decided many land use cases that raise racial discrimination problems. Cases raising this problem are usually brought in federal court. The state exclusionary zoning cases are not based on federal equal protection doctrine. They are usually based on the state constitutions, which are interpreted in a relatively different way. Therefore, it is important not to confuse or equate the federal equal protection standards described in this section with state exclusionary zoning cases.

I might also point out that major group home cases in such states as California and New Jersey are based on special state constitutional provisions. In California, for example, the court relied on a fundamental right of privacy it found imbedded in the state constitution. Because this constitutional right is fundamental, the state court reversed the presumption of constitutionality and placed the burden to justify the restriction on the local government, just as the federal courts do when they apply strict scrutiny judicial review. But this is not the same thing as applying federal equal protection standards and the special judicial doctrines that have grown up around them.

The "Anything Goes" Test?

Siemon: I agree with Dan that it is important for planners to understand the three tiers of federal equal protection review. I would emphasize that equal protection comes into play in a very limited set of circumstances in land use regulation. By and large, if a regulatory program or governmental decision meets due process standards and does not violate any incorporated constitutional principles, then it is unlikely that equal protection will come into play. There are, to be sure, certain limited circumstances where a regulatory program has no rational basis for its discriminatory purpose. But look at the rational basis standard established by the U.S. Supreme Court in *City of New Orleans v. Dukes*, 427 U.S. 297 (1976), where the Court exempted one class of hot dog vendors from a proscription against sidewalk selling because it had eight years of experience in selling hot dogs. I think Judge Goldberg of the Fifth Circuit Court of Appeals was correct when he described this first tier equal protection test as the "anything goes" test.

Blaesser: But there still are limits even to the relatively relaxed standard applied by the courts when assessing land use regulations under the equal protection clause. For example, the equal protection clause can be used to invalidate a zoning regulation that differentiates among uses so as to effectively exclude a business altogether from a zoning district in which other businesses that are not that different from the excluded business are permitted. Of course, if the zoning regulation is racially motivated or infringes on a fundamental constitutional right, the strict scrutiny test, rather than the rational relationship test, applies.

Other Forms of Discriminatory Land Use Regulations

Schulman: I think that there are many forms of nonracial discrimination that are widely practiced by planners. For example, what about a zoning ordinance that sets aside residential land uses by income category, or by form of ownership, such as rental or condo or cooperative? What about regulations based on age limitations such as senior citizens only, or no children under 18? What guidance does the equal protection clause give us in these circumstances?

Mandelker: In these cases the courts may well decide that a fundamental constitutional right is infringed or that the classification is suspect. They would then apply a heightened standard of equal protection review and might invalidate the regulation. These examples indicate that the equal protection clause still has bite in land use cases.

Schulman: Does the equal protection clause require that all commercial areas be equally treated and regulated?

Blaesser: No. Now you are speaking about the basic fact that zoning involves the classification of property, and, where there is any reasonable basis for classification, the courts will generally uphold the regulation. For example, the courts have rejected equal protection challenges to regulations that distinguish between shopping centers and other retail stores, or between chain stores and other stores.

Schulman: What about taxation? Can a tax be applied in a discriminatory manner, for example, increasing the tax rate in one area as against the rest of the municipality, so as to achieve a desired planning goal? The planning goal could be to channel development into one area while reducing development pressure elsewhere. That goal could be achieved by using different tax levels to either induce or inhibit development.

Mandelker: Most state constitutions contain a uniformity of taxation clause similar to the equal protection clause. The uniformity of taxation clause requires a uniform tax rate throughout the jurisdiction. Some courts have upheld tax abatements for redevelopment projects, but this is done by lowering the tax assessment, not the tax rate.

SECTION 6:
PRINCIPLE 6:
JUST COMPENSATION (THE TAKING CLAUSE)

◆ **6.01 The Fifth Amendment**

The Fifth Amendment provides in relevant part:
"[N]or shall private property be taken for public use, without just compensation." ◊

Comment on Eminent Domain

The discussion that follows is primarily concerned with the issue of whether planning and other regulatory decisions can result in a taking of property, even though there has been no formal transfer of title to the government. This taking of property indirectly through the impact of regulation is different from the taking of property through the formal exercise by government of eminent domain. Eminent domain is exercised pursuant of a plan which recommends the acquisition of title to particular property through the negotiation of price with the landowner; if such negotiation proves unsuccessful, fair market value for the property interest to be taken is assessed and awarded through a judicial proceeding.

Because recent Supreme Court decisions may increase the likelihood of regulation being characterized as a taking requiring compensation, planners in certain cases may wish to consider the direct exercise of formal eminent domain proceedings to ensure a successful planning outcome. The use of eminent domain for most planning objectives is likely to be upheld, since courts give substantial weight to legislative determinations in this area. In particular, the public use requirement for the exercise of eminent domain is now viewed by the Supreme Court as coterminous with the scope of a local government's police power. An actual use by the public is no longer required; it is enough that there be a benefit to the public.

Caselaw

Hawaii Housing Authority v. Midkiff, 467 U.S. 229 (1984) [V-2.18]
Berman v. Parker, 348 U.S. 26 (1954) [V-2.03]

Eminent Domain Illustration No. 1

A city condemns a landowner's property in order to stem the extension of urban blight. The city intends to clear the land and resell it to another private owner who is willing to construct new commercial space. If the legislature believes this will benefit the community, it will be accepted by the courts as an appropriate subject for the exercise of eminent domain.

Eminent Domain Illustration No. 2

A city condemns a private site for a parking garage to be constructed by the city and leased to a private operator. The operator is free to set parking rates at any level and may use part of the property for a restaurant. A federal court would likely defer to the city's legislative judgment. However, because of the sometimes more demanding view of public use required under state law, the presence of the private enterprise and the fact that the city lacks control over the parking rates, might cause a state court to invalidate the city's action.

Comment on Regulatory Taking

Having distinguished formal exercises of eminent domain, the remainder of this section focuses on determining when a land use regulation becomes a taking. The Supreme Court has indicated that there is no set or precise formula for this determination. Rather, the Court balances a number of what it has called *ad hoc* factors. Seldom is any single factor dispositive.

One such factor is the character of the government's regulatory action. Here, the Court is particularly sensitive to whether the regulation can be fairly said to be designed to prevent harms, rather than extract benefits from the landowner. The distinction between harm prevention and benefit extraction is seldom precise, and there is sharp disagreement on the Court over this issue.

A factor that is less controversial on the Court is the factor of permanent physical occupation. In the Court's words, a permanent physical occupation is a *per se* or automatic taking. If a regulation authorizes this type of physical occupation, the Court views the intrusion as serious, whether or not such physical interference causes a substantial economic loss or serves an important public purpose. In a recent case, the Court has seemingly expanded the types of physical interferences which may give rise to a *per se* taking, putting less emphasis on the permanence of the occupation.

Another factor considered by the Court is whether the landowner's investment was reasonable in light of his knowledge of the regulatory program. The Court has not been particularly clear about this reasonable investment-backed expectation factor, but it would appear to be less significant than either the character of the regulation, as discussed above, or the economic impact of the regulation, discussed below. In fact, in one of its recent cases, the Court expressly disavowed the notion that unilateral notice by the government can diminish private property rights as opposed to government benefits or privileges.

Most regulatory taking claims are triggered by the perceived economic impact of the regulation. This is another of the factors balanced by the Court. In assessing the impact of a regulation on what the Court calls economic viability, the Court views the property as a whole. Thus, if the regulation takes the mineral rights underlying a parcel of land, the fact that economically viable uses can be made of the surface and air rights is a significant fact which may preclude the finding of a regulatory taking.

There is one recent decision which suggests that a total abrogation of an essential stick in the bundle of property rights can lead to a regulatory taking. Only one such stick has thus far been identified: the taking of the right, at one's death, to pass on property either by will or under statutory rights of interstate succession.

A final consideration for the Court is whether the regulation can be said to provide reciprocal benefits to the regulated party. If the regulated landowner is no more harshly treated than anyone else and if he, like all others, receives what is said to be an "average reciprocity of advantage," then no taking may be said to result. This last consideration is something of a summation of the Court's entire approach. It also reveals the ultimate objective of the Fifth Amendment, which is to prevent the local legislative body from burdening one individual with costs that should be borne by the community as a whole.

Caution: As in any area of the law dominated by constitutional considerations, there is sometimes less consistency in the application or statement of the above factors in the Court's decisions than the summary here may suggest. Moreover, while the Court is careful to observe precedent, changes in personnel, and the mere passage of time, ultimately yield differences in approach and emphasis.

Caselaw

Nollan v. California Coastal Commission, 483 U.S. 825 (1987) [V-2.32]
Hodel v. Irving, 481 U.S. 704 (1987) [V-2.19]
Keystone Bituminous Coal Association v. DeBenedictis, 480 U.S. 470 (1987) [V-2.21]
Loretto v. Teleprompter Manhattan CATV Corp., 458 U.S. 419 (1982) [V-2.23]

Penn Central Transportation Company v. City of New York, 438 U.S. 104
(1978) [V-2.34]
Pennsylvania Coal Company v. Mahon, 260 U.S. 393 (1922) [V-2.36]

◆ 6.02 Regulatory Taking Defined

A regulatory taking may be found to have occurred in light of the following considerations or factors. With rare exception, no single factor is dispositive: (1) a land use regulation does not relate to a legitimate state
interest; or (2) assuming a legitimate state interest, the regulation does not
substantially advance that interest; or (3) the advancement of a legitimate
state interest places the disproportionate burden of securing a benefit
upon a single landowner when it is more properly borne by the general
community; or (4) the regulation entails a permanent physical occupation;
or (5) reasonable investments were made prior to general notice of the regulatory program; or (6) the economic effect of the regulation deprives the
landowner of all, or substantially all, beneficial use of the property, and
there are no off-setting reciprocal benefits; or (7) the regulation abrogates
an essential element of private property. Because these factors require factual inquiries, it is unlikely that the mere enactment of a law or the promul-
gation of a regulation will result in a regulatory taking.

A regulatory taking may be either temporary or permanent, with compensation required for the period the regulation is in effect. The economic
impact of the regulation is determined in relation to the entire property interest owned by the regulated party, which can range from a nonposses-
sory easement interest to a fee simple absolute. The nature, validity, or
definition of property interests is determined by state law, even in federal
court. Regulatory taking principles are not applied where the regulation
can be fairly characterized as necessary to prevent a harm or a nuisance. ◊

Comment

For a considerable period of time, there was some doubt as to whether the
government was required to compensate for the period prior to an ordinance being declared invalid as a regulatory taking. That doubt has now
been eliminated. Where government's activities have already worked a
taking, no subsequent action by the government can relieve it of the duty
to provide compensation for the period during which the taking was effective. In short, temporary takings are not different in kind from permanent
takings, and both clearly require the payment of compensation under the
Constitution. Thus, if a local government adopts a regulation in May of

1989, which, under the U.S. Supreme Court's multifactored taking analysis is found to be a taking in September of 1989, compensation is required for the period from May to September and for such additional period, if any, that the regulation remains in effect beyond the court's taking judgment.

Temporary takings may not occur merely as a result of normal delays in the permitting process. However, if delays are used in a deliberate manner to forestall development, such action may be treated as a *de facto* determination by the regulatory body for taking purposes. The Court has not addressed the specific question of moratoriums in this context. For example, if during a moratorium a landowner can demonstrate the presence of one or more of the above taking factors, especially the deprivation of all, or substantially all, economic viability during the moratorium period, it could be argued that this constitutes a temporary taking requiring compensation.

Caselaw

First English Evangelical Lutheran Church of Glendale v. County of Los Angeles, 482 U.S. 304 (1987) [V-2.12]

Hodel v. Irving, 481 U.S. 704 (1987) [V-2.19]

Keystone Bituminous Coal Association v. DeBenedictis, 480 U.S. 470 (1987) [V-2.21]

Loretto v. Teleprompter Manhattan CATV Corp., 458 U.S. 419 (1982) [V-2.23]

San Diego Gas and Electric Co. v. City of San Diego (Brennan, J. dissenting), 450 U.S. 621 (1981) [V-2.40]

Penn Central Transportation Company v. City of New York, 438 U.S. 104 (1978) [V-2.34]

Pennsylvania Coal Company v. Mahon, 260 U.S. 393 (1922) [V-2.36]

Mugler v. Kansas, 123 U.S. 623 (1887) [V-2.30]

Taking/Moratorium Illustration No. 1

A landowner's property, which is adjacent to the municipal airport, is zoned residential. By all accounts, the classification is ill-suited to the property and has largely been used by the local government to keep the property undeveloped and in a *de facto* holding zone. The landowner petitions for a rezoning, but is denied, having been informed that the city has placed a formal moratorium on all rezonings for two years in order to study the appropriate uses for the property. A temporary regulatory taking may be said to have occurred if the landowner can show that the existing classification does not substantially advance a legitimate state interest or that the effect of the existing classification is a deprivation of all, or substantially all, economic value. In all likelihood, the two-year moratorium on rezonings is not an excusable normal delay. This is an uncertain result, however, since the U.S. Supreme Court's temporary taking analysis has yet to be applied directly to moratoria of this nature.

Taking/Moratorium/Illustration No. 2

The facts are the same as in Illustration No. 1 above, except now the landowner is informed that the moratorium will be lifted and a rezoning granted if he will donate a third of his land to the city for airport parking. The landowner agrees, but only under protest, stating his intent to bring a court action to challenge the exaction. The municipality has an established protest procedure, which allows a partial rezoning to be granted pending the judicial challenge. The landowner is successful in having the exaction declared a regulatory taking on the ground that it impermissibly places a burden on a specific landowner that should be borne by the general public. Damages for the regulatory taking may be less in this case because of the availability of a procedure to obtain a rezoning and construction permits for at least a portion of the parcel while the matter was in litigation.

♦ **6.03 Judicial Standards for Determining a Regulatory Taking**

1. Regulation Unrelated to a Legitimate State Interest. In most cases, the courts will defer to legislative judgment. Thus, if under any reasonable conception the regulation can be said to promote the health, safety or welfare of the community, it will be presumed to have a rational basis. However, in rare cases, a land use regulation may be so irrational in design that the regulation will be declared invalid on its face. Alternatively, the regulation may be facially valid, but applied in a manner which does not advance the public interest. ◊

Comment

Courts do not have a license to judge the effectiveness of legislation or its policy wisdom. However, courts sometimes do examine the operative provisions of a statute, not just its stated purpose, in assessing its true nature. While this substantive due process scrutiny is more common in state court, the Supreme Court has stated that a taking may result where the extent of the public interest is shown by the statute to be limited. One member of the Court has suggested that a regulation which does not promote a legitimate state interest might not be a taking because of the absence of public use, but might nevertheless give rise to an action for money damages under 42 U.S.C. §1983, which provides a remedy for deprivations of civil—including property—rights.

Caselaw

Keystone Bituminous Coal Ass'n v. DeBenedictis, 480 U.S. 470 (1987)
[V-2.21]
Nectow v. City of Cambridge, et al., 277 U.S. 183 (1928) [V-2.31]
Village of Euclid, Ohio v. Ambler Realty Company, 272 U.S. 365 (1926)
[V-2.49]
Pennsylvania Coal v. Mahon, 260 U.S. 393 (1922) [V-2.36]

Facial Challenge Illustration

The state legislature enacts a law whose stated purpose is prohibiting mining that causes subsidence. However, a review of various provisions in the
law reveals that the law is for the special, private benefit of a few landowners. For example, the affected landowners are expressly authorized to
waive the provisions of the law, notwithstanding the fact that such waiver
could result in negative environmental externalities being imposed on the
community-at-large. A court would very likely declare such a law invalid
on its face because it does not further any public purpose.

As Applied Challenge Illustration

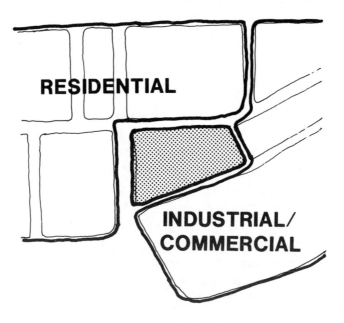

A landowner's property is placed in a residential district. The property is bordered on the south and east by industrial/commercial development and to the north and west by residences. The evidence in the record suggests that the natural development of the property would be industrial and that no practical use can be made of the land in question for residential purposes. The residential zoning is invalid because the governmental power to interfere by zoning regulations with the property interests of a landowner by restricting the character of his use is not unlimited, and such restriction cannot be imposed if it does not bear a substantial relation to the public health, safety, morals, or general welfare.

◆ **2. Failure of Regulation to Substantially Advance a Legitimate State Interest**

A regulatory taking results if the regulation or prohibition does not substantially advance a legitimate state interest. There must be a clearly established nexus between the regulatory means and the end sought to be achieved. This is a higher standard of review than the court employs in its general review of economic regulation, outside of the regulation of property. ◊

Comment

Most land use regulation affects solely economic interests. However, the judicial standard of review for a regulatory taking claim is different from the standard applied to due process or equal protection claims. The Court has required that the regulation substantially advance a legitimate state interest—not that a court could view the state as having rationally decided that the measure adopted might achieve some state objective. Thus, the court views the Fifth Amendment's taking clause "to be more than a pleading requirement, and compliance with it to be more than an exercise in cleverness and imagination." In short, judicial scrutiny of governmental justifications in taking cases is *more* strict than that used to review other economic regulation, although less strict than that used when regulation affects speech or religion [see Part II, Sections 7 and 8]. Some members of the Court dispute the appropriateness of this higher standard of review in challenges to land use regulation, and it remains to be seen how conscientiously it is applied.

Caselaw

Pennell v. City of San Jose, 108 S.Ct. 849 (1988) [V-2.35]
Nollan v. California Coastal Commission, 483 U.S. 825 (1987) [V-2.32]
Agins v. City of Tiburon, 447 U.S. 255 (1980) [V-2.01]

"Linkage" Illustration No. 1

A developer of office space for high-income professionals is required, as a condition for development permits or other zoning approvals, to contribute fees to a low- and moderate-income housing fund. The municipality has little empirical evidence demonstrating the relationship between office development, especially office development for high-income professionals, and increased demand for low- and moderate-income housing. Moreover, unlike parks and streets, housing is, with some exception, provided through the private market. Thus, the empirical evidence establishing the requisite nexus is weak, both because it fails to demonstrate that the development was the cause of the demand and because the housing supply is less static, given the entry of private suppliers, than is the case with traditional municipal services. The validity of this type of linkage fee under the above circumstances would be open to serious challenge.

"Linkage" Illustration No. 2

A factory developer in a community with a severe housing shortage is required to make a contribution to a low- and moderate-income housing fund. The funds will be kept in a separate account and used as subsidies of various kinds to develop low- and moderate-income housing within the purchase range of the factory's anticipated workforce and within a reasonable geographic distance of the factory site. The municipality is better able to empirically show the nexus between this type of development and the desired housing than in "Linkage" Illustration No. 1 above. Moreover, some effort is being made to have most of the benefits of the regulation return to the regulated party. Again, however, since housing supply is not directly a function of municipal, rather than private, activity, this may suggest that the municipal objective to increase supply is more properly borne by the community generally. The validity of this type of linkage fee under the above circumstances is more likely to survive judicial review, but it is not certain to do so.

♦ **3. Improper Singling Out of One Landowner to Bear a Community Objective**

A legitimate state interest is not substantially advanced if it singles out a particular landowner to bear a burden which should be borne by the public as a whole. ◊

Comment

Closely related to the nexus required between regulatory means and ends discussed in Section 6.03 [2] is the nexus required between the regulatory end and the particular regulated landowner. Most members of the U.S. Supreme Court agree that avoiding the singling out of a landowner for a burden which is more properly accomplished through general tax and spending mechanisms or other generally applicable laws is the primary objective of the Fifth Amendment's just compensation requirement. The sufficiency of this nexus is also likely subject to the Court's heightened scrutiny, discussed in Section 6.03[2] above.

A regulation truly aimed at preventing harms, rather than securing community benefits, will more readily be found to satisfy this aspect of the Court's nexus requirement and is subject to more deferential judicial review. Thus, if a particular use can be fairly characterized as nuisance-like or injurious to health and safety, the character of the government's action in regulating such a use may largely insulate the government from regulatory taking concerns. While one or more members of the Court have from time-to-time downplayed the significance of the harm—benefit distinction, the issue remains very much alive in the Court's cases.

Of course, one person's harm may be said to be another's benefit. Thus, Justice Brennan characterized landmark preservation in one case as avoiding a harm; whereas, Justice Rehnquist viewed it as the placement of an affirmative duty. Despite the unresolved nature of this issue, it is fair to state that planning activity which is directed and characterized in terms of harm avoidance is more likely to be upheld, and far less likely to give rise to a successful claim for damages.

Caution: Even if a regulatory requirement satisfies the nexus requirements discussed in Sections 6.03 [2] and [3], it may still be found to be a regulatory taking if other factors, such as economic nonviability or physical occupation, are found to exist by virtue of the regulatory program, and these factors in the Court's balancing process are, in a given case, weighed more heavily (see the Illustrations in Section 6.03 [6] discussing the inter-relationship of taking factors).

Caselaw

Pennell v. City of San Jose, 108 S.Ct. 849 (1988) [V-2.35]
Nollan v. California Coastal Commission, 483 U.S. 825 (1987) [V-2.32]
Agins v. City of Tiburon, 447 U.S. 255 (1980) [V-2.01]
Penn Central Transportation Company v. City of New York, 438 U.S. 104 (1978) [V-2.34]
Goldblatt v. Town of Hempstead, 369 U.S. 590 (1962) [V-2.15]
Hadacheck v. Sebastian, 239 U.S. 394 (1915) [V-2.17]

Off-Site Road Improvement Fee Illustration

A landowner's residential development will generate a significant number of trips, of varying lengths, to and from the new houses. These trips will place a burden on the existing road system external to the development. A traffic engineer using accurate measurement techniques ascertains the number of trips to be generated; planning officials and civil engineers determine the necessary road improvements to accommodate the additional trips; and the cost of the improvements is assessed as a fee per house based on the plat submitted by landowner.

Assuming the imposition of the fee will not deny economic viability, it is apparent that it serves a legitimate governmental interest. Provided the landowner is given an adequate opportunity to challenge the fee calculation, and further provided that the fee does not reflect capital improvements unnecessary to meet the needs generated by the landowner, the road improvement fee should survive the requirement of a nexus between this landowner and the regulatory fee.

Exaction for "Cultural Center" Illustration

A residential developer is required to make a per dwelling unit contribution to the village cultural center. Again, there must be a showing of a nexus between the activity of this developer and the regulatory fee. Unlike the road improvement fee in the above example, however, the need for additional village cultural activities generated by any particular development may be impossible to quantify. More significantly, the absence of cultural activities is hardly attributable to this developer. For this reason, this fee is likely to be improper. The village cultural center should be financed with a general finance mechanism.

Parking Exaction Illustration

A coastal commission requires a restaurant owner to dedicate land for beach parking as a condition for the restaurant's improvement permit. The condition is largely unrelated to the activity of this landowner, and more intended to provide a general community benefit. Under the court's heightened scrutiny in taking cases, the parking requirement would likely be a regulatory taking by reason of the absence of a causal nexus between the requirement and this landowner.

School Fee Illustration

In order to secure permits, a residential developer is required to make a contribution to the local school system on a per dwelling, flat fee basis. The developer argues that much of the development, by virtue of the location and size of the units, will appeal substantially to unmarried individuals and couples with nonschool-age children. Moreover, there is no limitation on where the fees can be spent. Because the fee could have been calculated on a per bedroom or square foot basis and limited in a manner to benefit this development, it is open to greater challenge under the Supreme Court's heightened scrutiny.

◆ **4. Character of Government Action/Physical Occupation**

A taking will more readily be found when the interference with property can be characterized as a physical invasion by government. Such physical occupations are said to always be takings, and they are called *per se takings*. Moreover, it does not matter whether the physical invasion is by the government itself, or by those authorized by the government, or that the invasion accomplishes an important public benefit, or that it may be minimal. ◊

Comment

As a body, the Supreme Court is intolerant of regulations accompanied by physical occupation, even when such are relatively minor in size or scope. In this regard, even one member of the Court who has been highly deferential to planning and regulatory prerogatives has stated, "The Fifth Amendment draws no distinction between grand larceny and petty larceny." The Court has established this *per se* rule because of the serious nature of the property infringement entailed by an invasion—effectively destroying all of the landowner's rights (to use, exclude, or alienate for true value) the affected property.

Caselaw

Nollan v. California Coastal Commission, 483 U.S. 825 (1987) [V-2.32]
Loretto v. Teleprompter Manhattan CATV Corp., 458 U.S. 419 (1982) [V-2.23]
Kaiser Aetna v. United States, 444 U.S. 164 (1979) [V-2.20]
United States v. Causby, 328 U.S. 256 (1946) [V-2.43]

Municipally Authorized Cable Installation Illustration

A city passes an ordinance which requires that a landowner permit the physical installation of relatively small cable television wires and connections by a third party upon payment of an established nominal fee. The city's authorization of the permanent physical occupation is always a taking, even though the tenants may view the availability of cable favorably, and the installations require only minor physical attachments.

Required Donation of Beach Easement Illustration

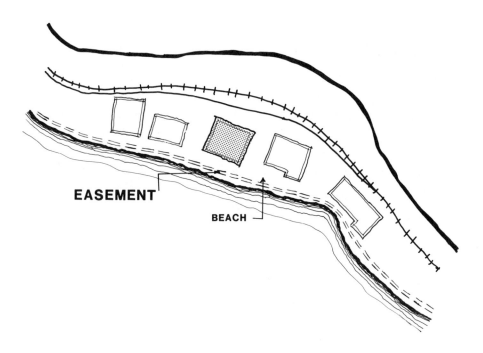

A coastal commission requires a landowner to grant a lateral beach easement for use by the general public. This is a "permanent physical occupation" within the terms of the rule, against physical occupations, since "individuals are given a permanent and continuous right to pass to and fro, so that the real property may continuously be traversed, even though no particular individual is permitted to station himself permanently upon the premises."

◆ 5. Reasonable Investment-Backed Expectations

The concern under this factor is whether the landowner was aware, or given notice, of the regulation prior to substantial and reasonable investment. ◇

Comment

What constitutes a reasonable investment-backed expectation is not clear. This factor has not figured prominently in the Supreme Court's decisions, although the Court does mention the factor. The importance of this factor has been further clouded by a recent case which suggests that the unilateral public announcement of a regulation does not authorize the government to interfere with private property rights. The factor is more relevant where the right claimed is a governmental benefit, such as a license or marketing privilege. However, the Court has stated: "The right to build on one's own property—even though its exercise can be subjected to legitimate permitting requirements—cannot remotely be described as a 'governmental benefit.'"

The concept of an investment-backed expectation is somewhat analogous to the acquisition of what is loosely termed, in the state cases, a vested right. While the Supreme Court has not equated vested rights and reasonable investment-backed expectations, it can be stated as a general matter, that unilateral action by the landowner is not sufficient to acquire a vested or protected right; rather, the landowner, in good faith, must substantially rely on the representations of, or permits issued by, the regulating body. Again, however, it should be remembered that the presence or absence of reasonable investment-backed expectations is but one factor in the Court's taking determination.

Caselaw

Nollan v. California Coastal Commission, 483 U.S. 825 (1987) [V-2.32]
Ruckelshaus v. Monsanto Co., 467 U.S. 986 (1984) [V-2.39]
Kaiser Aetna v. United States, 444 U.S. 164 (1979) [V-2.20]

Notice of Regulation Prior to Purchase Illustration

A landowner with an option to purchase property is informed that she must donate a lateral beach easement in order to obtain a construction permit. While the notice before actual investment is a relevant factor in determining whether or not a taking exists, it does not preclude the finding of a taking. For example, if the required easement donation constitutes a permanent occupation or does not substantially advance a legitimate state interest or results in a deprivation of substantially all of the property's economic viability, it may well be treated as a regulatory taking, notwithstanding the notice prior to the actual exercise of the option to purchase.

Reliance Upon Governmental Assurances Illustration

A landowner connects a previously nonnavigable pond to a navigable body of water in order to construct a private marina after receiving governmental assurances that this construction is permissible. If the government later asserts public rights of access in the marina, contrary to the previous assurances given, such action would be a deprivation of the landowner's reasonable investment-backed expectations, and would be one factor in determining the existence of a regulatory taking.

◆   **6. Deprivation of All, or Substantially All, Economically Viable Use**

The principal concern underlying this factor is that economic burdens of public actions not be disproportionately concentrated on a few persons. ◊

Comment

The deprivation of substantially all economically viable use of land is a heavy burden to satisfy. In addition, the concept of economic viability has not been defined by the Supreme Court with mathematical precision. The Court has upheld regulations that have diminished the value of property by as much as 90 percent. State courts, by contrast, seem to ascribe more importance to this diminution factor. A party whose property value has been diminished by more than 50 percent will often allege a regulatory taking, and such claims will be seriously considered in many state forums.

Even though taking claims often arise because of the economic impact of regulation, it is important to remember that diminution in value is only one of the Court's many taking factors. These factors, when considered together in a given case, may persuade the Court that a regulatory taking exists. Thus, the fact that there is a well-defined nexus between the regulatory means and end may not preclude the finding of a taking based on the economic impact of the regulation or the lack of justification for imposing the regulatory burden on the particular landowner. Alternatively, a regulation with little economic impact may still be found to lack the requisite nexus, and hence, result in a taking. However, the Supreme Court has stated that diminution of value in itself is not determinative.

In calculating the economic impact, the landowner may not divide a single parcel into discrete segments and attempt to determine whether rights in a particular segment have been entirely abrogated.

Caselaw

Nollan v. California Coastal Commission, 483 U.S. 825 (1987) [V-2.32]
Keystone Bituminous Coal Ass'n v. DeBenedictis, 480 U.S. 470 (1987) [V-2.21]
Penn Central Transportation Company v. City of New York, 438 U.S. 104 (1978) [V-2.34].
Pennsylvania Coal v. Mahon, 260 U.S. 393 (1922) [V-2.36]

Economic Impact, Standing Alone, Not Usually Determinative—Illustration

A city enacts a zoning ordinance which has the effect of requiring a local brickworks to terminate much of its operation in what has become, over time, a residential section of the city. The ordinance results in close to a 90 percent diminution in the value of the property. However, because the ordinance is substantially related to avoiding a harm caused by this landowner, it does not constitute a regulatory taking, notwithstanding its economic impact.

Calculation of Economic Impact Mitigated by Average Reciprocity of Advantage Illustration

A city enacts a sign control ordinance which applies evenly to all similarly situated landowners. While there is an adverse economic impact, there is also an implicit advantage in knowing that this general law will preclude a neighboring landowner from erecting a large or otherwise bothersome sign. Since the adverse economic impact is more than exceeded by the value of the regulatory control, it negates the use of economic impact as a taking factor.

Relationship Between Economic Viability and Other Taking Factors Illustration

A landowner's property is in a residential zone allowing one house per ten acres. Assume that the impact on the economic viability of the property is substantial and that the nexus between this large lot zoning and a legitimate governmental interest is so tenuous that based on these two factors alone, the zoning would be considered a regulatory taking.

The planning commission informs the landowner that the density can be increased to an economically viable level if the landowner makes a monetary contribution to the community park fund, or alternatively, dedicates land on the site of the proposed development for park purposes. The new development will increase the number of families and the fee or dedication requirement is precisely matched to the needs created by the landowner.

In all likelihood, despite the established nexus between the dedication requirement and the landowner's activity, a regulatory taking will still be found. This is so because the underlying ordinance resulted in a taking on the basis of economic impact and the lack of nexus between the large lot zoning and a legitimate governmental interest. Even though the condition is valid in itself, the taking is not excused by allowing the landowner the option of buying back property interests which were improperly taken by the ordinance in the first place. On the other hand, if the underlying ordinance was *not* a taking by reason of these other factors, then the nexus for the park dedication or fee appears well established and should survive judicial scrutiny.

Calculation of Impact in Relation to Whole Parcel Illustration

A city enacts a landmark preservation ordinance, the effect of which precludes a landowner from constructing an office tower in the airspace above the property. The existing economic operations on the surface of the parcel are unaffected and produce a reasonable return on investment. The landowner is unable to claim that the ordinance deprives him of all economic viability because that is determined not just in reference to the economic impact on the value of the airspace, but in reference to the property as a whole. The consideration of the whole property refers to the entire property owned by that landowner. Thus, had the landmark ordinance been applied to someone who owned only the airspace, the loss of economic viability would be near total and would constitute a far stronger taking claim.

Calculation of Impact in Relation to Whole Parcel Even if State Separately Identifies Elements of the Parcel Illustration

A state enacts a law to prevent subsidence from mining activity. A landowner owns substantial subsurface rights and, in addition, a separately recognized support estate under state law, ownership of which allows the landowner to cause subsidence by mining activity without liability. The new state law preventing subsidence abrogates the value of the separate support estate; but for taking purposes, the economic viability calculation will be done in relation to all the regulated property owned by landowner. Since the regulation left valuable subsurface rights unaffected, there is no regulatory taking.

◆   **7. Abolition of a Core or Essential Property Right**

A regulatory taking may result where legislation effectively abolishes one of the most essential elements of property. ◊

Comment

This factor is a recent addition to taking analysis, and it is not entirely clear what its scope or application will be. In particular, it is not known which elements of property will be considered by the Supreme Court to be most essential. To date, the Court has been sensitive to interference with the right to exclude, hence the *per se* taking test for physical occupations, and the right to pass on property at death. In contrast, the right to sell property has been prohibited where the remaining rights of use and disposition were deemed substantial. This principle has been largely articulated in contexts outside of land use regulation—notably with respect to Indian land. In this respect, its direct applicability to general land use matters is not fully apparent.

Caselaw

Hodel v. Irving, 481 U.S. 704 (1987) [V-2.19]
Kaiser Aetna v. United States, 444 U.S. 164 (1979) [V-2.20]
Andrus v. Allard, 444 U.S. 51 (1979) [V-2.02]

Restraint on Power to Sell Illustration

A regulation prohibits the sale of artifacts of historic value. Owners retain the right to possess, donate, or devise the artifacts. The abrogation of the power to alienate the property is only one of the strands of the property bundle, and the aggregate of the bundle must be considered before a taking will be found.

Abolition of the Power to Dispose at Death Illustration

A statute is passed, completely abolishing the descent and devise of a particular class of Indian property in order to facilitate the consolidation of fractional interests. Even though investment-backed expectations were low and the economic impact was not substantial, the abolition of an essential property right which has been part of "the Anglo-American legal system since feudal times" is a taking. The abolition is also suspect because it does not directly foster, in all cases, the regulatory objective of the consolidation of property interests. Therefore, its means-end nexus is weak.

◆ 6.04 Comparison to State Law: Overview

Virtually every state has a provision in its state constitution which parallels the prohibition in the Fifth Amendment against uncompensated takings. Many state constitutions prohibit damagings of private property as well. In state jurisprudence, the claim is also frequently characterized as a deprivation of due process. However, in view of the Supreme Court decisions which are clearly applicable to the states, which recognize an action for money damages under the Fifth Amendment's taking clause, that claim is now better characterized as a taking. However described, the requirements of the federal Constitution are a floor, not a ceiling. In other words, state provisions may extend (and frequently do extend) more generous protection to property, but not less. (See discussion in Part I, Section 1.) Because a federal floor based on *ad hoc* factual inquiries is not always predictable, and because few state decisions are actually reviewed in federal court, there is considerable variation among judicial approaches taken in the state decisions. Nevertheless, the following characteristics can be gleaned from existing state law on the subject of regulatory takings:

  1. Like other legislative action, land use laws are presumed valid, even if the law may be open to some doubt or is fairly debatable. ◊

Comment

The presumption of validity normally shields land use regulation from serious judicial reexamination in terms of whether the regulation concerns a legitimate state interest or whether that interest is promoted by a reasonable means. On its face, state law is not significantly different from the federal rule explained above. As applied, however, a number of state courts show a greater willingness to question the ends and means of regulation than the federal courts. It is clear as a matter of constitutional law that the extent to which state courts question the ends and means of regulation can be no less than that required by the U.S. Supreme Court.

◆ 2. The landowner must be left with a reasonable use, but not necessarily the highest and best or most profitable use. ◊

Comment

This state consideration mirrors the *ad hoc* considerations articulated by the Supreme Court. However, some state courts are far more willing to find a denial of reasonable beneficial use than would a federal court.

◆ 3. Some state courts engage in a balancing of benefits and burdens in resolving a regulatory taking claim. ◊

Comment

Balancing the loss to the landowner against the gain to the public is unpredictable and, it may be argued, contrary to the judicial (as opposed to the legislative) function. Judges are asked to adjudicate controversies in the application of law, not to pass on the wisdom of particular land use planning enactments. The second-guessing of the planning process merely increases unpredictability. In a state predisposed against the landowner, it may produce results which slight the minimum requirements of the Fifth Amendment. In states favorable to development, it yields results more generous than would be required federally.

6.05 Symposium Discussion

Kmiec: In my reading of the cases I discern three elements to the Supreme Court's discussion of what constitutes a regulatory taking. The first element concerns the question: Is there a public purpose at all? There are not very many cases that turn on this issue alone. This question resurrected itself in the *Keystone* case where the court struggled to distinguish

Pennsylvania Coal. The distinction that the Court lit on was that the Kohler Act in *Pennsylvania Coal* was really not protecting anyone other than a few private landowners, while in *Keystone* the Subsidence Act was expressly directed at a number of community purposes, including maintaining property for development, taxation, and more generally, a good environment for investment. So the difference was that the act was invalid in *Pennsylvania Coal* because there was only a private purpose, but the act was valid in *Keystone* because there was a public purpose. So one challenge that can theoretically be brought under the general rubric of regulatory taking is a facial challenge alleging an absence of a public purpose. This is theoretical because there are few successful cases under this element. However, this type of challenge is not likely to be successful in the future because of the difficulty of proving a taking merely on the fact of the regulation itself.

The second element is derived from *Nollan* v. *California Coastal Commission.* The case suggests that where there is a legitimate public purpose, the regulation may still be deemed a regulatory taking if it does not substantially advance that interest. That is a higher standard of review than I think the Court previously applied in taking cases. It is certainly a far higher standard of review than the Court applies when it reviews economic regulation generally. What does this nexus standard mean? It means two things. First, there must be a demonstration of a nexus between the means, i.e. the regulation, and the end sought to be achieved. Notice that the Court in *Nollan* maintained the adjective, legitimate, before the word, end, suggesting that there is a category of things that are illegitimate. The Court didn't explore what those illegitimate things were—if anything, in the context of the case, the Court suggested that the police power was very broad—instead, the Court focused on whether the regulation truly advances the goal chosen by the community under the police power. The second meaning of the *Nollan* nexus standard concerns whether or not a particular landowner is singled out to bear a disproportionate burden that should be borne by the community generally. Is the landowner being asked to rectify problems that were largely generated by others? This was not something that was argued in *Nollan,* but it's very important to the Court and at the heart of the Fifth Amendment. The Court requires a nexus not just between the regulation and the legitimate end, but also a nexus between the particular landowner and the particular government objective.

The third or additional principal element of the Supreme Court's regulatory taking examination is derived primarily from *Penn Central*—a set of considerations the Court calls *ad hoc* factors. These factors question whether the regulation causes a deprivation of substantially all economically viable use; whether there is an interference with reasonable investment-backed expectations; and finally, some consideration of the nature or character of the government's activity. Is the regulation preventing a harm, or is it a benefit-exaction disguised as a regulation? Is the regulation a physical invasion? The *Loretto* case illustrates that if regulation results in physical occupation of property, it doesn't matter what the public purpose is, or that the occupation is only *de minimis*, it's a *per se* taking. Curiously, the Court in my judgment, took some of that back in *Nollan* when it suggested that a permit could be conditioned on a concession of property rights. That doesn't quite square with its *Loretto* holding, so it remains to be seen what, if anything, it means.

Tarlock: My approach to takings issues is, in many ways, similar to Doug Kmiec's approach but I arranged some things a little differently. I start by asking two questions. First, what is the purpose of the takings clause? Next, what are the clear cases when a city can regulate without paying compensation? Only after you answer these two questions do you get to which judicial remedy—having to pay compensation or having the ordinance invalidated when it violates the Fifth Amendment—places a city at the higher risk.

Starting with the purpose question, I think there are two points. One is you have to realize that real property is different from other economic interests that are subject to regulation for the reason that Doug suggested, namely, that there is the risk of a landowner or small groups being singled out, so that triggers greater judicial scrutiny. The second point is that the taking clause is a checking function against certain exercises of government power. It's really the same one behind the First Amendment.

Then you go to the second question: What are the easier cases of regulation? There are basically three. One, of course, is nuisance prevention. Then there is the case where there is a clear reciprocity of advantage, to use Holmes' phrase. I think that type of analysis is still important because it validates a lot of conventional zoning. And finally, there is the much misunderstood doctrine of notice to property owners which grew out of a particular water law doctrine, navigational servitude. But now this idea of notice has been merged into the investment-backed expectations test.

Then you get to what's left, Don Hagman's wipeout idea, that's the destruction of value, and you ask the destruction of value of what?

Distinction Between Federal Federal and State Law?

Bauman: The fundamental problem I have with this discussion on the takings issue is the distinction that is made between federal and state law. In my judgment there is absolutely no distinction between the two. Planners who are out in the field are interested in knowing what standards to use to determine when there is a regulatory taking. It doesn't matter if it's a federal or a state law, because it's the same thing. There may be distinctions between federal and state law if you're talking about substantive due process. But when you're talking about takings law, the Supreme Court has handed down these general principles, and it effectively said in *Hamilton Bank,* "You will go litigate these things in the state courts; please don't come to federal court if at all possible." So these basic principles that are set out in Section 6.02 are applicable in the state courts.

A Dissenting View

N.Williams: Let me address some specific points in the text of Section 6. First, the U.S. Supreme Court has dealt with about 20 cases in the last 15 years and one in the previous 46 years. The state courts turn out about 600 opinions per year. It's my view that the Supreme Court's takings decisions may not last. Second, it is suggested in the Comment under Section 6.01 that planners now should give increased consideration to eminent domain and public ownership. I'm not that ardent an advocate of public ownership of a whole lot of land with the responsibility of maintenance and everything else. I would suggest instead increased attention to what many of us have been talking about for a long time, that is, some intermediate solution between the extremes of full public ownership and private ownership, combining some regulation with partial compensation. There is an enormous field there, part of which has been explored. Third, I am concerned with the comment under Section 6.01 that interprets the *Midkiff* case as abolishing all concern about condemnation and suggesting that all you have to show is some public benefit, some substantial public benefit. My reading of the case suggests that they've been pointing strongly in that direction but they refuse to say that flatly. As a matter of fact I think it's just as well they haven't, because any of us who have had dealings with the urban renewal program know that a lot of hanky-panky was going on there in the 1950s and well into the 1960s. There was no reversal of judicial attitudes, because we ran out of urban renewal cases. The program got killed. For that reason, and for that reason only, we never saw a change in judicial attitudes towards urban renewal, towards a more critical judicial review on urban renewal, which we have clearly seen in the state courts on zoning and subdivision regulation. I'm uncomfortable with the notion that you can take A's land and turn it over to B and have no judicial review. That's been shown to be a major source of corruption.

Forrest: I, for one, applaud the discussion of the eminent domain concept under Section 6.01 but I think we might go farther than it has gone. I believe that many communities are looking at eminent domain, and if they use eminent domain for economic development support purposes, and codevelopment purposes, they will likely win those cases on public purpose grounds.

Predictability in Taking Cases

N.Williams: Also, in my view, the text in Section 6.02 is quite misleading on the whole question of predictability in taking cases. I would summarize the situation as follows. First, in Twentieth century American land use litigation, many major issues have been worked through at length, with significant results—as, for example, recognizing the importance of a regional perspective, reversal of the normal presumption of validity as to a few favored uses (churches and schools, affordable housing, and certain quasi-family arrangements), a constitutional right against land use regulations which are totally confiscatory, etc. The Supreme Court (except for Justice Stevens) is largely ignorant of the complex issues involved in land use litigation, many of which have been worked out at such length in the states (e.g., the significance of a regional perspective). Moreover, the Court's opinions show no interest in learning from the long, rich state experience. Perhaps because of all this, several recent decisions have reversed long-settled law. Naturally, this has created great confusion; no one knows how far this Court is willing to go.

In the taking cases, the Court has invoked about a dozen phrases, as if these were ruling criteria which decide the cases. In fact they are not; many are so vague that they do not point directly to any result—"general propositions do not decide concrete cases." To the limited extent that they have any meaning at all, most overlap to some extent with several others, and yet point in a quite different direction from still others. Moreover, and worse yet, there is no way of knowing which of these phrases will be invoked in any given future case; certainly the relatively few Supreme Court cases give no guidance as to this. There is enough precedent available pointing in both directions so the Court could go either way, depending (presumably) on gut reactions.

Almost all the recent cases have been either 5-to-4 or 6-to-3. The present membership of the Court is deeply divided on a number of basic issues: whether there is a presumption of validity (or strict scrutiny or intermediate scrutiny); whether (and when) the impact of a regulation is to be evaluated in terms of its effect on a particular right or on the whole bundle; whether there is broad power over land use or merely a narrow nuisance exception to free-marketism; to what extent regulatory takings are similar to or quite different from physical takings, and so on. There is even a basic split as to which constitutional principle should be invoked in these cases—substantive due process or the taking clause—and whether the applicable criteria are the same in these two, or different. So we really don't even know what part of the constitutional law we are talking about. What I am suggesting is that, while there has been quite a lot of predictability in the amiable chaos of state land use law, the Supreme Court's intervention has largely destroyed that.

To complicate matters further, the Supreme Court is no longer the accepted leader in American constitutional interpretation. In several fields closely related to our concerns here—exclusionary zoning, zoning for quasi-families, and school financing—the state courts obviously either have been evading Supreme Court review, or have gone directly contrary to Supreme Court policy. We should no longer act as if we thought the Supreme Court's writ still runs in American land use law; often it does not.

In my view, much of the text in Section 6 on just compensation, particularly in the illustrations, reflects the world view of the Rehnquist-Bork-Scalia school of thought, which is clearly trying to repeal much of the progress in constitutional law of the last 50 years—both as to the broadening of acceptable purposes of environmental protection, and as to the implications of the *Carolene Products* footnote generally. There is plenty wrong with the land use control system, about which a lot of us have written at length; but, in quite a lot of firsthand planning experience, I have not observed this world view to be an accurate representation about how people usually behave. Nor are the problems raised the important ones which do arise.

One of the very few certainties in the present situation is that in the coming years there will be major changes in the membership of the Court. The future of the law, therefore, depends quite simply on who appoints the next judges; and we don't know much about that—though it seems quite unlikely that they will all be a bunch of mini-Borks. Just consider the recent role of historical accident—how different American public law would be if, say, Carter had made four appointments in his first term, and Nixon none. No doubt, in 1906—one year after *Lochner*—someone wrote an essay explaining that happily, American constitutional law was now all settled. In the present situation, it does not seem sensible for us to follow such a precedent.

Mandelker: As Justice Rehnquist once said, I agree with much of what Norman Williams has said.

Exactions and the Taking Issue

Bauman: Why did the Court do what it did in *Nollan?* The *Nollan* case was never presented to the Supreme Court as a regulatory taking case. That's what we got, but the case was put to the Court as one of physical taking. The case was hung entirely on the physical takings cases, such as *Kaiser* and *Loretto.* The briefing to the Court about development exactions, impact fees, and subdivision requirements, was done by the local governments and their briefs in particular described to the Court what would happen if the Court questioned those kinds of exactions in any kind of a ruling that reversed the California ruling. Twenty-six states were before the U.S. Supreme Court saying such exactions are entirely reasonable. Nobody asked the Court to do what it did after page six of its opinion. What happened in oral argument was that several justices, including Justice Marshall—and one reason he was interested was because he has property just like the Nollans'—could not understand where the connection was between the condition imposed on the Nollans and the stated governmental purpose. That's what led to the last ten pages of the opinion.

N.Williams: Two other points. First I don't think we know what's going to happen on the question of nexus after *Nollan.* I would guess that we're heading toward a series of situations where the municipal insistence on developer contributions to infrastructure is going to cause a lot of trouble. I think Justice Scalia quite misstated the present state of law on those required contributions. Second, in the discussion of state law, there is repeated reference to the fact that some states are a lot stricter on their insistence on developer rights than you get in the federal law. Obviously there are a lot of states which are a lot more pro-municipal as well.

Eminent Domain Purposes versus Police Power Purposes

Kmiec: I accept your last point Norman. Some states can be more prone to the municipal interests to the extent that they don't go beneath the floor of federally protected rights. Moreover, I agree the concept of *public use* still does have teeth at the state level. Nevertheless, I read Justice O'Connor's statement in the *Midkiff* case that public purpose is coterminous with the police power as basically opening the door to virtually anything that has a public benefit. However, I think if I were to assert that position in front of the Indiana courts, for example, they would smile at me and suggest I go home and rethink that position. Dan Tarlock mentioned the harm-benefit distinction and the corresponding objection that one man's harm can be another man's benefit. The two have been confused. Nevertheless, eminent domain was intended to secure public benefits and the police power was provided to prevent harms. But gradually, as the public use element on the eminent domain side of the equation became more generous to the municipality as to what purposes could be achieved under it, eminent domain became more like the police power and *vice versa*. It's the *vice versa* that is troubling because it is one thing to say that the community can do virtually anything under eminent domain so long as it pays; it is quite another to say a community can do virtually anything under the police power and not pay.

Now, the police power isn't just used to prevent harms; it is used to acquire things and achieve benefits, which were once thought to be the exclusive province of eminent domain. It took a while for the Court to recognize that communities were using the police power in place of eminent domain, but when it did, *First English* and *Nollan* resulted. In effect, the Supreme Court is saying that if you're going to use the police power in the way you previously used eminent domain, you're going to have to apply eminent domain principles; namely, compensation will have to be paid under some circumstances, and, of course, it's those circumstances which we are struggling to define.

Date from Which the Calculation of
Damages Is Made

Meck: Assuming there is a regulatory taking, does the calculation of compensation date from when you find out the regulation applies to you or when the regulation is actually enacted?

Kmiec: It's from the time of enactment.

Babcock: So I can sit back, Doug, for three or four years after the ordinance is passed and then still claim that the taking is measured from the time of its enactment and, not from the time I first knew about it?

Kmiec: Dick, that is a very important analytical point that the Supreme Court has only indirectly addressed. The point has special force to the landowner who sits on his hands knowing the impact of the regulation and only much later seeks damages. To what degree, if any, should damages be reduced because of the landowner's delay in notifying the regulator of his claim? Since the Court says a planner must know the requirements of the Constitution as much as a policeman, perhaps that means communities will be required to bear damages which flow from facially invalid regulation, regardless of the timeliness of the notice or claim from the landowner. Arguably, the community received the benefit of the invalid regulation during that entire time. All of this assumes, of course, that the regulation is truly a taking. As a practical matter if the landowner is so disinterested that he delays even filing a claim, that may suggest an absence of reasonable investment-backed expectations, which may dispose of the taking claim altogether.

Bauman: If the Court ever addresses the question, the property owner has to put the government on notice that he believes the taking is occurring. The questions are when do you do that and in what form. The Court didn't want to deal with it because all that the Court was interested in establishing in *First English* was the general principle of compensation for a regulatory taking. It has left to the lower courts to determine those questions in terms of timing.

Babcock: Yes, but Gus that still doesn't answer the question. If it's up to the states, what are the states going to say and what should they say?

Bauman: I think what the states would say and should say is that if an owner feels his property is being taken he's got to let the government know that. He can't sit on his hands, and I think the courts will take that position, too.

Siemon: My problem with that is that if I own a parcel of land and the government puts a dam on the river and the water comes up over my property and two years later I discover it, if I bring a lawsuit, the taking isn't the date I tell them that they occupied my land; the date is the date it came on my property. So if it's good for the goose it seems to me it's good for the gander.

Bauman: No. That isn't necessarily true because one case involves a regulatory taking where it doesn't make any difference because you had no expectations or plans, and it may have been relatively unencumbered; whereas the other case is a taking by physical invasion which, as Doug Kmiec suggests, has always put government under a greater burden.

Siemon: The whole justification in *First English* is that they are the same.

Bauman: No.

Siemon: The source of the law is the same.

Bauman: The courts use physical invasion cases as analogies, but they really view them as entirely different cases.

Tarlock: I think analytically the only way you can make sense out of the *First English* is that inverse condemnation has been extended to regulatory taking so there's got to be some connection.

Strong: There is another, related point which Justice Stevens makes in his dissent in *First English* which I think is persuasive: Simply because an ordinance is held invalid as a taking, its effect during the period of litigation is not necessarily also that of a taking. He also points out that a temporary taking does not necessarily result from an ordinance which, if kept in force, would constitute a permanent taking. A court must examine the limitations on use, the amount of property affected, and the duration of the temporary restriction to make that determination.

Delogu: I've always found it useful when talking with planners about the location of the dividing line between permissible regulation and regulatory taking to try to shift their focus from what it is they don't want to what it is they're willing to permit. In other words, what use opportunities remain. It seems to me you're in a much stronger position to have a regulation sustained if you think as much about what you will allow to be done, and to try to give as much emphasis as possible to the economic utility of those activities so that a court can perceive that there is, in fact, a viable range of permitted uses or activities.

The second point I wanted to make is that I think you should never allow those who would challenge an ordinance on regulatory taking grounds to structure the argument in terms of the area subject to the ordinance or regulation. Focusing on a small area can have a more immediate and devastating impact. For example, a case in Maine involving a state agency dealing with an unorganized territory; the agency penciled in some deer yards and imposed restrictions on timber cutting that made the viable economic options in the deer yard areas almost nonexistent. But, in fact, the total parcel involved 25,000 contiguous acres of land owned by the same landowner. In reality the area that the regulations severely restrainted concerned less than 1.2 percent of the total 25,000 acres. If the court were to accept the plaintiff's argument, there isn't a setback provision in the world that would be satisfactory because within the area set back you could do nothing, you just literally watch the grass grow. So planners should not allow taking issues to be cast in the narrowest terms. You have to look at the total picture or parcel.

Also, I must agree with those who suggest that the prohibition against the taking of A's land to give to B is almost totally dead at the state level. In many states the public purpose requirement is satisfied if, in fact, a sufficient public benefit can be shown. A handful of states, North Carolina, for example, still hold the line on more traditional public purpose, public use concepts. But, I think the shift in state law is clear.

Mandelker: I tend to think there's more uncertainty in the taking doctrine than the statement in Section 6.02 indicates. In fact, what we now have is a set of totally opposed tests. For example, we were told by the U.S. Supreme Court in the *Penn Central* case that it was not going to adopt a set formula but would apply a balancing test. Then we were told in *Keystone* that there is, in fact, a set formula—the legitimate governmental interest and the reasonably viable use test, except that Justice Stevens also talked about investment-backed expectations. There are other inconsistencies. If I own a huge railroad station and I want to build an addition to it and I'm told I can't, I don't have any complaint because the Court said in *Penn Central* that it looks at the economic viability of the whole parcel, not just a little part of it. But if I own an apartment house and the state authorizes somebody to put a little box on my apartment house, that's different because that's called a physical taking. That's the *Loretto* case. This inconsistency has to be indicated. I don't know if it's ever going to be clarified.

Schulman: There is a way to give the property owner relief short of direct monetary compensation and that's through the tax system. For example, there is a New York statute called protection of historical places, buildings, and works of art, and it provides in part: "[S]uch measures . . . if adopted in the exercise of the police power shall be reasonable and appropriate to the purpose, or if constituting a taking of private property shall provide for due compensation which may include the limitation or remission of taxes." I present it to you because it's the only example I know where the taxation power is used as a mechanism for compensation. I think that planners ought to be told about doing things like that. There isn't a track record on this approach but we ought to deal with it.

Diminution in Value

Meck: Is there a way of evaluating a regulation economically so that you know when a taking occurs? As a planner, the language in *Penn Central* and these other cases is simply verbiage. I view the value of a piece of property as representing a discounted stream of income from the future. And if a property does represent that stream of income, are there cases that indicate the range of reduction in value that would give you some idea of when the value of property is so substantially diminished, whether that be 50 or 81 percent, that a taking occurs?

Kmiec: Two things. First I don't think that a shorthand exists. A federal court could uphold a 75 percent diminution in value. But if you go to the state cases you can find diminutions in the range of 40 and 50 percent that are found to be takings. So there really isn't any scientific precision other than the feel you get from state practice in terms of knowing your courts. The second point is that for the Fifth Amendment test, it's not solely a question of diminution in value. The Supreme Court made that very clear in *Penn Central* and now *Nollan*. The landowner may have a substantial diminution in value as a result of regulation that initially might seem to be a taking. But perhaps if the landowner was on notice before he invested, and if the character of the government's action is seen as related to the prevention of harm as we discussed earlier, the regulation may very well survive the takings challenge when all of the elements of the Supreme Court's test are applied.

Bauman: I agree that there is no clear answer. It's going to be fought out in the state courts. However, by way of guidance, planners can look at the factors outlined by the courts and ask the question: Is there real use left in this property, not just for a Christmas tree lot in December, but some reasonable use? Nine times out of ten a responsible government can get just what it wants and still leave reasonable use in the property.

An interesting angle on this is the *Keystone* case. The important thing to remember is that *Keystone* was a facial attack on the statute, rather than as applied to the property of a particular owner. The percentage of the take in *Keystone* was 50 percent and so the owners claimed that 50 percent on its face is a taking. Now the difference in outcome between *Keystone* and *Nollan* was Justice White. He's a real pragmatist. It dawned on him that the case involved a facial attack, and the Court doesn't like facial attacks under the takings clause. That's an important rule for any planner to know. And, if you're faced with a facial attack, the property owner, at least in federal court, had better be able to demonstrate a substantial loss of value not just 50 percent of the investment-backed expectation. So I think we can tell planners that loss of property value has to be in the upper ranges, and you can determine that.

Downzoning

Lamont: I have a question concerning downzoning and the taking issue. Los Angeles last year held a referendum to require the government to downzone multifamily zoning that existed throughout the city. The city is now in the process of trying to downzone. Will that raise taking issues? To be more specific, let's say that since 1956, 13,000 single-family houses have been in zoning districts that allow 150 to 250 units per acre, depending on the district. Clearly, you could argue a mistake was made with the comprehensive plan and the zoning because the areas are basically single family. A lot of investment-backed decisions were made in acquiring property in those multifamily zones, but few developments beyond single family occurred. You go back now and you revisit the question and you say, wait a minute, there was an error in the original zoning and the comprehensive plan. You revise the comprehensive plan to show that it should not be multifamily zoning. Then you go back and take the next step and try to rezone that property to eliminate the 150 to 250 units per acre. Do we have a taking issue?

Bauman: I don't think so. I would like to have one of the homeowners be able to demonstrate with facts how they made investment-backed expectations based on that multifamily zoning, except for the fact that they bought the home.

Lamont: There probably are a number of property owners who can demonstrate that they did and are waiting for the market to turn around.

Delogu: That's an as applied argument then as opposed to a question of the facial validity of the regulation. If there is evidence that comes out of preliminary discussion between purchasers, developers and city officials that demonstrates that most of the properties in the area were bought and sold in accord with land values associated with single-family residential development, I don't think you have a taking problem if you downzone the area to single-family residential zone. Alternatively, a less dramatic downzoning that might permit townhouse type development compatible with a single-family residential neighborhood, or that allows some multifamily development units on at least in-fill properties would also stand a good chance of avoiding successful taking challenge.

Mee: What if the land has been exchanged at commercial land values, notwithstanding the fact that there's residential use. Then what happens? I think planners need help with determining what the true value is. Is it the market value based on uses today? Is it speculative prices that people are paying based on future uses which the zoning district does allow? That's where we need help. What is the value?

Delogu: Where the market has run ahead of zoning change, and has begun to value property in excess of its present use market values, you certainly have the possibility of an expectations argument being made. But I wouldn't say it will necessarily succeed merely because developers started acquiring land and bid the value of that land up in anticipation of presenting the city at some point with a rezoning proposal for land areas which, they would then assert, are in the process of transition. However, if the higher density zoning is already there, I think you have a much closer case. Where there's beginning to be a transition of uses and there are some actual multifamily developments that have been put in at the higher permitted densities and other adjacent properties are beginning to change hands in expectation of higher use, I think a downzoning that doesn't allow for either a transition period or some of that expectation value to be realized may be in jeopardy. That's a lot closer case.

Siemon: Let's say a community adopts a comprehensive plan, designates an area—usually its single family—and the housing in that area is not the best but currently is a reasonable source of affordable housing. The community decides it wants to redevelop that area and zones it for commercial or high density residential. The community then realizes that is not only inconsistent with their overall community development, but also, if the area is redeveloped for higher density use, a large reservoir of existing affordable housing will be lost. So the community decides to prevent reinvestment in those single-family dwellings on shotgun lots. It again revises its comprehensive plan, and rezones to save its residential area. In many of those areas the landowners are not owner occupiers. They are people who invested on the basis of an anticipation of that higher zoning. I don't believe that that kind of broad policy change, if supported by a rational planning process, has any serious risk of being found to be a taking, even though there may be a tremendous wipeout in those investment values.

Blaesser: Let's take away the comprehensive planning antecedents before you do that downzoning. Would you still come out with the same analysis? In other words, there is a zoning regulation in place but no comprehensive plan.

Siemon: If they're doing the rezoning on an area wide basis, then I think it will carry along all the baggage of the plan. But, if it's a small portion, say three acres, and the owner lets it be known that he's got a development plan, and all of a sudden his three acres gets downzoned and there's not a comprehensive response, I think there's likely to be a different outcome.

Delogu: If what's being said, though, is that the only people who can win these cases are those who've advanced their planning to the stage of having a vested right, I disagree. That ignores all of the arguments predicated on reasonably based investment expectations which can be found in the case law. You may be right, but I wouldn't count on it. I think there's at least an argument to be made that where the downzoning is abrupt, where the acreage involved is significant, where it seems to have no predicate in a comprehensive planning document, and particularly if there is any hint of it being retaliatory, then it is a taking. I'd take that developer's case and whether I'd win or lose, it would at least be a horse race.

G.Williams: I think that point really needs to be clarified. If, because somebody had invested in land at a higher value, the locality is precluded from adjusting the density to a more appropriate level, then I think you significantly inhibit the ability of cities to deal with the growth issues because that's where most of us are. We're overzoned, and our response to these pressures is to downzone.

Livingston: We have to do it properly, beginning with a comprehensive plan which concludes that the density permitted under the preexisting zoning is excessive.

Hack: The tradition in many eastern cities is very different. The plan consistency requirements have never quite found their way to most eastern cities, so you have a situation such as Boston's where they downzoned virtually the entire center of the city. There is no plan in Boston, and a whole lot of commercial investors have found themselves and their expectations significantly diminished.

Tustian: This is a topical question for all present. Is the consensus here that if you have large, commercial employment areas that have been in their present zones for a long time, people have bought this land, prices have gone up, the owners have expectations, and if we come along now and revise a master plan so as to downzone them, using appropriate procedural due process, and if we have some rationale so it also has been provided with substantive due process, is the consensus here that that's okay? Or are we at risk?

Tarlock: Obviously, the more land involved the more of an analogy there is between downzoning and taxation. The broader the distribution of the cost and benefits I think the harder it is to attack constitutionally.

Carey: I think your question hypothetically assumes that you have a legitimate state interest and you will provide adequate procedures. The question then becomes when you will pass the economically viable use test with regard to the application of the new ordinance, to the properties involved.

I think the simple answer is that you'd probably run a severe risk of being sued, but to the extent that you've been careful in your planning process with respect to highly restrictive zones to provide for some uses which at least look as though they could make some money for the land owner, and leave the property marketable, you're going to be in pretty good shape.

◆ **6.06 Ripeness**

The ripeness doctrine states that a land use proposal must be sufficiently pursued through available administrative procedures and state court proceedings before a federal court will consider a landowner's claim that a local government's refusal to approve the development proposal constitutes a regulatory taking. The doctrine is applied to both questions raised by a regulatory taking claim: 1) whether the regulation has gone so far that it has taken a landowner's property; and 2) whether compensation for the regulatory taking available through state procedures is just. When a court reviews the first question, it evaluates the local government's decision to determine if it was sufficiently final to enable a proper assessment of whether the regulation went too far. This is frequently referred to as the finality requirement in the ripeness doctrine. In considering the second question of a takings claim, the court inquires if the landowner sought and was denied just compensation through the state's inverse condemnation procedures, or if the procedures are inadequate or simply not available. ◊

Comment

The justification in the takings context for requiring a final decision is that it is impossible for a court to evaluate the economic impact of the challenged regulation and the extent to which the regulation interferes with reasonable investment-backed expectations until the local government has made a final definitive determination on how it will apply the challenged regulation to the particular land in question.

Even if a plaintiff asserting a regulatory taking claim can demonstrate that the local government reached a final decision on the type and intensity of development that it will permit on a plaintiff's property, the plaintiff has the additional burden of demonstrating that compensation for the alleged regulatory taking was sought through a state inverse condemnation procedure that was inadequate, or that such a procedure was not available.

The ripeness doctrine can be avoided altogether if the plaintiff brings a claim challenging the regulation on its face and in its entirety, that is, alleging that the regulation results in a taking of *all* property to which it applies, including the plaintiff's. The U.S. Supreme Court has cautioned that a plaintiff who brings a facial attack on a regulation as a taking faces a difficult task.

Caselaw

Keystone Bituminous Coal Ass'n v. De Benedictis, 480 U.S. 470 (1987) [V-2.21]
MacDonald, Sommer & Frates v. Yolo County, 477 U.S. 340 (1986) [V-2.24]
Williamson County Regional Planning Comm'n v. Hamilton Bank, 473 U.S. 172 (1985) [V-2.52]
Agins v. City of Tiburon, 447 U.S. 255 (1980) [V-2.01]

Ripeness Illustration No. 1

A property owner's land consists of an undeveloped 1,200 acre parcel zoned under a county residential use classification which permits a density of one dwelling unit per acre. Before the property owner submits any development proposal to the county, the county rezones the parcel to an agricultural zoning classification which permits one dwelling unit per 60 acres. The property owner sues the county alleging that the rezoning as applied to her property constitutes a taking without compensation. The court will dismiss the takings claim for lack of ripeness on the ground that the property owner never submitted any application for development to the county.

◆ 6.07 The Finality Requirement: Administrative Relief; Reapplication

Before bringing a taking claim in federal court, a property owner whose development proposal is denied by a local government must first pursue available means of administrative relief, such as variances or exceptions under the local ordinance, which would enable the development proposal to be approved. Second, if the administrative relief that is sought on the first development proposal is unsuccessful, the property owner must submit additional applications sufficient to determine the type and intensity of development that the local government will permit on the property. These steps are necessary in order to satisfy the finality requirement of the ripeness doctrine, which requires that the plaintiff property owner demonstrates that the administrative agency has reached a final, definitive position regarding the development proposal. ◊

Comment

The requirement that a property owner pursue available administrative relief from the denial of a development proposal in order to satisfy the finality prong of the ripeness doctrine is not the same as exhaustion of administrative remedies. Exhaustion of administrative remedies refers to the use of administrative and judicial procedures *after* a final adverse decision by the local government in order to seek review of that decision and obtain a remedy if the decision is determined to have been unlawful. The U.S. Supreme Court has held that exhaustion of administrative remedies is not required in addition to satisfying the finality requirement where the property owner brings a taking claim in federal court under 42 U.S.C. § 1983.

Caselaw

Felder v. Casey, _____ U.S. _____, 108 S. Ct. 2302 (1988)
Williamson County Regional Planning Comm'n v. Hamilton Bank, 473 U.S. 172 (1985) [V-2.52]
Patsy v. Board of Regents of State of Florida, 457 U.S. 496 (1982)

Ripeness Illustration No. 2—Finality

A planning commission rejects a plat of subdivision because it contains dwelling units in excess of the number permitted under a newly adopted zoning ordinance, places dwellings on slopes where construction is prohibited, and does not comply with road grading standards. The developer sues in federal court alleging that the rejection of the plat constitutes a taking of property.

The court will dismiss the complaint for failure to satisfy the finality requirement of the ripeness doctrine. Before bringing the taking claim in federal court, the landowner should have applied for appropriate variances or exceptions authorized under the subdivision and zoning ordinances in an effort to overcome the commission's objections. Even if the requested variances or exceptions had been denied, the court still would not consider a taking claim unless the developer could demonstrate that the submission of further applications to determine what level of development would be acceptable to the local government would be futile.

◆ **6.08 Exception to Finality Requirement: Futility**

Reapplication following denial of a development application is not necessary to satisfy the finality requirement if the landowner can demonstrate that such reapplication would be futile because the original application was meaningful within the context of the existing regulations and the denial constituted a final and authoritative decision that exposed the nature and intensity of development that would be permitted. A landowner may also be able to satisfy the futility exception where it can be demonstrated that development approval procedures are unfair and result in unnecessary delays. ◊

Comment

The U.S. Supreme Court has indicated that a meaningful application does not mean an "exceedingly grandiose" development proposal. Rejection of such a scale of development proposal does not, according to the Court, imply that less ambitious plans will suffer the same fate. Therefore, the futility exception to the finality requirement cannot be satisfied unless a landowner can demonstrate that a meaningful formal application was submitted to the local government and rejected. This futility test has been difficult for the lower federal courts to apply, and no single case has yielded any reliable method for determining when an application is truly "meaningful" and reapplication is not necessary for a takings claim to be ripe for consideration.

Caselaw

MacDonald, Sommer & Frates v. Yolo County, 477 U.S. 340 (1986) [V-2.24]
Williamson County Regional Planning Commission v. Hamilton Bank, 473 U.S. 172 (1985) [V-2.52]
Hoehne v. County of San Benito, 870 F.2d 529 (9th Cir. 1989)
Lake Nacimiento Ranch Co. v. San Luis Obispo County, 830 F.2d 977 (9th Cir. 1987), *cert. denied,* ____ U.S. ____ (1988)
Corn v. City of Lauderdale Lakes, 816 F.2d 1514 (11th Cir. 1987)
American Savings & Loan Ass'n v. County of Marin, 653 F.2d 364 (9th Cir. 1981)

Ripeness Illustration No. 3—Futility Exception

A landowner submits to the planning commission a development plan application accompanied by a request to rezone his property from single-family residential to multifamily. Following a hearing on the application, the planning commission recommends to the city council that it deny the application. Before the planning commission's recommendation is forwarded to the city council for action, the landowner requests and receives permission from the planning commission to withdraw his application without prejudice in order to discuss alternative development plans which might be acceptable to the city. During the next six months, the landowner engages in numerous discussions with planning commission staff and submits an informal, conceptual application to elicit staff and commission reaction. On the basis of the negative reaction of the staff and commission to his conceptual proposal, the landowner concludes that further application would be futile and sues the city on a taking claim in federal court. Unless the specific statements and/or actions of the staff and commission during the six month period persuade the court that another formal application would be futile, the court will dismiss the taking claim as unripe because an informal application does not constitute a meaningful application for purposes of satisfying the futility exception to the finality requirement of the ripeness doctrine.

Ripeness Illustration No. 4—Futility Exception

A county enacts a moratorium on all development within a planning district which includes the property of a landowner who had just completed, but not yet submitted, an application for development approval. The ordinance imposing the moratorium does not provide for any exceptions. The landowner sues the county in federal court alleging a regulatory taking. Because any request by the landowner for an exception to the moratorium would be futile under the terms of the ordinance, it is likely that the court would find that the landowner had satisfied the futility exception to the finality requirement of the ripeness doctrine.

Ripeness Illustration No. 5—Futility Exception

A landowner submits an application to develop land at a relatively high density, consistent with the applicable zoning requirements. The local government denies the application, explaining that all development of the property will be barred under its interpretation of the zoning ordinance. The landowner does not pursue any administrative avenues for relief from the decision. A court would probably find that the futility exception to the finality requirement is satisfied, since further applications or efforts to seek administrative relief from the government's decision would be fruitless.

◆ 6.09 Scope of Application of Finality Requirement

A property owner's claim that the application of a governmental regulation, in addition to resulting in a taking of property, violates substantive and procedural due process and equal protection under the Fourteenth Amendment, may also be subject to dismissal on the ground of lack of finality where the basis for these claims is identical to that of the takings claim. ◊

Comment

The finality requirement as articulated by the Supreme Court focuses on the question of whether a regulation as applied to a particular parcel results in a taking of property. Related claims of substantive and procedural due process and equal protection may be viewed as so intertwined with the application of the regulation to the property that these claims will also be ruled premature by the courts.

In the case of an action that asserts an inverse condemnation claim and claims based on related injuries that are alleged to have resulted from denial of equal protection or denial of procedural due process because of unreasonable delay or failure to act under mandated time periods, a court may reason that such claims are also not mature until the appropriate governmental body has made a final determination of the type and intensity of development it will permit. However, not all federal courts have reached the same conclusion. For example, some federal courts have held that the *reapplication* requirement of the finality test is irrelevant to substantive due process, equal protection, and procedural due process claims because these claims address the local government's specific actions during a particular application process and do not require speculation as to what forms of less intensive development might have been permitted.

Caselaw

Keystone Bituminous Coal Association v. DeBenedictis, 480 U.S. 470 (1987) [V-2.21]
Williamson County Regional Planning Comm'n v. Hamilton Bank, 473 U.S. 172 (1985) [V-2.52]
Herrington v. County of Sonoma, 834 F.2d 1488 (9th Cir. 1987), *amended and reh'g denied*, 857 F.2d 567 (9th Cir. 1988)
Kinzli v. City of Santa Cruz, 818 F.2d 1449 (9th Cir. 1987)
Boothe v. Manatee County, 812 F.2d 1372 (11th Cir. 1987)

Carroll v. City of Prattville, 653 F. Supp. 933 (M.D. Ala. 1987)
Oberndorf v. City and County of Denver, 653 F. Supp. 304 (D. Colo. 1986)

Ripeness Illustration No. 6—Scope of Finality Requirement

A municipality adopts an ordinance which imposes new density limitations on a landowner's property. The landowner submits an application for development approval requesting a use variance that would enable her to develop the property at the density that had been possible prior to the adoption of the ordinance. The planning commission denies the use variance request, and the landowner appeals the denial to the board of zoning appeals and is denied. She then brings suit alleging that the new ordinance as applied to her property constitutes a taking of property without compensation and is violative of her rights to substantive due process and equal protection. If the court determines that the landowner failed to obtain a final determination of the nature and intensity of development that the city would permit on the property, it will dismiss her taking claim and may also dismiss the related substantive due process and equal protection claims.

Ripeness Illustration No. 7—Scope of Finality Requirement

A developer sues a county, alleging that the county's failure to act on its preliminary plat application within the statutory time period constitutes a denial of procedural due process and equal protection and a deprivation of property without just compensation. If the court finds that the developer's taking claim is not ripe for adjudication, it may rule that the related procedural due process claim based on the county's failure to act under the mandated time period is ripe because the reapplication requirement under the test for finality is not relevant in assessing whether the county's specific actions during the particular application process violated procedural due process.

6.10 Symposium Discussion

Blaesser: The doctrine of ripeness is derived from the case or controversy provisions of Article III of the United Constitution and the Fifth and Fourteenth amendments. In all cases, not just land use cases, the federal courts don't want to render an advisory opinion or decide matters that are muddled for a lack of clear factual foundation. That's what ripeness is really all about. Should a court take the matter before it, or is it not really ripe for adjudication? In land use controversies, the doctrine of ripeness is applied to the two components of a regulatory taking: (1) whether the regulation has gone so far that it has taken a landowner's property and (2) whether the compensation for the regulatory taking that's available through state procedures is just within the meaning of the just compensation clause of the Fifth Amendment. When a court reviews the first component of a regulatory takings claim under the ripeness doctrine, it asks whether the local government's regulatory decision as applied to the property was sufficiently final to enable the court to properly assess whether the regulation went too far. This first component is usually called the finality requirement.

I want to focus on the finality requirement of the ripeness doctrine because it has the most significant implications for planning practice. I describe it in terms of steps or thresholds. The first threshold is that the landowner has to actually apply for some sort of development approval. He or she can't, as in the *Agins* case for example, merely say I don't like the regulation as I think it might apply to my property and then challenge it. The landowner first has to attempt to get some sort of economic use under the regulation. The second threshold is that the landowner who is turned down by the local government then has to use whatever administrative procedures are available to try to obtain some sort of an exception that will allow a development to go forward that is similar to what he or she originally proposed. However, in the Supreme Court case, *MacDonald, Sommer & Frates v. Yolo County*, 477 U.S. 340 (1986), the Court used language which has created confusion for developers and planners alike.

The case involved the denial of a specific subdivision proposal, and the Court adopted language from the California appellate court decision which stated: "The refusal of the defendants to permit the intensity of development desired by the landowner does not preclude less intensive but still valuable development." The Court also said: "Our cases uniformly reflect an insistence on knowing the nature and extent of permitted development before adjudicating the constitutionality of the regulations that purport to limit it." Well, these are very broad statements and the implications of this quoted language, it seems to me, are at least two. First, it means that a developer has to be prepared to submit various proposals for lesser intensities of the use he or she would like to do. And, if those are turned down, he or she will have to come back with proposals for other kinds of uses that might be possible on the property. The second is that planners, in turn, can either assist in helping to define what their local government believes is reasonable for a site, or they can engage in what I

would term a less than good faith attempt to try to create a very complicated, time-consuming process that holds out the continued possibility
that the landowner might get something if he or she comes in with one
more application. I find that to be a very dangerous part of the finality requirement. One approach which I think serves the interest of both government and the private sector is to require, as part of the application process,
that an alternative use feasibility study be done.

Sullivan: I agree generally with everything that Brian Blaesser has said. I
think the genesis of the doctrine of ripeness is part of a very studied effort
on the part of the U.S. Supreme Court to get most of these cases into the
state court system and not have them tried in the federal system. I think
you also have to make a distinction under the takings clause between challenges that are facial versus challenges that are as applied. A landowner
has a real uphill battle if he brings a facial challenge, in other words, arguing that the regulation is invalid under any set of circumstances. He is almost never going to be successful.

Exhaustion and Ripeness Distinguished

I also want to make sure we all understand that there is a difference between exhaustion of remedies and this notion of ripeness. Exhaustion
means that you got a final decision and the issue is whether you have to go
through judicial review of that decision. The courts say no, you don't have
to do that. But the ripeness doctrine says you've got to at least make an application to the local government to find out what uses are permitted on
the property before you can advance a claim that there is no reasonable
economic use left on the property.

What's the Planning Issue?

G.Williams: I have a little trouble seeing ripeness as a real planning
issue. It's more of a litigation strategy and what hoops a potential litigant
would have to go through.

Forrest: Except that planners might try to use a lack of ripeness strategi-
cally by making decisions on only one part of an application and then, at
the same time, clearly articulating a basis under which a reapplication or
an amendment could perhaps, without promising, result in a more favorable decision. As Brian Blaesser noted, planners might get the idea that

they can string out the decision-making process, which would be a mistake.

Mee: I have a couple of comments. I think that the idea that the developer would prepare a feasibility study of alternatives is the last thing they'd want to do because then it might show that they could do significantly less than what they're proposing to do. The second point is that planners do regularly give developers alternatives; at least we do. Somebody files something and they come in and meet with us. We always tell them what we think is a reasonable use and what would be allowed, including what intensity. I think that it is part of our job to do that.

An Invitation to Erect Discretionary Barriers?

Mandelker: One interesting point that the ripeness cases raise, which I think feeds into our statement of other constitutional principles, is whether planners and communities have responded to the invitation implicit in *Hamilton Bank* to erect more regulatory discretionary barriers to approvals. I wonder if Is Stollman, from his national perspective at APA, has seen any such reaction.

Stollman: I haven't observed any specific reactions. It may seem peculiar for planners to worry about the developers' problems, but the question of ripeness sometimes creates opportunities for public abuse—not, of course, by planners, but by planners' bosses. That is, saying you have to take this step, and after you take that one you have to appeal, and after you appeal you have to maybe go back, and so forth, does lend itself to the kinds of abuses which I don't think are advantageous to the community or to the developer or the planner.

Whose Burden to Prove?

Tustian: I wonder if there is anything in the law that puts a burden on the plan or on the government when these cases get litigated. Or do I conclude from what's been said that the burden is essentially on the applicant, and, if all the use alternatives haven't been fleshed out the first time, he is simply sent back to come up with another one, and if this doesn't work, then another one, and so on, until he can bring them to that point.

Blaesser: The legal posture as it is right now, is that the burden is on the applicant to demonstrate that he or she did everything reasonably possible to look at use alternatives that were available at the time and obtained a final or definite decision as to those alternatives. It's pretty hard to shift the burden to the planner's or government's side, probably because the standard is so nebulous, and infinite possibilities can be raised by a planning department. I think I disagree with Joy to the extent that she suggests that the local government planning process is helpful or effective in identifying the potential alternatives for applicants. There always are these discussions, but you rarely find anyone in that ministerial role or advisory process as you get ready to propose a development project who is going to say, well, I'm quite confident that you will get this density approved. Instead, developers receive informal comments on which they often rely to their detriment.

Tustian: We have an incentive zoning ordinance that provides for the doubling of density in central business districts in return for the provision of amenities through site plan review approval by the planning board, which has considerable discretion. Amenities ultimately are whatever the board says they are. Developers come in and as long as they are within the density limits, the board can say we like it designed this way or that way. One of the questions that has troubled us is the amount of time and effort that goes into the process. The board often doesn't quite know what the preferable design alternative is unless it sits down and does a lot of work to redesign a project. If we just recommend denial, then the developer says you haven't given me any alternative of what would be acceptable. Are we justified in just saying, well, come back and tell us when you've got something else, or do we have the obligation to say, well, here's how you could redesign it to make it acceptable?

Mandelker: I think the circumstance you describe raises a problem in the sense that the finality rule does shift the burden to the developer, but the futility exception may have the effect of shifting it back to the municipality in some way or another. It is these intermediate situations that are difficult.

Tustian: I would respond that we rarely just say denial. We say that staff recommends denial of the proposal as filed, but at the same time we identify what we would recommend. We would even propose a whole host of stipulations, which we would review with the developer prior to the hearings. We're pretty precise and it's in writing, and it's part of the public record.

Hack: We do that also. It costs a lot to do that, and in the interest of efficiency it would be nicer, in some sense, when somebody is coming in with something that's patently very bad, to just say that's bad, go back and invent something better. We'll give you some guidelines, but we're not going to do it for you specifically.

Mandelker: One of the questions is whether these ripeness cases allow a municipality to require developers to think and think and rethink their proposals.

Blaesser: They do at this point.

Bauman: This is an easy thing for the government because the burden is on the applicant and it's hard to prove futility.

Avoiding Immediate Judicial Review

Siemon: It seems to me if we're trying to give planners guidance, the only real message in this is that if you do what Joy does—you tell a developer what alternatives they can do—you potentially set yourself up to go to court as a result of the developer being able to argue that the local government's decision is ripe for consideration by a court on the merits. For example, in Florida under the development of regional impact (DRI) process, when you deny a developer, you're obligated by law to specify those changes and conditions which would make the applicant eligible for development. For that reason, there is no ripeness issue in regard to decisions under the 380 process. Some people want to remove that so that local governments who make a decision under that provision don't find themselves automatically in court. So it seems to me that the advice to planners is that if you do what Joy does, you're giving up the opportunity to avoid an immediate judicial review.

Schulman: Somebody used the words precision versus discretion and all of us bounce back and forth between those extremes. On occasion, whether as a municipal planner or even as a developer's planner, you'd like to have greater precision. I have an oxymoron that I'd like to offer to you, "precise discretion." That's the lesson we have to get across to planners. After all, don't we want a site plan review procedure that has well written standards? Then you're not acting capriciously or arbitrarily.

In many new ordinances, everything is approved through a special permit or site plan review procedure except single family housing. But such procedures, and related standards, still can have a high degree of what I call precise discretion. We should underscore the importance of doing things that way. There should be some flexibility—but don't use the word flexibility as if you don't understand what virginity means.

SECTION 7:
PRINCIPLE 7:
FREEDOM OF SPEECH

◆ 7.01 The First Amendment

The First Amendment states in relevant part: "Congress shall make no law . . . abridging the freedom of speech, or of the press; or the right of the people peaceably to assemble, and to petition the Government for a redress of grievances." ◊

◆ 7.02 Freedom of Speech

The guarantee of freedom of speech prohibits the government from interfering with freedom of expression. It is important to note that while the text of the First Amendment speaks in absolute terms—"Congress shall make *no* law"—the Supreme Court has rejected a literal reading of the text and has adopted the view that speech may be subject to certain forms of regulation.

1. Government normally may not impose direct restrictions on the communicative aspects of speech and other forms of expression, except in those instances where the courts have determined that the type of speech involved is not protected by the First Amendment. ◊

Comment

Speech may have both communicative and noncommunicative aspects. For example, a noisy street demonstration both communicates ideas and creates noise and traffic problems, the latter two being noncommunicative aspects of this form of speech. When government seeks to regulate the communicative aspects of speech—in the example above, by imposing criminal penalties for statements advocating particular ideas—the courts will strike down such a direct governmental restriction on free expression unless the speech in question is not protected by the First Amendment. Among the types of speech that courts have held are not protected by the

First Amendment are defamatory falsehoods, obscenity, and speech that presents a "clear and present danger" of a serious and substantial evil that rises far above public inconvenience or unrest.

Caselaw

Collin v. Smith, 578 F.2d 1197 (7th Cir. 1978), *cert. denied*, 439 U.S. 916 (1978)

Freedom of Speech Illustration No. 1

A municipality enacts an ordinance which would prohibit all public demonstrations that could incite "violence, hatred, abuse, or hostility toward a group of persons by reason of reference to religious, racial, ethnic, national, or regional affiliation." When a neo-Nazi group seeks permission to march through a predominantly Jewish neighborhood, the municipality denies permission based on the ordinance. The court will strike down the ordinance because it makes a crime out of creating a dispute or arousing anger based on the ideas to be communicated by the demonstrators.

◆   **2.** Government may impose indirect restrictions on speech and other forms of expression in the course of attempting to regulate noncommunicative types of conduct so long as these restrictions do not unduly limit freedom of expression. ◊

Comment

Often, government action that attempts to control noncommunicative acts will have an indirect effect on communication or the dissemination of information. In these instances, the courts will balance the government's interest in regulating the noncommunicative activity against any incidental restriction on freedom of expression and will uphold the regulation so long as the speech affected is not unduly limited. In many instances, this balancing is undertaken with reference to a judicial test set out by the U.S. Supreme Court in *United States v. O'Brien*, 391 U.S. 367 (1968).

The *O'Brien* test allows government regulation that incidentally restricts speech if: (1) such regulation is within the constitutional power of government; (2) it furthers an important or substantial government interest; (3) the government interest is unrelated to the suppression of free expression; and (4) if the incidental restriction on alleged First Amendment freedoms is no greater than is essential to the furtherance of that interest.

Where government does attempt to regulate expression based on its communicative aspects, the regulation will be found unconstitutional unless the speech involved falls within one of the categories that have been found not to enjoy First Amendment protection, such as obscenity.

Caselaw

Young v. American Mini-Theatres, 427 U.S. 50 (1976) [V-2.53]
United States v. O'Brien, 391 U.S. 367 (1968).

Freedom of Speech Illustration No. 2

A municipality places restrictions on adult entertainment businesses that prohibit more than two such businesses from locating within 1,000 feet of any other adult business or certain other specified businesses such as taverns and pool halls. The municipality's stated purpose for the restrictions is to prevent the neighborhood deterioration that has been shown to accompany the concentration of two or more such businesses in a given neighborhood. These restrictions are prospective only—they will not be applied to existing businesses—and will allow a reasonable opportunity for such businesses to operate in the community.

The U.S. Supreme Court found a substantially similar set of locational restrictions to be valid, although it could not agree on a single rationale for its decision. Four members of the Court upheld the restrictions because they furthered a substantial governmental interest in preventing neighborhood deterioration and did not have the effect of suppressing freedom of expression. They argued that the ordinance was aimed at the "secondary effects" of adult entertainment businesses—neighborhood deterioration —and not the content of adult entertainment itself; and, since the locational restrictions could not be shown to diminish the availability of adult entertainment in the community in question, the ordinance was valid. These members of the Court also argued that adult entertainment was a form of expression that did not command as much First Amendment protection as, for example, political speech. A fifth member of the Court agreed that the ordinance was valid, but for the reason that the locational restrictions really did not regulate speech at all, and, since in his view the ordinance met the *O'Brien* test, it should be upheld.

♦ **3.** Government may place "time, place, or manner restrictions" on speech so long as these restrictions do not make distinctions based on the content of the speech or unreasonably limit expression in a traditional public forum. ◊

Comment

Government may be permitted to place restrictions on when, where, and how individuals exercise their free speech rights. When a court examines such restrictions, it tries to determine whether government is seeking to restrict the free flow of ideas under the pretext of regulating the manner in which the speech occurs. The nature of this examination can vary depending upon whether the challenged restrictions seek to regulate speech in a location that can be considered a "public forum": an area traditionally open to the public for assembly and debate. Public streets and parks, for example, would normally be considered public forums. The courts will be more demanding in their examination of time, place, and manner restrictions that seek to regulate speech in public forums because of the vital role they play in providing individuals and groups with an inexpensive means to convey ideas and messages to the public.

Historically, the courts' concern with the issue of content neutrality in relation to time, place, and manner regulations stemmed from the many cases in which government used such restrictions to bar certain groups or individuals from exercising their First Amendment right to freedom of expression. Scholars have pointed out that most of these cases actually are better understood as involving viewpoint neutrality—i.e., government's use of time, place, and manner regulations to bar certain points of view.

The difference between content neutrality and viewpoint neutrality can be understood by considering the following example. Government's use of a facially neutral time, place, and manner regulation to bar all political groups from holding meetings in a public park would be viewpoint neutral —since *all* political expression would be treated equally—but not content neutral since a certain type of expression, that concerning politics, was singled out for disparate treatment. By contrast, if government selectively enforced these same regulations against only one political group—followers of Lyndon Larouche, for example—while allowing other political groups to hold meetings in the park, the government's actions are better described as violative of viewpoint neutrality.

U.S. Supreme Court opinions in First Amendment cases involving time, place, and manner restrictions generally state that such restrictions must be content neutral. However, in recent land-use cases involving time, place, and manner restrictions, the Court has both upheld and struck down ordinances that seemed to violate content neutrality, but which, arguably, were viewpoint neutral.

For example, the Court struck down a municipal ordinance that, with certain exceptions, banned both commercial and noncommercial off-premises signs and billboards while permitting commercial on-premises signs and billboards. The regulations were certainly not content neutral, since it was the content of the message—i.e., whether it was commercial or noncommercial or fell within one of the exceptions to the ban on off-premises signs—that determined the treatment of any particular sign, but they were viewpoint neutral. Even though the ordinance could not in any way be seen as an attempt by government to suppress certain points of view, four members of the Court held that the ordinance was unconstitutional, in part because the exceptions to the ban were not content neutral. By contrast, in a later sign control case, a majority of the Court, after making note that the ordinance in question was viewpoint neutral, upheld a ban on attaching signs to certain public property even though the ordinance provided for certain exceptions to the ban based on content.

In cases involving adult entertainment regulations, the Court has upheld ordinances that singled out certain theaters for disparate regulatory treatment based on the content of the films they exhibited. In these cases, however, the Court found that the regulations were aimed at preventing the secondary effects caused by the presence of these businesses—neighborhood deterioration—rather than being a veiled attempt to suppress speech. Under these circumstances, the Court found that government could properly identify the subjects of regulation by reference to the content of the films and books available for sale on the premises.

When government attempts to regulate the time, place, and manner in which free speech rights may be exercised in a traditional public forum, it must show that its restrictions are content neutral, are narrowly tailored to serve a significant governmental interest, and leave open adequate alternative channels of communication. This standard can be difficult to administer, requiring courts to determine the relative significance of the governmental interest asserted to support the restriction on speech, whether the restrictions are narrowly tailored to serve that interest, and what constitutes an adequate alternative.

Caselaw

Young v. American Mini-Theatres, 427 U.S. 50 (1976) [V-2.53]
Metromedia, Inc. v. City of San Diego, 453 U.S. 490 (1981) [V-2.26]
Members of the City Council of Los Angeles v. Taxpayers for Vincent, 466 U.S. 789 (1984) [V-2.25]

City of Renton v. Playtime Theatres, Inc., 475 U.S. 41 (1986) [V-2.10]
Frisby v. Schultz, 108 S. Ct. 2495 (1988) [V-2.14]

Freedom of Speech Illustration No. 3—Public Forum

A municipality received numerous complaints after persons opposed to abortion began to picket the residence of a doctor who performed abortions at his clinic in a neighboring town. In response, the municipality enacted a total ban on all picketing "before or about" private residences, stating that the purpose of the ban was to protect the peace and privacy that individuals expect to enjoy in their own homes.

The U.S. Supreme Court viewed the ban as a restriction on speech in a traditional public forum, ruling that public streets, even in a residential neighborhood, have traditionally been used for assembly and debate. The Court also found, however, that the preservation of the peace and tranquility of the family home is a significant governmental interest, that the ban was narrowly tailored to serve that interest because it only barred picketing that attempted to disrupt the tranquility of the home, and that adequate alternative channels of communication were available, including marches in residential areas, door-to-door information campaigns, and mail or telephone contacts. Based on these findings, the ban was upheld.

Freedom of Speech Illustration No. 4—Public Forum

A municipality prohibited the posting of signs on public property, including utility poles and lampposts, in order to further a governmental interest in aesthetics and traffic safety. The ordinance was challenged by a candidate for elective office who had posted campaign signs that were later removed by public employees. A majority of the U.S. Supreme Court found that the signs and poles were not a traditional public forum and that the ordinance made no distinctions based on the content of signs attached to public property. Based on these findings, the majority scrutinized the ordinance under the *O'Brien* test and held that the restrictions were valid because aesthetics and traffic safety are significant governmental concerns and the restrictions regulated the posting of signs no more than was necessary to achieve those goals.

Freedom of Speech Illustration No. 5—Content Neutrality

A municipality enacts a sign-control ordinance that bans all off-premises signs, with certain specified exceptions, and allows only commercial on-premises signs. A plurality of the U.S. Supreme Court found that this ordinance violated content neutrality in two ways. First, it distinguished among on-premises signs based on their content, allowing signs with a commercial message while prohibiting noncommercial messages. Second, the exceptions to the ban on off-premises signs were also content-based.

◆   **4.** The First Amendment protects both commercial speech and noncommercial speech from improper regulation by government. ◊

Comment

Courts provide greater First Amendment safeguards for noncommercial speech that addresses political, social, or philosophical concerns than for commercial speech that merely advertises a product, service, or business. Even so, commercial speech does receive some limited First Amendment protection. A court will analyze a governmental restriction on commercial speech based on the test for commercial speech established by the U.S. Supreme Court in *Central Hudson Gas & Electric Corp. v. Public Service Commission*, 447 U.S. 557 (1980). That test first requires that a court determine whether the type of expression in question is protected by the First Amendment. For commercial speech to have First Amendment protection it must, at a minimum, concern lawful activity and not be misleading. Next the court will determine whether the asserted governmental interest advanced by the regulation is substantial. If the answer to both of these questions is yes, then the court will determine whether the regulation directly advances the asserted governmental interest and whether the regulation is more extensive than is required to achieve that interest.

The First Amendment land-use cases that involve the distinction between commercial and noncommercial speech have involved sign and billboard controls. While the law in this area is still evolving, certain principles have emerged. A majority of the members of the U.S. Supreme Court have agreed that municipalities may justify sign and billboard controls by citing the strong governmental interest in aesthetics and traffic safety, and, further, that a municipality need not provide any proof that sign and billboard controls further this interest, but can rely on the common sense notion that signs and billboards are both an eyesore and a potential traffic hazard.

A majority of the Court has also found that a municipality may either ban commercial signs and billboards entirely or impose only a partial ban—for example, barring commercial billboards and signs off-premises while permitting on-premises commercial signs used for identification or advertising. This distinction between the treatment of on-premises and off-premises commercial signs has been approved by the Court because a municipality may reasonably conclude that both businesses and the public have a stronger interest in identifying business locations and advertising the products and services available there than the municipality has in incrementally furthering its goals of aesthetics and traffic safety by banning on-premises commercial signs.

It is not clear whether a majority of the Court would uphold a total ban on all signs and billboards, both commercial and noncommercial. The plurality opinion in the *Metromedia* case was contradictory on the issue, and the majority opinion in the *Vincent* case, although upholding a total ban on political signs posted on public property, did not reach the issue of a total ban on all signs. Two Justices who dissented in both *Metromedia* and *Vincent*, while theoretically supporting the concept that a total ban could be valid, indicated that they would impose such a stringent test on a municipality attempting to use the technique. Thus, there is little likelihood that a municipality could justify a total ban on all signs.

The plurality in the *Metromedia* case also ruled that the San Diego sign ordinance was unconstitutional in part because it permitted commercial on-premises signs while prohibiting noncommercial on-premises signs. In the view of the plurality, this constituted an impermissible attempt by government to show a preference for commercial speech over noncommercial speech.

Caselaw

Members of the City Council of Los Angeles v. Taxpayers for Vincent, 466 U.S. 789 (1984) [V-2.25]
Metromedia, Inc. v. City of San Diego, 453 U.S. 490 (1981) [V-2.26]
Central Hudson Gas & Electric Corp. v. Public Service Commission of New York, 447 U.S. 557 (1980)

Freedom of Speech Illustration No. 6—Signs and Billboards

A municipality enacts significant restrictions on both commercial and noncommercial signs and billboards. All off-premises signs and billboards are banned, while on-premises signs are limited to the display of commercial messages. Although the distinction in the ordinance between on-premises and off-premises signs is valid, and the ordinance could legitimately ban all commercial signs and billboards, because the effect of the ordinance is to place greater restrictions on noncommercial than on commercial speech, this ordinance is invalid.

♦   **5.** Even when government may legitimately regulate expression, an ordinance may be invalid if it is so vague that it is unclear what type of expression is actually regulated or if it is so broadly worded that it has the effect of restricting speech to an extent greater than is required to achieve the goals of the regulation. ◊

Comment

These two principles—termed *void-for-vagueness* and *overbreadth*—seek to ensure that government regulation of expression is sufficiently precise so that individuals will know exactly what forms of expression are restricted and that laws which legitimately regulate certain forms of expression do not also include within their scope other types of expression that may not permissibly be regulated. These two principles are quite closely related and courts often find that an ordinance violates both.

Caselaw

Schad v. Borough of Mount Ephraim 452 U.S. 61 (1981) [V-2.41].
Purple Onion v. Jackson Inc., 511 F.Supp. 1207 (N.D. Ga. 1981).

Freedom of Speech Illustration No. 7—Void-For-Vagueness

A municipality enacts an adult entertainment ordinance. The definition of an adult business in the ordinance is so vague that it could be applied to any private home that might have a copy of *Playboy* magazine, downtown hotels that exhibit movies on cable television, and even the federal courthouse since adult movies and magazines, which are evidence in lawsuits, could be found there. The ordinance is invalid for both vagueness and overbreadth.

Freedom of Speech Illustration No. 8—Overbreadth

In an effort to bar an existing adult entertainment business from exhibiting live topless dancing, a city adopts an ordinance that can be interpreted as prohibiting all live entertainment within the city's boundaries. This regulation is overbroad because it has the effect of totally suppressing an important form of expression and there is no reasonable justification for such a serious infringement on freedom of speech.

♦   **6.** Laws that have the effect of prohibiting or limiting speech unless or until the speaker has obtained the approval of government constitute a prior restraint on freedom of expression and are generally presumed to be unconstitutional. ◊

Comment

Courts view any attempt by government to condition the right to freedom of expression on receiving the prior approval of a governmental official as posing a particularly serious threat to the values embodied in the First Amendment. Such attempts are termed prior restraints and call for the strictest judicial scrutiny. Where a court finds a prior restraint, it will reverse the traditional presumption of validity accorded to the actions of government and presume that the prior restraint is unconstitutional. In order to overcome the presumption that a prior restraint is unconstitutional, government must show that the licensing or permitting scheme is subject to clearly established standards that strictly limit the discretion of those officials administering the scheme. Courts also require that such schemes meet stringent procedural requirements.

In the land use context, requiring any type of permit or license as a prerequisite to engaging in activity associated with speech or expression would appear to have the potential for constituting a prior restraint; however, the U.S. Supreme Court limits the concept to permitting or licensing schemes that constitute a content-based regulation of speech. To date, the Court has not applied the prior restraint doctrine to commercial speech.

Caselaw

City of Lakewood v. Plain Dealer Publishing Co., _____ U.S. _____, 108 S.Ct. 2138 (1988) [V-2.08]

Freedom of Speech Illustration No. 9—Prior Restraint

A municipality adopts an ordinance that allows newsracks to be located in certain zoning districts subject to approval of an annual permit by the mayor. If the mayor denies a permit, he is required to state the reasons for the denial. If a permit is granted, it is subject to specified conditions, including design approval and obtaining liability insurance. It is also subject to such other conditions deemed necessary and reasonable by the mayor. The newspaper challenges the ordinance on the ground that it constitutes an unlawful prior restraint. A court would find that the portions of the ordinance that gave the mayor the unbridled authority to deny a permit application and unbridled authority to condition the permit on any additional terms he deems necessary and reasonable to be unconstitutional.

7.03 Symposium Discussion

Weinstein: After the U.S. Supreme Court's landmark 1976 decision in *Young,* many municipal governments saw an opportunity to use their zoning regulations to suppress adult businesses. In a large number of cases, municipalities enacted overly restrictive regulations that were eventually struck down by the courts. With the Court's 1986 decision in *Renton,* however, the rules of the game shifted dramatically in favor of stricter regulation. That case replaced the *O'Brien* test used by many courts to evaluate adult zoning ordinances with two reasonableness standards. The first, allowed a municipality to use information from other cities about the secondary effects of adult businesses to justify the need for adult zoning. The second requires that a city need only provide adult businesses with a reasonable opportunity to find a suitable location.

These new standards provide municipalities with much greater leeway in strictly regulating adult businesses. Interestingly, even with the increased judicial deference to adult business regulation following the *Renton* decision, some cases have shown the same pattern of municipal overreaching that followed *Young* and these ordinances have been struck down. In one case, the city offered no evidence whatsoever to support its regulations, not even bothering to cite another city's experience on the issue of secondary effects. Another defined what constitutes an adult business so stringently—the showing of a single adult film—that no secondary effects could possibly arise. Another instituted an outright ban on certain kinds of adult entertainment. So the old pattern that emerged after *Young* seems to be re-emerging once more. For planners, the great importance of the *Renton* case was that the Court recognized that the concentration of adult uses was an available constitutional strategy in addition to the dispersion scheme approved in *Young.* For lawyers, the greatest import of the decision was the rejection of the *O'Brien* test that had been enunciated in Justice Powell's concurring opinion in *Young,* and which had been used by a number of courts since Justice Stevens' plurality opinion was joined by only three justices.

Sign Regulation

In the area of billboard and sign regulation, I think the cases demonstrate that the regulations don't have to be comprehensive in the sense that the community does not have to address all of its aesthetic problems at once in order to address the area of sign regulation. But courts will strike down such regulations if they have no rational basis.

Siemon: I would underscore the point in the area of sign regulation that in determining whether the regulation substantially advances the governmental purposes a court is going to be greatly impressed whether the regulation is part of a comprehensive program or stands by itself. The probability of success in defending a fairly intrusive limitation on signs will stand a much better possibility of success if it is a part of a comprehensive program. If the court can look and say you selected this group out and there's no probability of any other program you may not be able to survive the requirement in *Central Hudson Gas & Electric Corp.* v. *Public Service Commission,* 447 U.S. 557 (1980) that the regulation substantially advance the governmental purpose.

Weinstein: Yes, I agree. The plan must be a comprehensive plan in the sense of good planning practice, but it need not be all-inclusive and regulate every possible aesthetic problem. Finally, running through all of these cases, whether they concern regulations affecting adult uses or billboards and signs, are the First Amendment concepts of time, place, and manner regulations and the vagueness and overbreadth doctrines. In case after case, where ordinances are vague or overly broad, they have been struck down.

Newsracks

Meck: One problem right now is newsracks. The U.S. Supreme Court just decided a case from Ohio, *City of Lakewood v. Plain Dealer Publishing Co.,* 108 S. Ct. 2138 (1988). The newspaper company's theory was that somehow they have been given a sort of eminent domain right through the First Amendment and that they can put newsracks anyplace on public property. They can also obstruct sidewalks, attach their newsracks as fixtures by bolting them to the concrete. The *Plain Dealer* was upheld by both the trial and appellate courts even though the city of Lakewood modified its ordinance to satisfy what they thought were the problems.

Blaesser: It was upheld in its challenge of the regulation against it?

Meck: The *Plain Dealer* was upheld initially in its challenge of the Lakewood ordinance. The city of Lakewood went back and corrected what they thought were the defects of the ordinance. The newspaper then again challenged that amended ordinance and won. Then it went to the Supreme Court, and the Court supported the newspaper.

Delogu: The thing that brought the *Plain Dealer* case to a head was a total exclusion. Didn't the first ordinance seek to ban these newsracks almost totally from residential areas? It's that action that put the town behind the eight ball. If what we're talking about is whether a collection of First Amendment purveyors can occupy 35 spaces at one subway exit point, the courts aren't going to have much difficulty saying "no." There must be some room made, but not 35 spaces. In sum, I think we can advise planners that reasonable performance standards will apply to certain collateral activities of religious groups and that the First Amendment rights of newsdealers, and others, are amenable to certain time, place (location), and manner of delivery restrictions.

Gerard: The most obvious problem is the one the court raised in the taxation of the press case. You can impose uniform business regulations on the press so long as you don't single the press out. If, for example, you do not permit the clothier to put out racks and sell ties, socks, etc., then in theory at least you can impose that same kind of restriction on the press. When the Supreme Court finally disposed of the *Plain Dealer* case last June, it resolved none of the novel issues raised by newsracks. The vote was 4-3, two justices not participating. The only disagreement between the majority and the dissenters was over whether the newspaper was entitled to challenge the constitutionality of the ordinance on its face. This, in turn, depended on whether the ordinance should be characterized as a regulation of newspaper circulation (the majority's view), or only as the regulation of the placement of newsracks on public property (the dissenters' view).

The ordinance authorized the mayor to grant permits for newsracks under certain stated conditions and also "[to impose] other terms and conditions deemed necessary and reasonable by the Mayor." That language was held unconstitutional under the well-established principle that forbids the vesting in any official of unbridled discretion to permit or deny speech. The Court held that the quoted provision created a real risk of cen-

sorship of opinion, especially because the required permits had to be renewed annually, and therefore violated that principle. None of this was
anything new. The majority of four refused to rule on the question
whether newsracks could be banned from public property entirely; the
three dissenters thought they could be.

I think that one major point of interest did emerge from the decision.
The majority opinion stated: "Of course, the City may require periodic licensing, *and may even have spatial licensing procedures for conduct commonly associated with expression . . .*" [speaker's emphasis]. This makes it
clear that an ordinance dealing explicitly with newsracks—and thus singling the press out for special treatment—will not be held unconstitutional
for that reason alone.

Freedom of Association

Weinstein: Before we conclude our discussion of freedom of speech, it's
important to note that the First Amendment has been read in conjunction
with the due process clause of the Fourteenth Amendment to provide a
constitutional safeguard to certain rights of privacy and freedom of association. In the land use context, privacy and freedom of association have
been important issues in cases that challenge restrictive definitions of
"family" in municipal zoning ordinances. In *Belle Terre v. Boraas* [V-2.48],
for example, a majority of the Supreme Court rejected the claim that a
zoning ordinance that limited occupancy of single-family homes to any
number of persons related by blood, marriage, or adoption, or no more
than two unrelated individuals, intruded upon the privacy and
associational rights of the six unrelated students who occupied the house
in question. However, in *Moore v. City of East Cleveland* [V-2.29], a plurality
of the Court held that an ordinance that barred a grandmother, who lived
with her son and grandson, from taking in another grandchild—the first
grandchild's cousin—who had been orphaned, intruded too deeply into
the privacy of the family relationship. Although some state courts have relied on freedom of association and privacy to strike down family definition
ordinances, the majority of courts also have found violations of state constitutional guarantees of due process.

SECTION 8:
PRINCIPLE 8:
FREEDOM OF RELIGION

◆ **8.01 The First Amendment**

The First Amendment states in relevant part: "Congress shall make no law respecting an establishment of religion, or prohibiting the free exercise thereof. . . ." ◇

◆ **8.02 Freedom of Religion—Introduction**

The First Amendment's guarantee of freedom of religion addresses two separate aspects of that freedom. First, government may not take action that would effect "an establishment of religion." This is commonly known as the *establishment clause*. Second, government must not prohibit the "free exercise" of religion. This is commonly known as the *free exercise clause*. ◇

8.03 Freedom of Religion—The Establishment Clause

◆ The establishment clause prohibits government sponsorship of religion. ◇

Comment

When a governmental act involves religion or religious institutions, it must pass a three-part test to be held valid under the establishment clause: (1) it must have a secular purpose; (2) its primary effect must be secular; and (3) there must not be an excessive entanglement between government and religion.

A local government may violate the establishment clause when it delegates its own powers to a religious organization or shows preference for certain religions. On the other hand, government may legitimately undertake an activity for a secular purpose even though there is some incidental benefit to religion.

Caselaw

Larkin v. Grendel's Den, Inc., 459 U.S. 941 (1982) [V-2.22]
Lemon v. Kurtzman, 403 U.S. 602 (1971)

Establishment Clause Illustration No. 1

A local government provides basic municipal services, such as police and fire protection, to religious institutions. This would not be considered a violation of the establishment clause because such services have a secular purpose and effect, they do not involve excessive government entanglement with religion, and they benefit religion only incidentally.

Establishment Clause Illustration No. 2

A local government ordinance allows churches or schools to veto the grant of a liquor license for any premises located within 500 feet of the church or school. The ordinance would violate the establishment clause because it would create an excessive entanglement of government with religion. The ordinance would involve churches in the process of government and could allow churches to use their veto power for religious purposes.

◆ 8.04 Freedom of Religion—The Free Exercise Clause

Government may never take action that would prohibit an individual from holding any given religious beliefs; however, government action that incidentally burdens religious practices is permitted when such action involves the regulation of secular activities and the state interest in regulation outweighs the incidental burden on religious practice. ◊

Comment

Government does not necessarily violate the free exercise clause when it places a burden on the practice of religion. A government restriction or regulation that affects religion will be scrutinized under two tests. First, the court will inquire whether the government action substantially burdens the practice of religion. If a substantial burden can be demonstrated, then the court will examine whether this burden on the free exercise of religion is justified by an overriding governmental interest and, if the burden is justified, whether the religious belief could be accommodated without unduly interfering with the achievement of that interest.

Caselaw

Wisconsin v. Yoder, 406 U.S. 205 (1972)

Comment

1. *Houses of Worship in Residential Areas*   Potential conflicts between religious institutions and government arise in the land use context when municipalities seek to apply zoning restrictions to churches, synagogues, or other houses of worship. Such restrictions are often imposed because of the significant traffic and parking problems associated with houses of worship and the possible negative effect this may have on property values. Because of these concerns, communities often seek either to bar houses of worship from low-density residential neighborhoods or require that they obtain special permits.

States   Most state courts that have addressed this question do not explicitly consider the free exercise of religion issue. Instead, the courts generally base their analysis on substantive due process considerations.

A majority of state jurisdictions hold that it would be an unreasonable use of the zoning power—and thus a violation of due process—to exclude houses of worship from low-density residential areas. In these jurisdictions, zoning restrictions on houses of worship cannot be justified by such factors as potential traffic hazards, effect on property values, noise, and decreased enjoyment of neighboring properties, because the courts find that the "high purposes and moral values" of religious institutions far outweigh "mere pecuniary loss." In some of the majority jurisdictions, special permit requirements for religious institutions have been held invalid; in others although municipalities have been allowed to impose special permit requirements on houses of worship, the courts have invalidated those provisions that have the effect of unduly limiting houses of worship.

In the few instances where ordinances completely excluded houses of worship from a municipality, they have been declared invalid. Ordinances banning houses of worship from all residential areas have also been held invalid.

By contrast, a minority of state jurisdictions allow municipalities to treat houses of worship in the same manner as other nonresidential uses and thus to exclude them from residential areas. New York, which had previously been the leading jurisdiction espousing the majority view, has now joined the minority view. Religious institutions in that state are no longer presumed by the court to be in the public interest and can be excluded from residential neighborhoods if a municipality can show legitimate zoning reasons for doing so.

Federal

Few federal appellate court decisions have addressed the question of barring houses of worship from residential areas. In two cases, the federal courts upheld the application of zoning restrictions that had the effect of barring a particular house of worship from a residential area. These courts balanced the competing interests of municipalities and religious institutions and found that the zoning regulation in question did not unduly burden the free exercise of religion where it affected only the location of a house of worship, other sites were available to the congregation, and the city had legitimate zoning reasons for its decision. By contrast, the one federal court that has struck down an attempt to bar a religious institution on zoning grounds found that the city was attempting to ban the religious institution—an Islamic student center and mosque—by denying it permission to operate in areas where Christian houses of worship were permitted, and that the denials were based on spurious reasons. This attempt at a total ban did constitute an undue burden of religion and the municipality could not justify its actions.

Caselaw

Federal

Islamic Center of Mississippi, Inc. v. City of Starkville, 840 F.2d 293 (5th Cir. 1988)
Grosz v. City of Miami Beach, 721 F.2d 729 (11th Cir. 1983), *cert. denied*, 469 U.S. 827 (1984)
Lakewood, Ohio Congregation of Jehovah's Witnesses, Inc. v. City of Lakewood, 699 F.2d 303 (6th Cir. 1983)

State

Diocese of Rochester v. Planning Board of Town of Brighton, 136 N.E.2d 827 (N.Y. 1956) [Majority State Court View]
Corporation of Presiding Bishop of Church of Jesus Christ of Latter Day Saints v. City of Porterville, 203 P.2d 823 (Cal. 1949) [Minority State Court View]
Cornell University v. Bagnardi, 503 N.E.2d 509 (N.Y. 1986) [Minority State Court View]

Free Exercise Clause Illustration No. 1—Federal Court Approach

A local zoning ordinance allows construction of churches in 10 percent of the city. A congregation seeks to erect a church building in a district where churches are not permitted, but is denied zoning approval. The congregation claims this decision violates the free exercise clause. The federal court will examine the burden placed on religion by the zoning ordinance and the government interest served by the ordinance. The burden on religion is that the congregation must construct its church only in certain districts. Since such a burden does not deny persons the right to observe their religious faith but merely addresses the ability to construct a church building at a given location, the burden on religion is indirect, and there is no real impact on the practice of religion. The ordinance would be upheld.

Free Exercise Clause Illustration No. 2—Majority State Court Approach

A town board denies an application from a newly formed congregation to convert a single-family dwelling in a residential district into a church. The state court in a majority jurisdiction would overturn the denial on the grounds that religious uses are presumed to benefit the public health, safety, and welfare and thus may not be excluded from residential areas.

Free Exercise Clause Illustration No. 3—Minority State Court Approach

A municipality excludes a church from a single-family residential district. The church challenges the action. A state court in a minority jurisdiction would rule that a municipality may lawfully exclude churches from residential districts if the problems expected to be caused by traffic, parking, and noise from the church would be detrimental to property values and would disturb the quiet residential nature of the community. Such restrictions will not be found to be improper restriction on freedom of religion so long as the church may be constructed in some other zoning district.

2. *Religious Schools*   A number of courts have considered whether a parochial school may legitimately be subjected to more stringent zoning requirements than a house of worship. The majority hold that the more stringent requirements are justified because a school has a greater potential adverse impact on surrounding properties. The minority view holds

that a parochial school is an integral and inseparable part of a religious institution and may not be subject to more stringent requirements.

Caselaw

Seward Chapel, Inc. v. City of Seward, 655 P.2d 1293 (Alaska 1982)
[Majority State Court View]
City of Concord v. New Testament Baptist Church, 382 A.2d 377 (N.H. 1978) [Minority State Court View]

Free Exercise Clause Illustration No. 4—Majority State Court Approach

A zoning ordinance excluding nonpublic schools from a residential area is challenged by a church. A court in a majority jurisdiction probably would uphold the ordinance finding that it was based on a reasonable conclusion that a school may generally have an adverse impact making it incompatible with a residential area. Such an ordinance does not violate freedom of religion, because it simply requires that religious schools be located where their impact on surrounding properties is lessened.

3. *Home Worship* Cases involving attempts to restrict home worship usually arise when neighbors complain that a home is being used frequently by large numbers of persons for worship, with resulting parking and noise problems. Although some courts have upheld the imposition of zoning regulations to curb religious activities in the home, other jurisdictions find any restriction on home worship to be an infringement per se on freedom of religion.

Caselaw

Grosz v. City of Miami Beach, 721 F.2d 729 (11th Cir. 1983)
Farhi v. Commissioners of the Borough of Deal, 499 A.2d 559 (N.J. Super. L. 1985)

Free Exercise Clause Illustration No. 5—Home Worship

A local zoning ordinance limits the uses in all residential districts except one to private, noncommercial, single-family dwellings. Churches and other places of worship are permitted only in that one district. The owner of a single-family house in a residential district where houses of worship are not permitted holds religious services in his home and converts a portion of the house to accommodate these services. On weekdays, the 10 to

15 people who attend services use their automobiles. On weekends, when as many as 25 attend, there is little automobile usage because of the religious beliefs of the worshipers. The municipality seeks to enforce the zoning prohibition against houses of worship after the neighbors complain about parking problems and noise.

A federal court, upon weighing the burden on religious freedom against the municipality's interest in maintaining its zoning scheme, would uphold the municipality because, it found if there were sufficient alternative locations for a house of worship, there was no undue burden on religion and the municipality had a strong interest in maintaining its residential areas exclusively for homes. Some state courts have ruled, however, that the guaranty of freedom of worship contained in the state constitution forecloses any use of the zoning power to prohibit the free exercise of religious activity in the privacy of one's own home.

4. *Landmarks Designation*   Several New York cases have considered whether religious groups, which own houses of worship or other buildings that have been designated as landmarks, should receive preferential treatment in the administration of the landmark preservation scheme. These cases arise when the governmental authority that administers the landmarks law seeks to prevent a religious group from either demolishing or altering a landmark or prohibits new construction—typically a modern high-rise office or apartment building—above or behind the existing landmark structure.

The New York courts have ruled that when the religious group's use of a landmark building is secular in nature, there is no basis to distinguish religious groups from any other owner. In such instances, the religious group must prove that the landmark designation amounts to a taking of the property in order to avoid regulation. When, however, the use is for a charitable or religious purpose, the First Amendment curtails the permissible extent of governmental regulation and the religious group need only show that the landmark designation will seriously interfere with the carrying out of that purpose.

Caselaw

Society For Ethical Culture of City of New York v. Spatt, 415 N.E.2d 922 (N.Y. 1980)
Lutheran Church in America v. City of New York, 316 N.E.2d 305 (N.Y. 1974)

8.05 Symposium Discussion

Weinstein: In the free exercise area, the critical issue typically is whether or not religious uses are permitted in prime residential districts. Such uses would include formal churches and synagogues, or private homes used for religious observance. One obvious factor that emerges from the cases is that most of the litigation concerns denominations such as Seventh Day Adventists, the Jehovah's Witnesses, Pentecostal churches, synagogues, and a few Roman Catholic congregations. What you don't see are the mainline Protestant denominations. The benign explanation is that the more established churches predate zoning or came into the community before prime residential areas were fully developed. A less charitable explanation, is, of course, religious prejudice.

In the last few years there has been some very interesting movement in the law in this area. First, the three federal appeals courts to address these cases have adopted a First Amendment balancing test approach similar to that used by the U.S. Supreme Court. The states, by contrast, traditionally have utilized a substantive due process analysis in applying their state constitutions and are divided into minority and majority jurisdictions. The minority allow the exclusion of churches on general planning principles; the majority find churches to be a presumed beneficial use, which then requires government to shoulder the burden of proving why the church should be excluded.

The second emerging issue is the use of private homes for religious services. This is occurring primarily with fundamentalist Christian denominations and newly formed orthodox Jewish congregations.

The one federal court to consider this issue used a balancing test that weighed the restrictions on the free expression of religion against the government's interest in land use regulation and upheld the municipality. By contrast, in New Jersey, the courts view religious activity in the home as absolutely protected under the freedom of religion clause in the state constitution.

Tarlock: I think, particularly at the state level, that there is a real imbalance in the way that the courts approach zoning that touches on religious practice and orthodox First Amendment law. There certainly are a lot of state cases that simply do not reach First Amendment issues that are presented, and I think the real key is the type of religion involved. Second, one has to make the distinction between worship per se and religious related services. Most of the hard state cases are coming in the daycare schools program area.

Babcock: The First Amendment says "Congress shall make no law . . ." I think an argument can be made that very few local or state, if any, regulations are covered by the First Amendment. They generally dig into them at the Fourteenth Amendment. The *St. Barts* case is a fascinating case moving up through the state courts in New York. St. Barts, a church on Park Avenue, wants to sell off a portion of the community house and get $5 or 6 million even though it has been designated a landmark. The church has pled the First Amendment, and I think it's really going to come down to the Fourteenth Amendment. The question for me is whether that case would have a different outcome if it arose in the District of Columbia under federal law. I think it might. So I think you've got to be very careful about assuming that all of these cases involving state and local government are really First Amendment cases. I think they're more likely the Fourteenth Amendment.

Church-Related Activities

Mee: The issue with churches is not so much the churches themselves, the actual religious worship facilities. It's the baseball, basketball, the church-related activities and special events, and whether or not some reasonable performance standards can be placed on them.

Delogu: I think the cases indicate that there is a fundamental difference between the basic religious activity, whether its a Jehovah's Witness group or a mainline church, and the collateral activities, whether they be athletic, the daycare center, the school. The latter activities are amenable, if not to being precluded, at least to some reasonable restrictions in the nature of performance standards that address lighting, parking, hours, signs, and other aspects of such activities that may be incompatible with the residential neighborhood.

Berman: We have a proliferation in one block of six or eight churches and that really does impact the community. In residential neighborhoods where there were large homes in the past, churches are either remodeling them or demolishing them and rebuilding churches on large lots and conducting extracurricular activities along with their religious services. Just the traffic, parking, and the buses place an impossible burden on the residents.

Livingston: The church issue needs to be broken down into two subsets, one is the onsite activities, the school and the bus parking and all the things that go on, plus the raffles, etc. The other set concerns the social welfare activities conducted under church sponsorship off-site, which are fundamentally different from the church activities that occur on the actual church site.

Lamont: I would like Larry to clarify the issue as far as group homes, shelters, etc. operated by a church. I don't see what the issue is.

Livingston: The claim made frequently in communities where I have worked is that these activities are not subject to the general rules with respect to group homes and other types of social service activities because they are church-sponsored, church-owned, and church-operated. I disagree with those who make the claim, I think that they should be subject to all the same rules for the same uses that are not church-sponsored, but it comes up all the time.

The Establishment Clause

Gerard: Many of those earlier cases that gave special status to churches seem to me to be highly dubious under more recent Supreme Court establishment clause doctrine. It's perfectly clear that if by law you declare that it's up to the church to decide whether or not it's going to comply with the law, that violates the establishment clause.

Tarlock: Suppose you said that a place of religious worship has a lesser burden to meet under a special use permit?

Gerard: If you provide that by law, it flatly violates the three-prong test that the Court uses to determine whether there is an establishment clause violation.

Tarlock: What happens to a Catholic parish that says healing the sick is just as much a part of our religion as taking communion on Sunday, so that running a group home here is just as much a religious activity as Sunday services? Therefore, says the church, we're entitled to whatever First Amendment protection there is for churches for this activity.

Gerard: One of the things that's set forth in the statement on the free exercise clause in Section 8.04 is that the government must in some way be prohibiting or coercing the individual, either to refrain from following the tenets of his religion or to adopt the tenets of somebody else's religion. With respect to many of the cases we're talking about, which are free exercise problems, it is highly dubious that such a claim of coercion can be made.

Kmiec: Following up on that point, there is an historic distinction between conduct and belief, and perhaps, that's the point you're making. The free exercise clause has long been interpreted to preclude coercion or compulsion in terms of belief, but it has much different impact in terms of conduct. As a result, it is clear that even though the Mormons believe in polygamy, the state can have a substantial interest that outweighs their freedom to practice polygamy. Similarly, while Bob Jones University believed it was appropriate in certain circumstances to discriminate on the basis of race in its policy, the U.S. Supreme Court said that it was equally clear that the federal government had a substantial interest in overcoming racial discrimination and allowing the IRS to deny the university's tax exemption.

Weinstein: I want to point out one thing about the church-school cases. The clear trend in my view is that the courts are prohibiting schools attached to churches when the churches are allowed. That is because the churches are located in areas where schools are not generally allowed. We're not talking about the Sunday school in the church building. We're talking about the parochial school as a separate accessory use along with the church, the clear trend is that they can be excluded even though the church may be permitted.

Mee: What about communities that cannot regulate where schools locate? We can do less to public schools than we can do to churches.

Blaesser: That situation is governed by state statute.

Delogu: Even in the states that cannot bar schools from certain districts, it's my understanding that in a majority of those states, schools may still be subjected to reasonable performance standards. You may not be able to control them in the sense of placing them where you want, but you can control them in the sense of hours, of operation, lighting, parking spaces available, etc.

III

Planner Problem Solving Areas

Matrix 1: Relationship of Planner Problem Solving Areas to Constitutional Principles with Cross Reference to Supreme Court Cases

Constitutional Principles

Legend

- ● Relationship exists
- ●/2.01 Cross reference to applicable Supreme Court Case(s) in Part V

Planner Problem Solving Areas

	Delegation of Power [II-1]	Void for Vagueness [II-2]	Procedural Due Process [II-3]	Substantive Due Process [II-4]	Equal Protection [II-5]	Just Compensation [II-6]	Ripeness [II-6]	Freedom of Speech [II-7]	Freedom of Religion [II-8]	Establishment Clause [II-8]	Free Exercise Clause [II-8]
Discretionary Permitting [III-1]	●	●	●	● 2.32 2.49	● 2.05 2.49	● 2.01 2.12 2.32					
Downzoning [III-2]				● 2.32 2.40 2.49	● 2.05 2.49	● 2.01 2.12 2.32					
Specific Parcel Rezoning [III-3]				● 2.32 2.40 2.49	● 2.05 2.49	● 2.01 2.12 2.32					
Special Exception [III-4]	●			● 2.32 2.49	● 2.05 2.11 2.49	● 2.01 2.12 2.32	● 2.24 2.40 2.52				
Negotiated (Rezoning) Approvals [III-5]	●		●	● 2.32	● 2.05 2.11 2.49						
Development Exactions [III-6]				● 2.32		● 2.12 2.32					
Prohibition of Use: Adult Entertainment [III-7]		●		● 2.32 2.53	● 2.53	● 2.12 2.32		● 2.10 2.41 2.53			
Prohibition of Use: Religious Use [III-7]		●		●	●					●	●
Prohibition of Use: Housing for Mentally Retarded [III-7]				●	● 2.05						
Prohibition of Use: Multi-Family Residence [III-7]				●	● 2.47						
Growth Phasing [III-8]	●			● 2.32	● 2.49	● 2.12 2.32					
Interim Land Use Controls (Moratorium) [III-9]			●	● 2.32 2.49	● 2.49	● 2.12 2.32					
Resource Protection [III-10]				● 2.21 2.32	● 2.49	● 2.12 2.21 2.32					
Regulation for Aesthetic Purposes [III-11]	●		●	● 2.25 2.26 2.32	● 2.53	● 2.12 2.32		● 2.08 2.25 2.26			
Amortization of Nonconforming Use(s) [III-12]				● 2.32	● 2.49	● 2.12 2.32					

SYMPOSIUM DISCUSSION

Topical Index

SECTION 1:
DISCRETIONARY PERMITTING

1.01 Historic District Regulation: Fact Situation

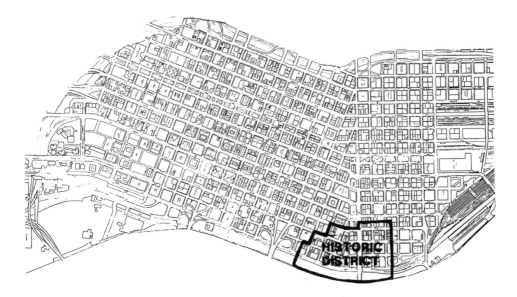

The planning board recommends historic district legislation that will require design and demolition review before a building or demolition permit may be granted. The historic district is a portion of the downtown business district comprising twenty square blocks of commercial buildings. The purpose clause of the proposed legislation states that it was enacted to preserve and protect the early architectural heritage of the city (on the edge of the Rockies) by protecting the many buildings constructed between 1860 and 1880. Most of the property owners in the proposed district oppose the legislation.

Under the proposed legislation, all new buildings must meet specific design criteria unless an exemption is granted by the design consultation board (DCB). The design consultation board is composed of five members appointed by the mayor. The membership must represent property owners from the area, the local chapter of the American Institute of Architects, a developer proposed by the board of realtors, and a member appointed from the landmark preservation commission. The purpose is to assure an expert board. Appeals from the DCB may be made to the city's landmark preservation commission (LPC).

The design review process begins with the planning board staff who provide an initial consultation, which is followed by a review by the design consultation board. Applications for a building permit are evaluated against the following general criteria:

1. The protection, enhancement, and perpetuation of buildings, sites, and areas located within the historic district.
2. The encouragement of rehabilitation.
3. Compatibility with the architectural heritage and character of the district in terms of: architectural style, massing, texture, scale, color, and materials.
4. Compatibility of contemporary design. (Contemporary design is not discouraged, but must be compatible.)

If the DCB denies a permit request, the applicant has a right of appeal to the LPC, which conducts a public hearing on the appeal.

The DCB also reviews any request for demolition of a contributing building. Contributing buildings, identified by a survey of the area, are buildings which add to the district's historical character.

When a demolition permit is requested, the design consultation board must consider the following factors:

1. Whether the building is imminently dangerous to the public.
2. Whether maintaining the building will impose a significant economic hardship on the owner (i.e., making it impractical to rehabilitate or reuse, as well as the economic feasibility of reuse versus the economic value of the proposed redevelopment).
3. Whether demolition of the building will impose a significant hardship to the public interest (i.e., significance of the building as related to the district, age of building, the extent to which the structure maintains continuity of adjacent contributing structures, etc.)

A public hearing is held on a request for demolition, which may be prohibited or approved. Postdemolition redevelopment plans for the site must accompany any request for demolition. If approved, the demolition permit will not be issued until a building permit is obtained for the new building. The burden of proof is the responsibility of the property owner. The DCB's decision may be appealed to the landmark preservation commission, but otherwise is final. From the landmark preservation commission, the appeal goes to the courts.

After designating the area and adopting the ordinance, the city council has no further involvement.

1.02 Discussion

Any legislation calling for a special permit to construct or to demolish and not providing for a final review by the local legislative body is at least suspect. Giving final decision-making to an administrative body without adequate standards may violate the **Delegation of Power [II-1]** doctrine. In this case there is no indication of the standards used by the design consultation board (DCB) to grant exemptions. Such an omission may leave too wide a discretion to the DCB and may be challenged as an improper delegation of authority by the city council. Generally, a standard is sufficiently definite if a reasonable person can understand what is required and a court can use the standard to determine whether a particular decision is arbitrary under the standard. The availability of an appeal to the landmark preservation commission (LPC) probably is not sufficient because it is also an appointed body.

There is also the probability that some of the standards may be challenged for **Vagueness [II-2]**. Criterion No. 3, "compatibility with the architectural heritage and character of the district," may pass the test, provided the purpose clause of the ordinance is clear regarding the intent of this historic district. Presumably the purpose is not to preserve architecturally significant buildings but to protect the ambience of a particular era—as is the case in some districts in Seattle. This in itself is not a basis for invalidating such an ordinance, but the purpose clause must be explicit regarding the goals of the ordinance. Criterion No. 4, "contemporary design is not discouraged but must be compatible," is more dubious. The terms *contemporary design* and *compatible* are both equivocal and may leave the applicant uncertain as to what he or she can do. A definitions section that deals with these phrases may help the ordinance.

The discretionary permitting process must satisfy the requirement of **Procedural Due Process [II-3]**. There is no provision for a public hearing and notice before the design consultation board for a permit request. Procedural due process requires that persons who wish to protest a proposal and who may be aggrieved by a decision be given an opportunity to be heard.

The ordinance may also raise a question of **Substantive Due Process [II-4]**, that is, whether the regulation bears a substantial relationship to the public health, safety, and welfare. In this case we do not know whether the 20 square blocks still contain a majority, a minority, or a balance between the number of old and new buildings. Presumably the city has conducted a survey and mapping of the area, and presumably a majority of the buildings are of the 1860–80 era. If they are not, then the city may be acting too late and a person who is turned down may allege that the decision is unreasonable and denies substantive due process.

An issue of **Equal Protection [II-5]** could also arise in this case because the ordinance does not require a written report either by the DCB or the landmark preservation commission. Usually, appointed bodies who make decisions are required to issue written reports setting out facts and the reasons why they reached a conclusion. Unless some written record is made, there is no basis to determine whether the design consultation board, in its decisions, is giving equal treatment to persons similarly situated.

The provisions for demolition are also disturbing. A denial of a demolition permit without compensation raises a taking issue under the **Just Compensation Clause [II-6]**. The design consultation board need only consider the three factors and, having considered them, presumably may deny the permit. Some of the vulnerability to constitutional challenge might be lessened were the final decision left to the city council. Most antidemolition ordinances do no more than delay demolition for a year or less to give an opportunity for buyers, either public or private, to come forward. Even then, however, depending on the circumstances, a temporary taking issue could arise.

SECTION 2:
DOWNZONING

2.01 Townhouse to Single-Family Detached: Fact Situation

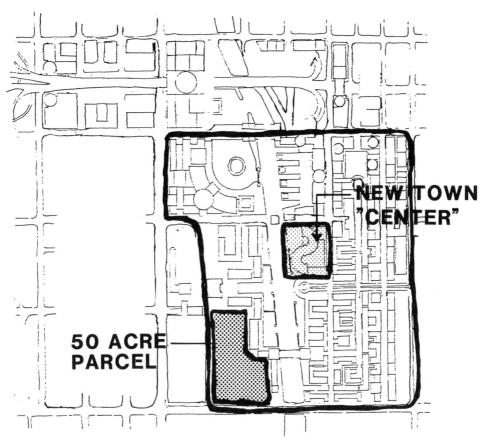

A 50-acre parcel of land in a suburban municipality was upzoned in 1975 from low-density residential (i.e., one dwelling unit per acre) to town-house density residential (i.e., 10 dwelling units per acre), by the munici-pality as part of a comprehensive zoning map amendment for a large area that was called a new town. No development has yet taken place on this parcel, but many other similarly rezoned parcels in the vicinity have been developed with townhouses.

The new residents of one of these townhouse developments complain that there are too many townhouses in their community, and that there is an inadequate supply of single-family detached housing. They argue that not only does this generate a second-class image for their community, but also that there is an inadequate supply of move-up housing available for people who currently reside in townhouses.

The planning commission agrees with the perspective of the new residents and recommends a downzoning of the 50-acre parcel to single-family detached residential at a density of two dwelling units per acre. It is noted by the commission that this property is further away from the center of the new town than the remaining townhouse zoning.

At the public hearing before the city council, the landowner, who purchased the property shortly after the upzoning, argues that she has been prevented from developing her land for townhouses since 1975 because the municipality has withheld the provision of sewer service as part of a staging program for the new town under which her land was designated for development at a later stage than others. She and the planning commission agree that her property can be adequately served in the future by planned roads and sewers, and that no environmental constraints exist that would prevent the townhouse density from being accommodated on the land.

After the public hearing, the city council approves the downzoning by a majority vote, without discussion, comment, or findings. The applicant appeals the decision to the circuit court on the grounds that there is no valid public purpose for the downzoning, and that she has been deprived of the opportunity to use her land under the previous zoning because of the action of the municipality in withholding sewer service.

2.02 Discussion

The downzoning in this case raises two **Substantive Due Process [II-4]** issues regarding the reasonableness of the city council's action: spot zoning and lack of stated reasons for the downzoning.

A specific parcel downzoning following a previous comprehensive rezoning raises the question of reverse spot zoning. This is especially the case where the master plan has not been amended to justify the later downzoning. In addition, surrounding properties have been developed at the higher, townhouse density and no public facility reason exists why the downzoning is necessary. Hence it appears that a property owner is being singled out for political reasons, i.e., the neighbors just don't like her zoning.

Second, the downzoning is this case appears to be flawed because no reasons or findings are in the record that support the city council's decision. For example, had the council based its decision on evidence in the record that a need now exists for a different type of residential land use, such a reason might constitute a sufficient public purpose to justify the rezoning. The general rule under the due process clause is that the government's action need only be rational. The fact that the parcel in this case is located further away from the new town center and, hence, should be of a lower density, appears rational. [*Editors' Note:* In a minority of jurisdictions, an individual rezoning of a single parcel of land is deemed a quasi-judicial or administrative action. This increases the burden on the government to justify its action, especially when it cannot be justified by the master plan.]

An **Equal Protection [II-5]** issue is raised in this case because other nearby properties zoned for townhouses at the same time as the 50-acre parcel were allowed to develop while that parcel was prevented from being developed, and then was downzoned. But for the government's actions preventing development from 1975 to the present, the owner apparently would have built her townhouses as the neighboring property owners did. The facts raise the question of whether a public facilities reason existed for the differential treatment. Equal protection challenges are rarely successful in land use disputes because the government can argue that the distinctions it made are rational and hence constitutionally valid. If the staging plan is deemed rational, and thus the change in zoning in response to the changed circumstances over the years is also deemed rational, the equal protection issue would likely fail.

The downzoning in this case also raises a taking issue under the **Just Compensation Clause [II-6]** issue. The economic impact of the council's decision is clearly substantial. The owner can argue that she has lost 80 percent of the value of her land due to the downzoning and that for 13 years she was prevented from developing, not for market or economic reasons, but because of a land use restriction, i.e., staging of infrastucture improvements. She can also argue that once she was ready to develop, having retained her property since 1975 based on the government-induced expectation, the government then changed the rules to her detriment. Unfortunately, however, under the facts neither argument supports a conclusion that there has been a taking of her property. Delays caused by the staging of infrastructure improvements, where supported by planning analysis, have been held constitutional. In this case, the facts suggest that the staging program is tied to the comprehensive zoning map amendment for the new town area. Also, the facts do not demonstrate that the property owner made any, let alone a substantial, expenditure of funds on plans and preliminary approvals in reliance on the local government's actions, only to have the rules changed by the municipality. Such facts would have to exist before a court would find that the property owner had a vested right to develop at the townhouse density. While the public purpose advanced by the city in this case is not well articulated, the need to stage development consistent with capital facility improvements is generally considered a valid public purpose. In response to a taking challenge, government must show a substantial advancement of a legitimate government interest to support the public purpose part of the taking equation. If the downzoning is found to serve a valid public purpose, a taking will only be found if the effect of the downzoning is to restrict substantially all use of the individual's property. The fact situation presented does not support such a conclusion.

SECTION 3:
SPECIFIC PARCEL REZONING

3.01 Residential to Commercial Zoning: Fact Situation

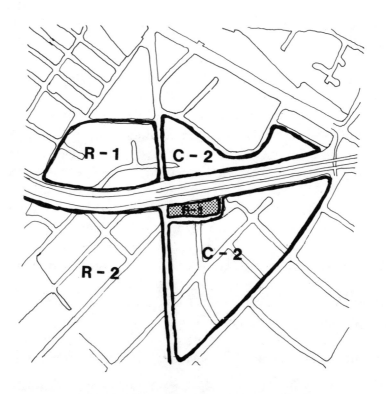

A developer applies to the city for rezoning from R-1 single-family residence to C-2 highway commercial for three lots on the south side of a major highway. The developer intends to erect a speculative commercial building on the lots, replacing three existing single-family residences. Properties to the northeast (across the highway) and directly to the southeast of the three lots are also zoned C-2 and are used for a variety of highway-oriented purposes. There are single-family homes directly to the northwest of the site, though most are renter-, rather than owner-occupied and rundown. There is single- and two-family residential zoning to the southwest.

The developer argues that the heavily traveled nature of the highway (more than 18,000 vehicles per day), the presence of commercial zoning on adjoining properties, and the changing character of the residential area to the northwest justify the rezoning. The zoning boundary, he says, is arbitrarily drawn and, in his words, should be squared off.

The city's planning staff recommends denying the rezoning change, pointing to the comprehensive plan, whose commercial area land use designation follows the boundaries of the C-2 zoning district exactly. According to the staff report, the rezoning would "perpetuate strip commercial development" and "increase the number of turning movements on an already congested highway corridor."

Following the unfavorable recommendation of the planning commission, the city council denies the zoning request.

3.02 Discussion

The developer could challenge the constitutionality of the zoning as applied, contending that the current zoning of the property violates the **Equal Protection [II-5]** requirements of the Fourteenth Amendment. This claim is typically brought in a line-drawing case such as this. The plaintiff objects to the configuring of the district boundaries on the zoning map, claiming that zoning regulations do not give similar treatment to persons similarly situated.

The fact situation does not state whether or not the commercial uses in the nearby C-2 district predate the comprehensive plan and the zoning, so that any previously nonconforming commercial uses became conforming ones. This could explain the difference in the zoning across the highway and to the southeast. Prior use—residential for the three lots in question and commercial for those southeast and east—may have been the sole rationale for the difference. If the municipality cannot show that the facts affecting these three lots are distinguishable from those governing the prior zoning for commercial uses, then the developer may well prevail with the argument that there was no rational basis for treating his land differently and that, therefore, he has been denied equal protection.

The developer could also argue that the refusal to rezone his lots is unreasonable, and therefore a denial of **Substantive Due Process [II-4]**. Courts tend to be more tolerant of introducing one more similar commercial use to an area already somewhat mixed in use between residential and commercial than of breaching a previously stable residential area. However, if the issue is reasonably debatable, the court is unlikely to question the city council's decision. For example, in response to the developer, the city might submit evidence that additional commercial use in the area would overload the area with commercial activity and create significant traffic impacts. The court is likely to defer to the judgment of the municipality if a reasonable rationale is offered.

The developer could also allege that there has been a taking under the **Just Compensation Clause [II-6]**. It is quite probable that the three lots have a far higher value for commercial than for residential use. That alone will not constitute a taking. However, it is possible that the strip commercial uses on one side and across the highway, the heavy traffic, and the rundown condition of nearby houses could render the lots unmarketable for residential uses. Since the current zoning permits only residential use, the economic impact of the zoning could be sufficient to satisfy the standards for a taking.

SECTION 4:
SPECIAL EXCEPTION

4.01 Multifamily Development: Fact Situation

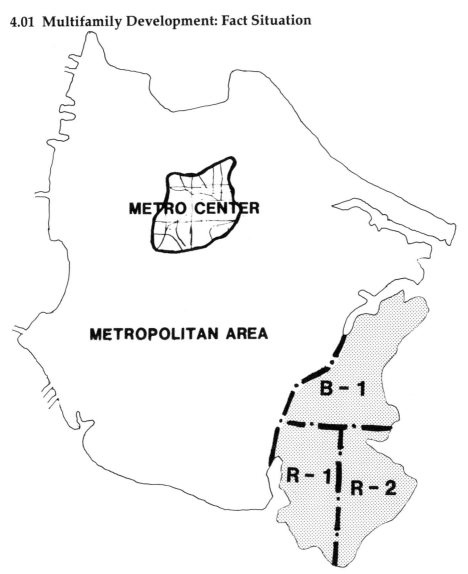

Suburban Smallville, a home rule municipality, is expecting significant growth due to the construction of a new rapid transit system to the metropolitan center some 30 miles distant. The community has a population of 38,000 and has the following characteristics: a major state university with all the related stimulating activities and diversions; a central business district with a 500,000 sq. ft. enclosed mall and adjacent public parking;

95 percent of the land area developed as single-family detached homes on 5,000–8,000 sq. ft. lots; excellent combined school and park system; tax rate lower than any city within 150 miles; excellent health facilities; and a population that is 60 percent caucasian, 35 percent black and 5 percent other. Smallville is still a desirable place to live and raise a family.

The city council passes its first zoning ordinance, which contains only three districts. The R-1 district permits only single-family detached dwellings as of right. Also permitted in the R-1 district by special use permit are:

> such other uses and expansion of uses as determined by the planning commission, at a public hearing, to be in harmony with the established character of existing uses and with the comprehensive plan which shall be adopted by the city council.

The same special use clause is repeated in the R-2 district regulations, which permit multifamily uses, and in the B-1 district, which permits retail and commercial uses. At the time the amendment is adopted, the city council announces that the purpose is to assure that any new development will not detract from the established character of the community, including its aesthetic quality, economic stability, and social equanimity.

A developer who has the option to purchase a 100-acre parcel subject to zoning approval is denied a special use permit in the R-1 district, based on a finding by the plan commission that the proposed use (an 800-unit, two story townhouse development, with a 30 ft. landscaped buffer surrounding it) is not in harmony with the surrounding single-family residential uses. The developer appeals to the city council and is denied a right to another hearing based on the planning commission decision and her refusal to request a zoning amendment to R-2. The developer elects to go to court instead of seeking rezoning.

4.02 Discussion

The ordinance raises a **Delegation of Power [II-1]** issue because the standards may be inadequate to guide the plan commission's determinations. The *in harmony with existing development standard* has been invalidated in a number of jurisdictions. In addition, the justification is largely aesthetic. This justification is accepted as a valid land use concern today by the majority of jurisdictions; however, it is one which is viewed with skepticism by some courts. The comprehensive plan, once adopted, will strengthen the application of the special exception provision.

A second **Delegation of Power [II-1]** concern is that there are only a few zones which have been legislatively determined—thus suggesting that the city council has merely passed the buck to the planning commission. However, it is not uncommon to have an administrative body, like the board of zoning appeals or a plan commission, determine the fate of special exceptions. Also, there is less chance of this ordinance being invalidated on overdelegation grounds once the comprehensive plan is adopted and used to guide the zoning decision for the three districts.

The language of the ordinance itself does not raise any **Substantive Due Process [II-4]** problem. However, problems could arise when specific conditions are placed on particular developments. Since this case involves an outright denial, the relationship between regulation and legitimate police power interests is more difficult to judge. In this case, it would be reasonable to expect the planning commission to document why the density, configuration, or location of the applied-for townhouses will undermine the open space and quiet nature of existing single family residences. Findings as to traffic, noise, and inadequate infrastructure would all be relevant to the court's review. Overall, it should be remembered that while courts are still likely to defer to what are legitimate legislative goals, they are becoming less tolerant of regulations which do not clearly advance those goals.

The fact that a large undeveloped tract exists in the city and is effectively restricted to the same uses that surround it without other considerations raises an **Equal Protection [II-5]** issue. In a few states, notably Pennsylvania and New Jersey, the facts presented might give rise to a state equal protection challenge alleging improper exclusionary zoning. However, even in these states, it is doubtful that the ordinance would be found to be exclusionary, given the fact that multifamily structures are permitted as of right in the R-2 zone. Of course, if only a small portion of Smallville's land area was zoned R-2 and special exceptions were rarely granted, an exclusionary zoning claim would be more credible.

Except where a suspect classification such as race is involved, the outcome of a federal equal protection challenge depends on whether the local government can establish a rational basis for its decision. This ordinance is likely to survive that deferential review. If similarly situated landowners have been treated differently, there is a stronger equal protection claim. However, even here, granting one townhouse development does not mean that all subsequent similar developments merit approval.

The developer might also bring a taking claim under the **Just Compensation Clause [II-6]**, although it is unlikely that she could win on these facts. The R-1 District, by definition, appears to leave the landowner's property with an economically viable use. The facts also do not clearly reveal that the landowner received the final determination of what would be allowed on her property. Therefore, a taking claim would likely be precluded on **Ripeness [II-6]** grounds.

SECTION 5:
NEGOTIATED (REZONING) APPROVALS

5.01 Downtown Commercial Rezoning: Fact Situation

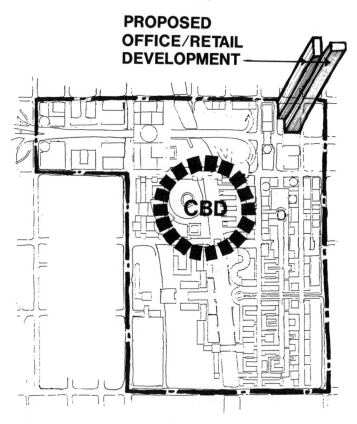

PROPOSED OFFICE/RETAIL DEVELOPMENT

The downtown area of a city is undergoing rapid expansion, with considerable pressure for construction of new office and commercial uses. Most of the perimeter of the commercial area remains zoned for multifamily housing or neighborhood commercial uses, neither of which will allow the scale of office and shopping complexes which developers are proposing. Several attempts by the city council to rezone the perimeter areas, promoted by the planning department, have failed because of public pressure over the displacement of low-income residents, loss of affordable housing, and impacts on older businesses. The city's plan is badly out of date and, thus, offers little guidance as to the desirable use of the perimeter of the downtown.

A developer proposes to redevelop a full block of the perimeter area for two office buildings, a parking structure and ground floor retail uses. The project would displace 10 housing units and have considerable impact on already congested streets in the area. After some negotiation with the planning department, the developer indicates his willingness, if his site is rezoned, to purchase 10 housing units elsewhere in the city and to sell those at considerably below market prices to the city's housing authority. He also agrees to make parking spaces available in his structure at preferred rates to residents of adjacent areas, thereby permitting the removal of parking lanes on several streets to smooth traffic flows in the vicinity of his project area. He indicates a willingness to make available up to 20 percent of the ground floor commercial uses to existing businesses owned by neighborhood residents at rents 40 percent below market. While some opposition to the project remains and is expressed at the public hearing, the site is rezoned by the city council and development is about to proceed.

Some other developers, heartened by the outcome of this process, begin similar negotiations with the planning department. Some nearby residential and commercial opponents of the developer's project bring suit to block the project and overturn the rezoning; they also seek to enjoin all similar negotiated rezonings.

5.02 Discussion

Negotiated rezoning approvals, where authorized by state statute or state court decisions, can be a useful and flexible tool for achieving legitimate governmental purposes. However, in most states such dealmaking constitutes illegal contract zoning. Furthermore, in most municipalities it is neither needed nor appropriate, but in those communities where development pressures are acute, and where there is an inherent complexity to the patterns of land use that overtax conventional planning strategies and zoning techniques, a negotiated approach to development approval can be a means to achieve a solution to a complex land use issue. This approach should *not* be undertaken for the first time by any state or municipality merely in reaction to some developer's proposal. Appropriate enabling legislation should first be adopted and safeguarding mechanisms should be put in place.

In circumstances such as those presented in the fact situation, the first question is whether state enabling legislation authorizes negotiated approvals, including negotiated rezonings to address: rapid downtown growth, perimeter areas in transition, and uncertainty as to the type and direction of movement of future developments in such areas. This may raise an issue concerning the extent of the state's **Delegation of Police Power [II-1]** if there are no clearly articulated legislative policies and standards to guide local governments in adopting ordinances which permit rezonings as part of negotiated development approvals.

In the absence of state enabling legislation, one must look to state court decisions to determine if those decisions have approved of what is termed *contract* or *conditional zoning*. Many state courts have invalidated rezonings which are approved as a result of a *bilateral* agreement between the municipality and the developer on the ground that a municipality cannot contract or bargain away the police power; hence the term *contract zoning*. Where there is no agreement by the city to rezone, but the developer has *unilaterally* agreed to make certain improvements reasonably required by the development, the courts in some jurisdictions have upheld the resulting rezoning as valid conditional rezoning. It is difficult to fit the contract zoning objection into any of the constitutional principles. However, it is possible to argue that a contract rezoning that bargains away the police power is a violation of **Substantive Due Process [II-4]**. If the rezoning by the city council is held to be legislative, then it cannot raise a **Procedural Due Process** problem. Neither would it raise a **Delegation of Power** problem.

By contrast, the delegation and procedural due process questions would arise if a court held that the rezoning was quasi-judicial. A state court might then hold that the failure to provide any standards for this type of rezoning was a violation of the principles of **Delegation of Power [II-1]**. There could also be a **Procedural Due Process [II-3]** objection. However, there is less likelihood that it would be raised in this case because the developer is satisfied with the rezoning he achieved through the negotiated development process. [*Editors' Note:* The remainder of the discussion of the fact situation assumes that there is either proper state enabling legislation or there is state judicial approval of this type of contract or conditional rezoning and it is held to be legislative rather than quasi-judicial.]

The ordinance could be subject to a **Substantive Due Process [II-4]** challenge on the ground that the discretionary rezoning process does not serve a valid public purpose. The fact situation only implies that there is a valid public purpose. It would be advisable, however, for both the state enabling legislation and the local land use ordinance to contain an express declaration both of the contexts in which this approach to rezoning is most useful, and also of the anticipated public benefits which the prudent use of this tool is intended to produce.

Another potential **Substantive Due Process [II-4]** problem is that the relationship between the discretionary rezoning and the public health, safety, and welfare is not apparent. There are some useful positive suggestions in this regard—the efforts to deal with low-income housing needs, parking problems, and small business relocation. On the other hand, the failure of the city to update its comprehensive plan, and the suggestion that the one approved rezoning and those that are still in the discussion stage may not be in accord with a comprehensive plan (and thus arguably inconsistent with the public's health, safety, and welfare), leaves the city open to challenge. Cities that rezone a parcel as the culmination of a negotiation process should spell out precisely the range of public health, safety, and welfare benefits which the particular project, the rezoning and developer quid-pro-quos confer.

Another key constitutional question is whether the rezoning constitutes a violation of **Equal Protection [II-5]**. This problem arises because a negotiated rezoning of this type can lead to differential treatment among developers. Some state courts invalidate zoning of this type because they believe that it leads to arbitrary treatment of landowners in similar situations, but the trend in the cases is in the other direction. This problem has not yet arisen in the federal courts, which may treat contract zoning as raising a state, rather than a federal, legal question.

Finally, it is important in this fact situation to note that the lawsuit is brought by third parties. This significantly changes the nature of the questions which a court will consider. A constitutional question, such as whether the requirements agreed to in the negotiated rezoning constitute a taking of property under the **Just Compensation Clause [II-6]**, will not come up because the landowner is satisfied with the rezoning and will not raise it. Problems could arise if the property were sold, because a purchaser of the property could object to the negotiated zoning and raise substantive due process and taking issues.

SECTION 6:
DEVELOPMENT EXACTIONS

6.01 Traffic Impact: Fact Situation

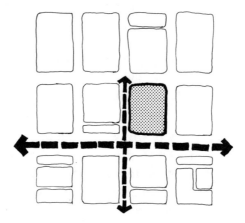

A proposed commercial development on a parcel adjacent to a busy inter-section is up for conditional use approval by the city council. The projected general growth in the community would cause an increase in traffic vol-ume necessitating the installation of a traffic signal at some unspecified time in the future. According to the city's traffic engineer, the proposed de-velopment will result in additional traffic that necessitates the installation of the traffic signal at the intersection now. The city council conditions ap-proval of the development on the developer providing the funds to pay the full cost of the traffic signal.

6.02 Discussion

The city may have trouble defending its decision against a taking claim under the **Just Compensation Clause [II-6]** in view of the U.S. Supreme Court's decision in the *Nollan* case. The major issue is whether there is a proportionality between the need created by the new development and the exaction. Before discussing this question, there are two subsidiary is-sues to be considered.

First, it may well be that the city could deny approval of the develop-ment altogether for a lack of infrastructure. *Nollan* appears to recognize that, if the development can be denied on such grounds, the approval of the development may be conditioned on provision of the facility. However, much depends on whether the law of the particular state authorizes the conditioning of development approval on such considerations.

Second, *Nollan* does not resolve the base-point from which need for the exaction is to be measured. A conservative view would measure the need in terms of existing development and the incremental need created by the proposal. However, a broader view would allow the city to base the exaction on future traffic generated by the site at full development. It will be easier to determine such justification in those states which have binding comprehensive plans which anticipate the traffic generated by the proposed use, as opposed to other traffic generators.

In the instant case, the city will probably have less trouble with the ability to condition approval than with the proportionality of the condition. The proposed development probably contributes only to some of the traffic requiring the signal. As such, even if that development has the incremental effect of requiring the new signal, it does not, by itself, cause the need for the new signal.

6.03 Neighborhood Revitalization: Fact Situation

The downtown area of a city is prospering economically, but several city neighborhoods are economically depressed and physically run down. A study shows that few of the new downtown jobs go to residents of such neighborhoods and the city council representatives from these neighborhoods argue that providing facilities and services for the downtown area drains funds that otherwise could be used in their neighborhoods. The city council decides that there should be a partnership between the downtown and the deprived neighborhoods and that hereafter new development in the downtown area will be required to make a contribution of $2 per square foot of new development to the partnership fund to be spent on facility and service programs in these neighborhoods. The only evidence presented in support of the $2 fee is a study which showed that the cost of construction plus the $2 contribution was well below the prevailing rents for newly constructed office space.

6.04 Discussion

This fact situation is on the frontier of land use law. It is the sort of linkage arrangement that has begun to receive scrutiny by the courts. It raises **Substantive Due Process [II-4]** issues and taking issues under the **Just Compensation Clause [II-6]**.

Again, the *Nollan* case provides some insights but also leaves some questions unresolved. To satisfy these constitutional standards, the city must demonstrate the relationship between the needs created by the proposed development—i.e., the diversion of funds which "would have gone" to depressed neighborhoods—and the assessments to the partnership funds. The relationship is not of the kind traditionally recognized (e.g., land or fees in lieu of land dedication).

The developer would argue that there is a lack of exact proportionality, or even a lack of rough proportionality, and that the partnership fund is a disguised attempt to raise more general tax revenues. The constitutional question of the level of proportionality will depend on whether a court applies a narrow or broad reading to the Fifth and Fourteenth Amendments under *Nollan*. It should be noted that Justice Brennan's dissent in that case accuses the majority of requiring an unduly exact level of proportionality.

This case would probably be decided either under state constitutional or statutory provisions, the most likely being the authority of the city to adopt the partnership scheme or the relationship of such a scheme to state constitutional or statutory limits on taxation.

6.05 Transit: Fact Situation

A city subsidizes its municipally operated transit system by making up out of general tax funds the difference between fares and grants and the cost of the system. The system has become increasingly overcrowded in the downtown area, particularly during the evening rush hours. As a result, there is increasing public objection to approval of new downtown office buildings. The city commissions a study which concludes that the costs of expanding current services and adding new services are directly proportional to the amount of peak-period city transit use generated by new development. It recommends that a fee be imposed that reflects the benefits to be conferred on new development by increasing peak-period capacity to accommodate passengers generated by the new offices.

To determine the cost of peak-period service necessary to serve new development, the study used generally accepted cost accounting methodology to estimate (1) the number of peak-period person trips generated annually per gross square foot of office use in new development and (2) the cost incurred by the city (after deducting estimated fare revenue and state and federal grants) in expanding and operating additional peak period transit capacity in the downtown area over the estimated life of new buildings. The cost was estimated to be $9.16 per square foot of office space. To be conservative and because a higher number was not politically achievable, the transit impact development fee was set by the city council at $5.00/sq. ft.

6.06 Discussion

The fact situation in this case is similar to that in San Francisco, which imposed a transit use fee on new downtown development to pay for the incremental cost of new transit facilities over and above that paid for by fares and subsidies.

It is important to note that the U.S. Supreme Court declined to review the San Francisco scheme after it had decided *Nollan*. The San Francisco transit fee may have well escaped such review because the city had done its homework and demonstrated the nexus between the need created for additional transit facilities and new downtown development. Properly done, such a fee can survive the **Substantive Due Process [II-4]** challenges and the taking challenges under the **Just Compensation Clause [II-6]** that could be brought under *Nollan*.

SECTION 7:
PROHIBITION OF USE(S)

7.01 Adult Entertainment: Fact Situation

A suburban city provides for three classes of retail shopping in its zoning ordinance: (1) neighborhood retail, (2) central area retail, and (3) general shopping center. All three allow book stores, video stores, art galleries, and pharmacies or drug stores. The ordinance prohibits in all retail zones the offering for sale or rent, or the displaying if any "printed materials, films, videos, photography, art works, or any merchandise dealing primarily with sexual activity" except as incidental to an otherwise permitted retail use. Incidental is defined as occupying no more than 3 percent of the total selling space and making no use of window display areas or of prominent interior display areas.

The proprietors of an art gallery challenge this limitation. They propose to open a shop devoted exclusively to the sale or rental of merchandise that comes within the prohibition of the ordinance. The shop, to be known as Graphic Graphics, will deal in sexually explicit posters, greeting cards, prints, sculptures, and other art works and will also sell pornographic videos and books. In recognition of community standards, the shop will limit its window display to a spare decorative effect that does not include any merchandise; it will also mount a prominent sign on the door to alert casual shoppers to the character of the goods and prohibit entry to underage children.

Graphic Graphics argues that free artistic expression is no longer free if government requires that it be offered to the public only if it is sufficiently diluted and veiled. The city argues its right to protect an overrriding community standard while making reasonable allowance for a minority interest.

7.02 Discussion

The ordinance infringes on the art gallery owner's right of free speech in three related ways. First, the ordinance's definition of prohibited materials is vague. The federal constitutional principle of due process requires that a person have a reasonable opportunity to determine in advance whether conduct complies or does not comply with the ordinance. An ordinance that fails to provide this notice may be **Void For Vagueness [II-2]**. The level of specificity required is a function of the interest at stake and a high decree of specificity is required when an ordinance restricts freedom of expression. States have interpreted their state constitutions to impose the same due process-based notice standards on local zoning ordinances. States are, of course, bound to follow a standard at least as strict as that imposed by the federal constitution. The standard is vague because it does not specify what materials deal "primarily with sexual activity," so that retailers have adequate notice that they may come within the terms of the ordinance.

Second, the ordinance infringes on the gallery owner's **First Amendment Right of Free Speech [II-7]**. The First Amendment protects the right to publish and sell sexually explicit material, i.e., pornography; however, obscene material—defined as material that is patently offensive to a reasonable person—is not protected by the First Amendment. The gallery owner is entitled to a judicial determination of whether the gallery's material is obscene. The content of each piece of allegedly obscene material must be compared to the federal standard. Attempts to define obscenity in advance are likely to be classed as a **Prior Restraint [II-7]** and invalidated because they chill (deter) the exercise of the First Amendment rights, especially where the definition is much broader than the current Supreme Court test for obscene material.

Nonobscene speech must be allowed in a community. The Supreme Court has held that the zoning power may be used to regulate the location of adult entertainment businesses in order to address such problems as crime and neighborhood deterioration. Communities are free to limit the location of adult businesses either by requiring that they be dispersed or by restricting them to particular areas of the community, but cannot totally exclude adult entertainment. Most courts have interpreted this to require each community to allow the level of adult entertainment demanded by the community. However, the ordinance in question is concerned more with exclusion than with location within the community. For this reason, the ordinance does not satisfy the First Amendment standards for the regulation of adult entertainment businesses.

7.03 Religious Building Accessory Uses: Fact Situation

A church building in a 40-year-old residential neighborhood was sold five years ago to the Church of Universal Atonement. The church now attracts congregants from throughout the metropolitan area. Its activities have begun to generate complaints from the neighbors.

The first complaints to city hall came when Sunday morning worship services were sometimes accompanied by an amplified brass quintet. Complainants were told that worship cannot be regulated. Neighbors later objected to the church's lighting its newly erected illuminated sign at night, but were told that the city's sign regulations do not apply to churches. As the number of church evening socials increased, parking problems developed. With the start of after-school religious classes, traffic problems grew.

The church responded to these problems by eliminating a thickly planted buffer strip surrounding a 50-car parking lot and expanding the paved area to accomodate 87 cars. The city responded to complaints about the loss of the buffer area by reporting that the plantings had been installed by the church voluntarily, and that there is no requirement that they be kept. The ordinance has been amended recently to require such buffers in residential areas.

The church has also initiated a bake sale and flea market on the parking lot every third Saturday of the month from 10 a.m. to 5 p.m. The lot is cleared of parked cars during this period, and the sale attracts more traffic and parking to all side streets.

The city notifies the church that the use of the parking lot for monthly sales is in violation of the zoning ordinance. The only ancillary uses permitted for a church in a residential area are parking, rectory, residences for clergy, and a school. Special requirements are stipulated for each of these. Retailing of any kind is not a permitted use. The city also notifies the church that the city was mistaken in dismissing the complaint about the removal of the buffer strip. While the requirement of buffers was not in the ordinance when the parking lot was first built, it was, in fact, enacted before the buffers were removed. The church cannot, therefore, create a new nonconforming element in the parking lot design. The church is ordered to hold no further sales on the parking lot and to restore the buffer.

The church seeks relief from the order, arguing that all merchandise sold is donated to the church, and all proceeds are retained by the church and used solely to meet church operating costs. Therefore, argues the church, the sale of merchandise is, therefore, not a business enterprise but a social activity that is part of the church's program to bring worshipers together.

The church points out that none of the analogous indoor activities of other churches—including annual auction sales, antique fairs, and lottery games—have been interfered with, presumably to avoid interference with religion. The church argues that the ordinance is being interpreted to permit these indoor church activities while prohibiting outdoor activity on the parking lot, and any such prohibition would be an unconstitutional limitation on the church's freedom to choose its forms of worship and communal activity.

7.04 Discussion

The fact situation raises a number of First Amendment issues. The **Free Exercise Clause of the First Amendment [II-7]** prohibits government interference with a person's choice of religious belief; however, government may regulate the exercise of religion for valid secular objectives, provided that the regulation does not infringe on the free exercise of religion. To balance the competing interests of the individual and society, the federal courts have drawn a distinction between regulation which infringes on *belief*, and regulation which only affects *conduct*. Federal courts have held that a city may exclude houses of worship from residential areas because the activity is too intense for a residential area, and such exclusion does not limit an individual's freedom to worship as he or she chooses, but only the locations where worship occurs. By contrast, the majority of state courts, using a due process rather than a First Amendment analysis, prohibit the exclusion of religious activities from residential neighborhoods.

The First Amendment applies to both core religious activities, such as worship, and ancillary activities such as education and social action. However, the more that the activity resembles a secular activity, the greater the city's interest in regulating the activity. Thus, an activity like a fleamarket may be regulated as a crowd- and traffic-generating activity.

The First Amendment also limits a city's power to apply its zoning ordinances to religious activities. Cities may apply accepted planning techniques, such as buffers, to religious activities because the activities may have an adverse impact on surrounding land uses; however, the standards may have to be varied to accommodate the **Free Exercise of Religion [II-7]**. For example, assuming that the church has to comply with the buffer requirement, some states hold that a city must interpret its ordinance to impose the least possible restriction on the exercise of religion. These states require the courts to reweigh the balance struck by the city between the exercise of religion and the minimization of the side effects of the use. The maintenance of the buffer could be found to be an unnecessary burden on the church, although most courts would find the requirement to be a minimal burden on the free exercise of religion compared to the benefits of the requirement.

If the ordinance did not require a buffer at the time the church installed its buffer voluntarily, the requirements of **Substantive Due Process [II-4]** may prevent the city from mandating retroactive compliance with a new ordinance standard. Ordinances generally apply prospectively, not retroactively. Principles of substantive due process generally require only compliance with standards in place when an activity is undertaken. Substantive due process does permit the retroactive application of zoning ordinances when the public interest is paramount and the landowner is given a reasonable period of time to comply with the new standard. If the ordinance does not apply to the church, the city probably cannot require immediate compliance with the buffer requirement.

The city's interpretation of the ordinance to preclude the operation of the flea market is subject to challenge as a misinterpretation of the ordinance and as a violation of **Equal Protection [II-5]**. The equal protection clause of the federal constitution requires the nondiscriminatory application of laws. If the church can establish that the particular interpretation of the ordinance has been applied only to this church, the ordinance may be invalidated as a violation of the right to equal protection.

7.05 Housing for Mentally Retarded: Fact Situation

Oakhurst is a suburb consisting primarily of single-family homes. Small areas of shops and apartments are included in the town, and there is negligible vacant land.

A recently completed comprehensive zoning study proposes a short list of refinements to address certain new issues, including the appearance of signs, the conversion of single-family dwellings into two-family dwellings, and the use of residences for occupancy other than by a family unit.

Mainstream Advocates, Inc. is refused an occupancy license to house six persons who are mentally retarded, plus one resident supervisor, in a single-family residence. MAI sues, asking that the limitation be declared invalid on its face as discriminatory. It sets a standard of occupancy that is not applied to other residences in the same district of the same size and has no apparent basis other than to make housing for the mentally retarded uneconomic or, at best, limited to the exceptionally well-to-do—thereby improperly excluding a class of people with no legitimate purpose in view.

Oakhurst responds that the occupancy limit has a rational basis in maintaining a good fit between the density of population and the provision of all public services, including street and highway capacities, water supply, sewage disposal, and recreation. As a basis for the proposed zoning amendments, the zoning study included a demographic analysis that showed average occupancy to be stabilized at 2.8 persons per residence.

7.06 Discussion

Municipal attempts to limit the occupancy of single-family dwellings to the traditional nuclear family face both federal and state constitutional challenges. Historically, cities have attempted to limit the occupancy of single-family dwellings by defining family to include only persons related by blood, marriage, or adoption. Nontraditional living groups have challenged these ordinances as violative of constitutional rights, such as **Freedom of Association [II-7]**. The Supreme Court has upheld the power of cities to limit single-family occupancy to blood, marriage, or adoption. More generally, there is no federal constitutional right to a self-chosen lifestyle; hence the First Amendment does not protect the associational right of the mentally ill to live together.

The refusal to issue an occupancy license may be attacked as discriminatory and thus a violation of the right to **Equal Protection [II-5]**. Proponents of deinstitutionalization have argued that the mentally ill are a suspect class. Regulations that adversely affect suspect classes, such as racial minorities, are subject to strict judicial scrutiny under the equal protection clause. Regulations that adversely affect a normal or nonsuspect class must meet standards of minimum rationality. The Supreme Court has refused to hold that the mentally ill are a suspect class. Local zoning ordinances that regulate deinstitutionalization facilities are thus not subject to strict scrutiny, but the refusal to issue the license may still be attacked under ordinary equal protection principles.

The Supreme Court has held that zoning ordinances excluding groups that have long been subject to prejudice will be scrutinized nonetheless to determine if there is a rational basis for the denial of a necessary permit. All of the traditional planning reasons offered by the city for the zoning classification can be reviewed independently by a court to determine if they rest on neutral grounds or are based on unjustified discrimination against the mentally ill. A court could conclude that group homes place no greater burdens on public facilities than do single-family residences. In addition to federal equal protection review, state legislatures may preempt local regulation of such facilities. Further, many state courts have recognized a fundamental right of groups of unrelated individuals to form familylike units and live in single-family residential areas.

7.07 Multifamily Residence: Fact Situation

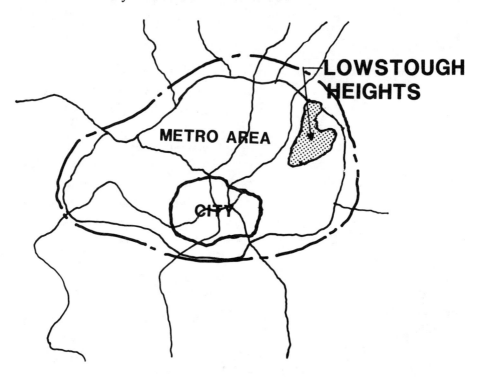

Lowstough Heights is a suburban municipality on the rim of a large metropolitan area. It has excellent access to the interstate highway network, but poor public transportation service to both the inner city and the downtown, as well as the shopping malls, office parks, and industrial zones of the surrounding suburban area. The residential zoning is almost entirely for single-family residences, with a few areas zoned for two-story, low-density apartments.

Pierce Builders proposes a new zoning district that would permit tall apartment buildings. Pierce could then construct apartments that are affordable to employees at the low-end wage scale in the vicinity. Rent supplement programs would further broaden the availability of the new apartments for low-income families.

Lowstough Heights refuses to create the new zoning category on the basis of its comprehensive plan that establishes policies for all future development, relating housing to transportation and other city services and establishing a role for the city within the total regional plan. That role calls for the city to continue its development as a single-family community.

Pierce Builders is joined by the regional housing coalition in seeking a court determination that the zoning policies of Lowstough Heights discriminate against low-income families and deny equal treatment to lower income jobholders who are invited into the community by the city's commercial development policies. If this zoning is allowed to stand, each suburban municipality will be allowed to adopt similar exclusionary practices and thereby exclude a substantial portion of the population from fair employment and housing opportunities.

Lowstough Heights replies that its policies are not exclusionary with respect to low-income residents. The city does not require expensive large lots for residences, does not require a large minimum floor area, and permits every variety of cost-cutting home building methods, including modular housing, manufactured and prefabricated housing, and even mobile homes if designed for installation on a foundation and in compliance with fire code requirements. The prices of homes in Lowstough Heights are the lowest in the region. Therefore, the city argues, it should be permitted to determine and shape its own distinctive character based on a methodically prepared plan.

7.08 Discussion

Local zoning ordinances that limit the construction of low-income multifamily residences have been attacked as a violation of **Equal Protection [II-5]** and the implied constitutional **Right to Travel**. The right to travel argument holds that persons have an absolute right to reside where they choose, and that zoning barriers to the construction of low- and moderate-income housing infringe on this right. The equal protection argument claims that poverty is a suspect class and thus zoning barriers should be subject to strict scrutiny. The Supreme Court to date has refused to create a federal constitutional law of exclusionary zoning. The right to travel does not require cities to adopt antiexclusionary zoning policies; and poverty, however defined, is not a suspect class. As a matter of federal law, therefore, a municipality's zoning ordinance may only be attacked on exclusionary zoning grounds if it constitutes racial discrimination.

By contrast, several states—notably New Jersey and Pennsylvania—have developed anti-exclusionary zoning doctrines that permit the state courts to invalidate low-density zoning policies and other barriers to the construction of low- and moderate-income housing. These doctrines require municipalities to devote some proportion of developable land to multifamily housing. However, a city's fair share may be assessed in relation to a regional need for the housing.

SECTION 8:
GROWTH PHASING

8.01 Growth Management Ordinance: Fact Situation

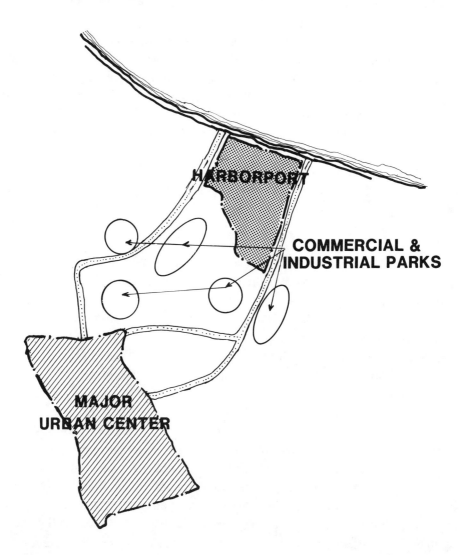

The city of Harborport, located near a major urban center, has experienced very rapid residential and commercial development since the early 1970s, growing in population from 40,000 in 1970 to over 100,000 today. Harborport's rapid growth is attributable to the exodus of affluent families from the urban center city, the completion of two major freeways connecting Harborport with the center city, and the development of large office and industrial parks within easy commuting distance of Harborport.

Harborport obtains its water supply from a metropolitan water district. While the water district has not refused to increase the city's water supply as it grew rapidly, there is no assurance that it will do so in the future. The city owns and operates its own sewage disposal system, which is now nearing its capacity.

Schools in Harborport are full but not yet overcrowded. In 1978, the local school district requested the city to require residential subdividers to contribute to a fund which would assist the district in purchasing or leasing portable classrooms. The city acceded to this request. In 1982, the school district asked the city to increase the exaction imposed on subdividers to assist in financing acquisition of needed new school sites and construction of new school buildings. The city also granted this request.

The two freeways and the arterial street systems in and near Harborport are now frequently congested. During evening peak hours, and on some summer weekend days, traffic congestion is severe. The city's traffic engineer describes the traffic situation as rapidly approaching gridlock.

With population growth, the city's cost of providing municipal services has risen rapidly. Under a statewide property tax limitation statute, real property taxes have been reduced approximately one half and the maximum permitted rate of increase is 1 percent annually. The city council anticipates a municipal financial crunch because the cost of providing public services is rising faster than the level of tax revenues and funding from external sources.

To counter the problems caused by rapid growth, the city amends its comprehensive plan to limit growth to no more than a 2 percent annual rate. A growth management ordinance is enacted, prescribing that no residential subdivision or development consisting of more than five units may be permitted unless the planning commission makes the following four findings:

1. Water supply is adequate to meet the projected need generated by the proposed development.

2. Sewer capacity is adequate to meet the projected need generated by the proposed development.

3. Public schools have adequate capacity to meet the projected need generated by the proposed development.

4. Real property taxes yielded by the development will be equal to or greater than the cost of necessary capital improvements and operating/maintenance costs of providing municipal services to the development.

In addition to the environmental impact statement (EIS) required by state law, the growth management ordinance prescribes that subdividers and other proponents of residential developers subject to the growth management ordinance reimburse the city for the cost of a fiscal impact study, which will be used to determine finding no. 4.

The growth management ordinance does not apply to commercial or other nonresidential developments because, according to the city manager, such development yields a fiscal surplus to the city, and limiting it would be counterproductive. If the ordinance were applied to commercial or industrial developments (which the city manager referred to as tax cows) they would be likely to locate in other nearby communities rather than in Harborport.

In the year following enactment of the ordinance, the House Development Corporation obtains an option to purchase a 30-acre site on which it proposes to build a 300-unit townhouse condominium project. The land is zoned for single-family residential use, but planned unit developments (including townhouses) are permitted on the granting of a conditional use permit. The property is surrounded on three sides by single-family residental subdivisions, with homes selling between $250,000 and $350,000.

When the Homes Corporation applies to the city for a conditional use permit, technical evidence presented to the planning commision shows that water and sewer capacity are adequate to accommodate the project but that the 300 units would generate significant additional traffic. The fiscal impact report concludes that real property taxes would yield a small deficit per unit.

At the public hearings on the conditional use permit, considerable opposition is expressed by residents of the surrounding subdivisions on the grounds that the development "will not pay its own way" and will lower the value of their properties. There is support for the project by civic organizations and a number of individuals in other parts of the city.

After the hearing, the planning commission makes the following findings: water supply and sewer capacity will be adequate; using the developer's required contributions, sufficient school capacity can be provided to handle the increased enrollment; the project will generate significantly increased traffic; and the real property tax yield by the development will not cover municipal service costs. The council denies the conditional use permit application.

Homes Corporation sues the city, asking the court to require the city to grant the permit application. The grounds for the suit are (1) denial of substantive due process because of the lack of definite standards to judge the adequacy of water supply and sewer capacity, school capacity, and freeway and arterial street capacity; (2) denial of procedural due process because of the fiscal impact report requirement and the decision based on it; and (3) denial of equal protection because the growth management ordinance applies only to residential development.

8.02 Discussion

The growth management ordinance may be challenged on its face as violating **Substantive Due Process [II-4]** guarantees on the ground that it bears no rational relationship to the public health, safety, and welfare. For instance, an application may be denied by the simple fact that the proposed development exceeds the 2 percent growth restriction. Substantive due process requires that such a growth limitation be rationally related to concerns for public health, safety, and welfare. Here, while some limitation can be easily justified on the basis of public health and welfare, the specific 2 percent requirement is more difficult to justify in that it does not appear on its face to be any more rational than a 4 percent or one percent limitation. This potential problem could be minimized by a declaration by the city council of the reasons why the 2 percent threshold was selected—i.e., studies demonstrate that if growth is limited to 2 percent, the projected tax revenues will be sufficient to provide necessary public service requirements.

Courts have traditionally given legislation the benefit of a presumption of validity in due process cases. However, recent cases have begun to look more carefully at the factual basis to test its rationality. Hence, the existence of studies, reports, and the like forming the basis of legislation is always desirable; and, if the current judicial trend continues, such studies and reports may become a functional requirement for defending due process challenges.

Homes Corporation could also challenge the decision of the planning commission on the grounds that the denial was irrational, arbitrary, and capricious because it does not appear to be consistent with most of the findings of fact. However, since the evidence presented was at least conflicting, such a challenge would probably not be successful under the usual standard that is applied; whether there existed evidence on which such a decision could be rationally based, not whether the decision was correct.

The growth management ordinance may also be subject to a constitutional challenge as being unconstitutional on **Delegation of Power [II-1]** grounds. For instance, the ordinance contains no standard by which to determine whether a new development will cause "a materially adverse impact" on traffic. Similarly, there are no standards by which to determine when Harborport's schools may be determined to have adequate capacity to meet the development's projected demand. In both instances, standards are available—traffic congestion indices, average vehicles per unit size, average school age children, average or desirable teacher/pupil ratios, and square footage per pupil. By utilization of standards, the ordinance will be less susceptible to arbitrary decision-making and at least partially (if not fully) insulated against a constitutional challenge on delegation of power grounds.

Third, because it applies only to residential development, the ordinance may be challenged on the ground that it violates **Equal Protection [II-5]**. Obviously, an industrial or commercial development will use water and sewer systems, add to traffic, and, necessarily, require other municipal services; yet applications for development of such nonresidential uses are not subject to the growth management ordinance. Generally, as in substantive due process, if there is a rational basis for the disparate treatment under the ordinance, it will withstand equal protection challenges, assuming that no suspect class (e.g., racial minorities) suffers disparate treatment. Here, for example, if the ordinance contained findings of fact based on reasonably reliable evidence, that commercial or industrial development would produce more than enough tax revenue to meet the additional public service requirements which they generate, then the disparate treatment of residential development would meet the rational basis test applied to equal protection challenges where no suspect class is involved.

There is a further **Equal Protection [II-5]** issue under the fact situation. It is conceivable that the ordinance, as applied, may well discriminate against low-income residential development; therefore, it may be argued, it discriminates against racial minorities. While demands on public services by low-income housing will be at least the same as that of moderately or highly priced units, assuming the same density, the tax revenues generated by such low-income housing will necessarily be lower. Hence, approvals under the ordinance are more likely for higher priced residential developments than for low-income developments.

The test for determining whether there is an equal protection violation where race, a suspect class, is involved is whether there exists a compelling state interest (as opposed to a rational basis) supporting the disparate treatment. Therefore, the application of Harborport's ordinance to the Homes Corporation could present an equal protection problem if a court is convinced that the ordinance will discriminate against racial minorities. Most, if not all, such potential equal protection problems are avoided by careful analysis of the impact of the ordinance on various classes of persons and by careful drafting to avoid any identified problems. For instance, the growth management ordinance clearly is neutral on its face. Moreover, approval or denial under the the ordinance is premised, to a large degree, on the size of the development, as opposed to the class of persons it is to serve. Hence, any equal protection claim may be defeated if it is clear under the ordinance that a reduction in density and/or a delay in the timing of development will probably meet the objectives of the growth management ordinance and result in approval.

The application of the growth management ordinance would no doubt be challenged as a taking of the developer's property in violation of the **Just Compensation Clause [II-6]**. First, Homes Corporation could allege that it had a vested right in site plan approval and that use of the ordinance to deny its application *after* it had been filed resulted in a taking of its property right to develop in accordance with that approval. The strength of this argument depends on whether it can be shown that, under state law, site plan approval would have been granted and that the use of the new ordinance to assess the pending application could not destroy the corporation's entitlement to that approval.

Homes Corporation could also allege that the denial of residential development on the basis of the growth management ordinance resulted in a taking of its 30-acre parcel of property. Certainly, such a denial will result in at least a temporary inability to develop the property in any fashion. Without considering any other factors, this would appear to amount to a taking for which just compensation must be paid. However, because any denial would necessarily be premised on considerations of the timing and density of residential development intended, the taking challenge would probably fail. The ordinance appears to substantially advance a legitimate public interest and even if an application is denied, *all* reasonable and economically viable use of the property is not destroyed. A reduction in density or a delay in development are the only actual impacts of the ordinance. At best, a temporary taking claim may be advanced but, because there is a substantial public interest in managing growth, particularly under the circumstances faced by Harborport, it is doubtful that even a temporary taking claim would be recognized, assuming that development of some sort is permitted within a reasonable period of time.

SECTION 9:
INTERIM LAND USE CONTROLS (MORATORIA)

9,01 Demolition Permits: Fact Situation

A city is about to begin conducting historic surveys in several mixed-use neighborhoods. A number of property owners, fearful of an historic district designation after the survey, obtain demolition permits and quickly tear down structures that might be designated as historic. The city council adopts interim regulations requiring a review of demolition permits for all structures over 50 years old in several specifically defined neighborhoods in which historic surveys are, or are about to be, underway. The defined neighborhoods are considered likely candidates for meeting the criteria necessary for the establishment of historic districts. The demolition review period is for six months, but may be extended by the governing body if the survey hasn't been completed or an historic district designated. There is a right of appeal to the city council if the planning department denies a demolition permit. There are also provisions for exempting properties if a public safety hazard or economic hardship can be shown, or if preserving a structure has no public benefit.

9.02 Discussion

This is a typical use of a moratorium to prohibit the demolition of buildings in an area a municipality is considering for designation as an historic district. The interim regulation requiring a review of demolition permits raises a taking problem under the **Just Compensation Clause [II-6]**. If the city refuses to issue a demolition permit, the owner of an historic structure will not be able to demolish his or her property during the time the historic surveys are conducted.

The city should be able to defeat a taking claim in federal court. The interim regulation advances the city's interest in historic preservation because it prevents the destruction of buildings that may be historically significant in areas considered likely candidates for designation as an historic district. The owner of an historic structure may not be able to demolish it while the moratorium is in effect, but the federal courts have upheld development moratoria when they are necessary to conduct studies of this type. These cases should apply in assessing a challenge to this ordinance. The city could defend the interim regulation against a taking of property claim in state court for the same reasons.

A number of features in the ordinance help protect it against a taking of property claim. The initial demolition review period is only for six months, and the city must justify its extension. There are also provisions for exempting properties from the demolition review prohibition. These exemptions include one for economic hardship, which is essential to avoid a claim that the ordinance prevents a landowner from making an economically viable use of his land.

The owner of an historic structure could also claim that the interim regulation violates **Substantive Due Process [II-4]**. The city would have to show that the interim regulation advances a legitimate governmental purpose. This showing is similar to the one it would have to make if the owner of an historic structure attacked the interim regulation as a taking of property. The city would not have much difficulty with the substantive due process challenge. The courts all hold that historic preservation is a legitimate governmental purpose. The interim regulation advances this purpose because it maintains the character of potential historic districts until necessary studies are completed and a designation made.

A property owner might also challenge the moratorium on **Equal Protection [II-5]** grounds, charging that certain properties are singled out for unfair treatment. This claim will not be successful. In the case of such economic regulation, the city need only show that it has a rational basis for its disparate treatment of property owners, and here the rational basis for the moratorium may readily be found in the perceived need to protect historic structures from demolition.

Finally, the moratorium could face a **Procedural Due Process [II-3]** challenge, but this too is unlikely to be successful, assuming that the ordinance contains such basic procedural safeguards as a right to appear before the planning department on a permit application, the right to be heard at any public hearing on the permit, and a right of appeal to the city council.

SECTION 10:
RESOURCE PROTECTION

10.01 Hillside Protection: Fact Situation

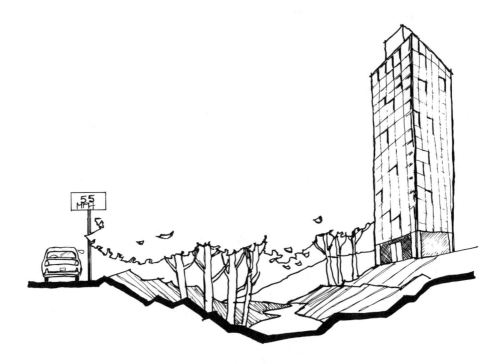

A developer seeks a building permit for a proposed high-rise residential building to be developed on a steep, environmentally sensitive hillside overlooking a river and a scenic parkway. The parkway is generally considered to be the best scenic drive in the city. The site's environmental features are fragile, tree-covered slopes and ravines. Soil and geologic conditions limit development based on studies of the area and incidents of landslides over a 10-year period. The site of the proposed development is located in a designated environmental quality district with special standards to be considered by the planning staff in making its recommendations and applied by a hearing examiner. The city has an excavation and fill ordinance for the protection of hillsides.

Neighborhood pressure—a response to the developer's announcement of the project—persuades the city to deny the developer's building permit application for the high-rise project and to rezone the site from multifamily to two-family uses. The rezoning is based on the following:

1. High-rise structures would be incompatible with existing uses in the vicinity of the site.
2. Excavation of the site for high-rise construction would seriously damage the hillside and adversely impact water drainage on site with resultant risk of landslide.
3. Views of the city's scenic hillsides would be dramatically altered by high-rise buildings.
4. Views from existing uses in the vicinity of the site would be obstructed by high-rise development.

The developer claims that because of the high cost of geotechnical investigation and engineering, only high-density development is economically feasible. In addition, the developer points to a popular theory that large scale development can provide hillside stabilization through engineering techniques. The developer claims that the city's decisions impose economically impractical limits on the use of her property and argues that the city has, in effect, taken her property.

10.02 Discussion

The city's action in rezoning the property to low-density residential and the denial of the application for a building permit raises the issue of the extent to which the constitution limits community choices in regard to legitimate public purposes—a **Substantive Due Process [II-4]** question. Second, it raises the issue of whether the restrictions are so severe as to raise a taking claim under the **Just Compensation Clause [II-6]**, depriving the developer of all economically viable use of her property.

The demonstrable impacts of erosion and increased surface water runoff that result from the intensive development of steep slopes, coupled with the incompatibility of high rises with neighboring uses, make it likely that a court would uphold the city's action as substantially related to the public health, safety, and welfare. It is important to note that while not necessary, it is desirable that evidence concerning such impacts be presented to the city when it rezones; it is enough, however, if the city can present the necessary evidence in court when the action is challenged.

As for the taking issue, it is now well settled that a regulation that limits the private use of property to the extent that it deprives the landowner of all economically viable use of property, violates the Fifth Amendment imperative for payment of **Just Compensation Clause [II-6]**. Given the city's action, the question becomes how much use is required to satisfy the constitutional mandate for an economically viable use. This question requires an essentially ad hoc inquiry by the courts, which look to the reasonableness of the landowner's expectations, the natural character of the land, and the uses which are permitted. Reasonableness is based on existing regulatory and economic conditions, that is, the developer's realistic expectations given applicable rules and economic facts. In other words, because of the characteristics of the site and its environs and the city's regulations, was it reasonable for the developer to assume that the city would allow high-rise development of the site?

Closely allied to the reasonableness of the landowner's expectations is the question of the natural character of the site. The supreme courts of several states have held, in the context of wetlands cases, that a landowner has no constitutionally protected right to development which requires that the natural character of the land be altered; and that, therefore, minimum economically viable use must be determined in the context of the natural character of the property. In other words, "if you bought a swamp, you have a constitutionally protected interest in using the property as a swamp." In that context, it seems probable that a court would find that the owner of a hillside parcel should have limited expectations for development and no constitutionally protected interest in the alteration of the natural character of the land in order to submit it to high intensity, urban development. If a court follows the lead of the wetlands cases, then economic viability will be based on the natural character of the site and not its theoretical, geotechnical engineered capacity for development. Just as wetlands can be made developable by dredge and fill, so also, at least theoretically, a hillside can be made developable with engineering solutions. But the measure of constitutional use does not take into account such alterations of natural conditions.

The final constitutional question with regard to the taking issue is the extent to which the permitted uses are actually viable. If it is physically possible and economically feasible to use the property for two—family units—that is, that the units can be used at an economic level consistent with the cost of the structures—then it is unlikely that the city's actions will be determined to have gone so far as to constitute a taking. The fact that the developer can make more money if she is allowed to build a high rise is not a significant fact in determining the constitutional validity of the city's actions.

SECTION 11:
REGULATION FOR AESTHETIC PURPOSES

11.01 Design Review: Fact Situation

The zoning ordinance of a midsize city requires special permit and site plan review processes for all uses except individual single-family houses. The city council then amends the ordinance, adding as an additional requirement a design review and approval process for all proposed buildings plans. The amendment provides that all special permit and site plan review approvals shall be conditioned on subsequent design review and approval of proposed building plans; that is, special permit and site plan approvals will have no validity unless and until the proposed building plans receive design review approval.

The amendment includes a statement of purpose, generalized citywide design review standards, and more specific design review standards for individual zoning districts and building types. The ordinance establishes an architectural review board to conduct the design reviews and issue approvals or denials. Site plan and special permit approvals remain the responsibility of the city council, planning board, or zoning board of appeals, depending on the particular use(s) and zoning district(s) involved. The amendment provides that the design review process will be governed by the same procedural rules that are currently applied to special permit and site plan approvals, with one exception: in the design review process, building plans may be disapproved only by a super-majority vote of the architectural review board, i.e., a majority plus one. As with site plan and special permit approvals, a failure to take action on the application for review within a stated time constitutes approval. A disapproval invalidates any prior special permit or site plan approvals.

11.02 Discussion

This ordinance raises a number of questions which fall within the **Delegation of Power [II-1]** category. For example, is the city authorized to enact such an ordinance? Also, is the city's delegation of regulatory authority to the architectural review board lawful?

Municipalities can only exercise their powers, including land use control, to the degree that such exercise has been authorized by the state through either constitutional or legislative grants of power to municipalities. Where cities do not have home rule powers, the primary source of municipal authority for land use controls is zoning enabling legislation.

Opponents of the proposed ordinance would likely assert that the municipality does not have the authority to enact these regulations, either because aesthetics is not a proper purpose under the police power or, more likely, because this citywide enactment exceeds the city's authority to regulate aesthetics. While courts have overwhelmingly upheld design review focused on maintaining historic districts or regulating signs and billboards, communitywide design review has normally been limited to single-family dwellings in predominantly residential suburbs. This ordinance, by requiring design review of all new nonresidential buildings wherever located, goes significantly beyond any judicial decision upholding design review.

The ordinance establishes a legislative policy regarding design review of proposed building plans, but then delegates administration of the review process to a nonlegislative body, the architectural review board. This raises concerns regarding delegation of power. The ordinance must be sufficiently clear and definite in its purpose and standards to avoid the charge that legislative power has been improperly delegated to another branch of government. Such clarity and definiteness can be problematic in a design review ordinance. The ordinance must establish standards of acceptable design that provide reasonable guidance to all applicants. This will probably be done best when the legislature clearly articulates the goals it seeks to accomplish through design review, but leaves some flexibility in setting the standards used for judging particular projects. Standards that are excessively specific regarding each building element limit the freedom of architects and designers and can result in unwanted uniformity of design. At the same time, overly general standards, which allow board members to vote their personal preferences, should be avoided.

These definitional concerns also raise **Delegation of Power [II-1]** issues. As opposed to design review for historic districts, where a fairly definite vocabulary of design elements can be derived from historical data, creating sufficiently definite standards for both the citywide and district/ building type elements of the ordinance could be difficult, particularly if the municipality is not entirely clear as to the purposes it seeks to accomplish through the ordinance. The ordinance can be made more definite by using standards that specify such design elements as materials, colors, shapes, orientation on lots, and treatment of facades. Ordinances have also relied on standards that either seek to achieve, or to avoid, similarity of design, depending on whether the legislative purpose was to avoid monotony or achieve compatibility. Generally, a standard is sufficiently definite if a reasonable person can understand what is required by the standard, and a court can use the standard to evaluate whether a particular administrative decision is arbitrary or capricious, given the standard and the reasons stated for the decision.

This ordinance also raises significant **Substantive Due Process [II-4]** issues regarding whether the legislation bears a substantial relationship to the public health, safety, and welfare. A principal concern here would be the reasons given for the citywide application of the design review process. For example, why is all current development uniformly in need of design review? Does the ordinance really require design review for industrial facilities, such as warehouses and factories? What about electric generating facilities or sewage treatment plants? If so, for what reason? Design review has often been justified on substantive due process grounds by reference to both purely aesthetic purposes as well as more quantifiable factors, including preservation of property values or creating attractive areas for tourists. The city will be pressed to convince a court what reasons justify design review for any structure located anywhere in the city.

The design review process must also satisfy the requirement of **Procedural Due Process [II-3]** by providing for a fair and timely design review procedure. At a minimum, this procedure must allow the applicant an opportunity to be heard and to provide written findings of fact which set out the reasons for the board's decision in each case. In the context of design review, the applicant's opportunity to be heard should include the right to present testimony, to introduce evidence, and to examine and comment on the exhibits and testimony introduced by others. In some states, the applicant may also have the right to cross-examine witnesses. Equally important to the procedural safeguards stated in the ordinance is the way that the procedures are carried out. Of particular concern would be the timeliness in which applications are decided on. The ordinance addresses this concern by mandating an automatic approval of an application if the board fails to take action within the prescribed period of time.

The ordinance may also give rise to **Equal Protection [II-5]** claims because it provides for differential standards for certain districts and building types. Governmental action must be consistent in its effects on similarly situated persons and property. While government may legitimately choose to treat similarly situated persons differently, different treatment must have a rational basis. If the ordinance clearly articulates the bases for treating certain building types and districts differently than others, it should survive a challenge on grounds.

A taking claim under the **Just Compensation Clause [II-6]** would arise if the ordinance is applied in such a way that a property owner is prevented from making any reasonable use of his property. The fact that the design review process may require the property owner to spend additional sums on building design or construction is not sufficient to establish a taking claim.

Finally, an applicant may claim that the design review process conflicts with his rights to freedom of expression under the **First Amendment [II-7]**. The theory of this claim is that design and architecture are forms of expression that deserve constitutional protection. However, to date the courts have not invalidated design review ordinances on such First Amendment grounds.

SECTION 12:
AMORTIZATION OF
NONCONFORMING USE(S)

12.01 Billboards: Fact Situation

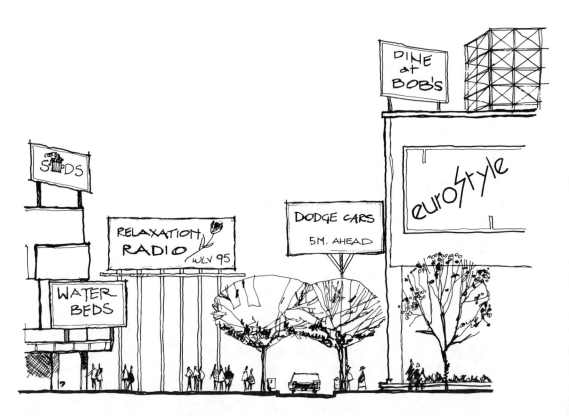

A city's zoning ordinance prohibits billboards in all commercial zones, including: local and neighborhood retail, central business, campus office, enclosed mall, and highway commercial districts. The ordinance defines *billboard* as "any free-standing outdoor sign structure with a display surface greater than 40 square feet."

After finding that each of the above districts contains one or more nonconforming billboards, the city amends its ordinance to require the termination of these structures over a period of time ranging from three years in local retail districts to 15 years in highway commercial districts. At the end of the applicable amortization period, the owner must cease displaying messages on the billboard and remove the sign structure. No compensation will be paid to the owners for either cessation of the use or removal of the structure.

12.02 Discussion

Amortization provisions will normally be upheld against a **Substantive Due Process [II-4]** challenge because of the long-recognized public interest in eliminating nonconforming uses.

The test for a taking challenge under the **Just Compensation Clause [II-6]** is the reasonableness of the amortization provisions. The basic standard for determining reasonableness in this context is a balancing of the gain to the public from eliminating the nonconforming use against the private loss to the person whose use is terminated. The major factor that courts have cited in making this determination is whether the amortization period is of sufficient length to allow the owner of the nonconforming use to recoup most of his or her investment. This will be judged by looking at the nature of the use in relation to the character of the neighborhood; the value and remaining use, if any, of improvements on the property; and the difficulty in removing the use to a properly zoned location. Courts have routinely sustained billboard amortization periods of three years and less under this analysis.

The **Equal Protection [II-5]** clause of the Fourteenth Amendment requires that governmental actions be consistent and that different results be based on a rational explanation. In this case, the city would have to provide a rational basis for applying different amortization periods to billboards located in different commercial districts. Most likely, the city would argue that these differing amortization periods reflect the varying level of concern with which it views nonconforming signs, depending on their location. The distinctions are thus related to the city's perception of the negative effects of the billboards on the surrounding area, with the most objectionable billboards being subjected to the shortest amortization period. Assuming that the city could produce some factual basis for its position this argument would most likely be accepted by the courts, as a rational basis for the differential treatment of billboards in different districts.

IV

Constitutional Analysis Tree

SECTION 1:
PURPOSE

The following outline provides planners with a form of constitutional decision tree for use in addressing the types of problem-solving areas presented in Part III of this book. The outline is not intended to be exhaustive of all issues that must be considered in preparing regulations addressing the specific problem-solving areas discussed. Rather, its purpose is to provide planners with a concise summary of the constitutional considerations discussed in Part III, which can be used in consultation with their legal counsel to identify possible constitutional issues in proposed land use regulations.

SECTION 2:
CONSTITUTIONAL ANALYSIS TREE

Discretionary Permitting

Delegation of Power

[a] Is there clearly articulated legislative policy as to the general circumstances when a discretionary approval is appropriate?

[b] Does the decision-making body have unfettered authority to determine when and if a discretionary permit should be issued?

Void for Vagueness

[a] Are there meaningful standards that alert a reasonably intelligent applicant to the criteria by which his application will be judged?

[b] Do the standards indicate the weight to be given to each of the criteria in making a discretionary decision?

[c] Are the standards for the issuance of a discretionary permit sufficiently definite that a court can review an individual decision and determine whether the decision was arbitrary and capricious?

Procedural Due Process

[a] Are there established procedures for the consideration of an application for a discretionary permit?

[b] Do the procedures provide for a reasonable opportunity for the applicant to present material and information in support of his application?

[c] If there is a public hearing, is notice of the hearing sufficient to alert affected persons of the hearing?

[d] Do the procedures afford the applicant a reasonable opportunity to respond to staff or citizen input in regard to the application?

Substantive Due Process

[a] Does the discretionary permitting process serve a valid public purpose?

[b] Is the relationship between the provisions authorizing a discretionary permit and the public health, safety and welfare apparent?

Equal Protection

[a] Do the standards ensure that similarly situated persons will receive comparable treatment?

[b] Are the standards such that any [classifications] are based on a reasonably logical and apparent basis?

[c] Are the standards such that no suspect class of persons (e.g. minorities) are singled out for disparate treatment?

Aesthetic Regulation

Delegation of Power

[a] Is there a clear grant of power from the state to the municipality authorizing it to regulate aesthetics?

[b] Is there a clearly articulated legislative policy regarding the purpose for both citywide and building or district specific design standards?

[c] Is the discretion of the architectural review board clearly limited by standards contained in the ordinance?

[d] Do the standards indicate the weight to be given to each of the criteria in making a design review decision?

Procedural Due Process

[a] Are there established procedures for consideration of an application for design review?

[b] Do the procedures provide for a reasonable opportunity for the applicant to present material and information in support of his application?

[c] Do the procedures afford the applicant a reasonable opportunity to respond to staff or citizen input regarding the application?

[d] Are applicants provided sufficient notice of the hearing on their application?

Substantive Due Process

[a] Does the design review ordinance serve a valid public purpose?

[b] Is the relationship between the standards, embodied in the ordinance and the public health, safety, and welfare apparent?

Equal Protection

[a] Do the standards ensure that similarly situated persons will receive comparable treatment?

[b] Are the standards such that any classifications are based on a reasonably logical and apparent basis?

Just Compensation (Taking)

[a] Do the standards, as written and applied, allow property owners to retain a reasonable use of their property?

Special Exception

Delegation of Power

[a] Is there clearly articulated legislative policy as to the general circumstances when a legislative approval is appropriate?

[b] Does the decision-making body have unfettered authority to determine when and if a special use permit should be granted?

Equal Protection

[a] Do the standards ensure that similarly situated persons will receive comparable treatment?

[b] Are the standards such that any classifications are based on a reasonably logical and apparent basis?

Special Exception (con't.)

Substantive Due Process ———————— **Just Compensation (Taking)**

[a] Does the special use permitting process serve a valid public purpose?

[b] Is the relationship between the provisions authorizing a special use permit and the public health, safety, and welfare apparent?

[a] Does the denial of the special exception requested still leave the property owner with a reasonable use of his property?

Negotiated (Rezoning) Approvals

Delegation of Power ———————————— **Substantive Due Process**

[a] Is there clearly articulated legislative policy as to the general circumstances when a rezoning of this sort is appropriate?

[b] Does the decision-making body have unfettered authority to determine when and if a discretionary zoning should be adopted?

[a] Does the discretionary rezoning process serve a valid public purpose?

[b] Is the relationship between the provisions authorizing a discretionary rezoning and the public health, safety, and welfare apparent?

Procedural Due Process ———————————— **Equal Protection**

[a] If quasi-judicial: Are there established procedures for the consideration of an application for a discretionary (negotiated) rezoning?

[b] If quasi-judicial: Do the procedures provide for a reasonable opportunity for the developer applicant to present material and information in support of his application?

[c] If quasi-judicial: If there is a public hearing, is notice of the hearing sufficient to alert affected persons of the hearing?

[d] If quasi-judicial: Do the procedures afford the applicant a reasonable opportunity to respond to staff or citizen input in regard to the application?

[a] Do the standards ensure that similarly situated persons will receive comparable treatment?

[b] Are the standards such that any classifications are based on a reasonably logical and apparent basis?

[c] Are the standards such that no suspect class of persons (e.g. minorities) are singled out for disparate treatment?

Prohibition of Adult Uses

Void for Vagueness

[a] Are the definitions in the ordinance sufficiently specific to alert a reasonably intelligent individual as to which products and publications are the subject of the ordinance?

[b] Are the definitions in the ordinance sufficiently definite that a court can review an individual decision and determine whether the decision was arbitrary and capricious?

Equal Protection

[a] Does the regulation discriminate between two or more similarly situated property owners?

Freedom of Speech

[a] Does the ordinance attempt to place a prior restraint on freedom of speech by defining certain products and publications as obscene and prohibiting their sale or exhibition?

[b] Does the ordinance attempt to exclude adult businesses rather than to regulate their location?

Substantive Due Process

[a] Does the regulation substantially advance public health safety and welfare?

[b] Does the legislation itself identify the public interest to be served and are their studies, findings, etc. forming the basis of the means selected to promote that interest?

Prohibition of Places of Worship

Substantive Due Process

[a] Does the ordinance apply retroactively in addition to prospectively?

[b] If the ordinance does apply retroactively, is there a strong public interest involved and is the owner of the subject property given a reasonable period of time to comply with the new standard?

Freedom of Religion

[a] If the ordinance totally excludes houses of worship from residential neighborhoods, is this permissible under state law?

[b] If the ordinance regulates religious activities for accepted planning reasons, do the benefits gained from the regulation greatly outweigh the burdens imposed on the religious activities?

Equal Protection

[a] Does the ordinance ensure that similarly situated religious institutions will receive comparable treatment?

[b] Are the provisions in the ordinance such that classifications are based on a reasonably logical and apparent basis?

Prohibition of Places of Worship (con't.)

Freedom of Religion

[c] If the ordinance regulates secular activities conducted by the religious institution, does the ordinance comply with constitutional due process and equal protection standards?

Prohibition of Group Homes

Equal Protection

[a] Do the standards in the ordinance ensure that similarly situated persons will receive comparable treatment?

[b] Are the standards such that any classifications are based on a reasonably logical and apparent basis?

[c] Do the reasons stated by the city for denying a permit rest on neutral grounds or are they based on unjustifiable discrimination against the mentally ill?

Downzoning

Procedural Due Process

[a] Did the property owner receive sufficient advance notice of the proposed rezoning?

[b] Was the owner afforded a fair opportunity to be heard on the issue and evidence before the rezoning authority?

Substantive Due Process

[a] Does the downzoning serve a legitimate public purpose?

[b] Does the master plan support the downzoning?

[c] Has the property been singled out and treated differently from similar adjacent or nearby properties?

[d] Does the public record state valid land use reasons for the downzoning?

Equal Protection

[a] Do the standards ensure that similarly situated persons will receive comparable treatment?

[b] Is the effect of the downzoning to zone out lower income people from the community?

Just Compensation (Taking)

[a] Does the downzoning substantially advance a legitimate governmental interest?

[b] Does the downzoning take away all reasonable use of the property?

[c] Is the owner's distinct, investment-backed expectations substantially destroyed?

Parcel Rezoning

Procedural Due Process

[a] Under the applicable state law, is rezoning considered a legislative act or an administrative or quasi-judicial act?

[b] Are there established procedures for rezoning and, if so, have they been followed?

[c] Is there a comprehensive plan? If so, does the rezoning conform to it, and have the planners participated in evaluation of the rezoning proposal in light of the plan?

Equal Protection

[a] Does the rezoning establish a classification of land which appears logical?

[b] Are landowners whose land has similar characteristics treated similarly?

Substantive Due Process

[a] Is there a valid public purpose underlying the rezoning? Does the rezoning advance the public health, safety, welfare, and morals? is the link between the public objectives and the rezoning evident?

[b] Is there a comprehensive plan? If so, does the rezoning conform to it? If the rezoning does not conform to the plan, have conditions in the area which would be affected by the rezoning changed materially since adoption of the plan?

[c] Would the uses allowed under the rezoning be harmonious with the current nearby uses? Is the area to be rezoned an island in the midst of another type of land use, or is it on a boundary between uses?

Just Compensation (Taking)

[a] Does the rezoning "substantially advance" a "legitimate state interest? Is there a strong link between the effect of the rezoning and the public purpose to be served?

[b] Would the rezoning so reduce the value of the parcel as to leave the owner with no reasonable economic use?

[c] Is the rezoning likely to be temporary rather than permanent and, if so, what reduction in value would occur as a result of this temporary restriction?

Interim Land Use Controls

Procedural Due Process

[a] Are there established procedures for the consideration of an application for a demolition permit?

[b] Do the procedures provide for a reasonable opportunity for the applicant to present material and information in support of his application?

[c] If there is a public hearing, is notice of the hearing sufficient to alert affected persons of the hearing?

[d] Do the procedures afford the applicant a reasonable opportunity to respond to staff or citizen input in regard to the application?

Just Compensation (Taking)

[a] Does the interim regulation deny property owners an economically viable use of their property?

[b] Has the interim regulation which temporarily denies property owners of all economically viable use of their property been extended without justification?

Substantive Due Process

[a] Does the ordinance serve a valid public purpose?

[b] Is the relationship between the provisions authorizing the moratorium and the public health, safety, and welfare apparent?

Equal Protection

[a] Do the standards ensure that similarly situated persons will receive comparable treatment?

[b] Are the standards such that any classifications are based on a reasonably logical and apparent basis?

[c] Are the standards such that no suspect class of persons (e.g. racial minorities) are singled-out for disparate treatment?

Resource Protection

Substantive Due Process

[a] Does the city's action limiting density/use on the property bear some substantial relationship to the public health, safety, and welfare?

[b] Does an explanation exist for why the city acted which can be said to "make any sense at all?"

[c] Is the explanation for the city's action based on reliable, believable information?

Just Compensation (Taking)

[a] Does the city's action leave the landowner with a physically possible use of his property?

[b] Is the physically possible use of the property economically feasible?

[c] Is the developer's proposed use consistent with natural character of the site or does the developer's proposal require that the site be altered to accommodate the proposed use?

Amortization of Nonconforming Use

Substantive Due Process

[a] Does the amortization provision serve a valid public purpose?

Just Compensation (Taking)

[a] Is the amortization period of sufficient length to allow the owner of the nonconforming use to recoup his investment?

Equal Protection

[a] Do the amortization provisions ensure that similarly situated persons will receive comparable treatment?

[b] Are the differing amortization periods supported by a reasonable policy that can be supported by facts?

Development Exactions

Substantive Due Process

[a] Does the regulation substantially advance public health, safety, and welfare?

[b] Does the legislation itself identify the public interest to be served and are there studies, findings, etc. forming the basis of the means selected to promote that interest?

Just Compensation

[a] Is there a demonstrable fit or "nexus" between the exaction imposed upon the property owner as a condition to granting a permit and the public need or burden created by the proposed development?

[b] Does the regulation substantially advance a legitimate state interest?

Equal Protection

[a] Do the standards ensure that similarly situated persons will receive comparable treatment?

[b] Are the standards such that any classifications are based on a reasonably logical and apparent basis?

Growth Phasing

Void for Vagueness

[a] Are there discernable standards in the regulation which
  [1] are rationally based and
  [2] adequately alert an applicant to
    the criteria to be used in applying the ordinance?

[b] Are the standards utilized sufficiently definite so that decisions may be reviewed on the basis of the application of the standards to a given proposal?

Substantive Due Process

[a] Does the regulation substantially advance public health, safety, and welfare?

[b] Does the legislation itself identify the public interest to be served, and are their studies, findings, etc. forming the basis of the means selected to promote that interest?

Growth Phasing

Equal Protection

[a] Does the regulation discriminate between two or more similarly situated people?

[b] If so, does it discriminate between a member(s) of a "suspect class" and others?

[c] If not, is the regulation rationally related to a legitimate public concern?

Equal Protection

[d] If so, is there a compelling state interest justifying the disparate treatment?

Just Compensation (Taking)

[a] Is the impact of the regulation on a landowner such that it either prevents any reasonable use of his property or denies a recognizable property right in the regulated parcel (e.g. the right to exclude others)?

[b] If so, does the regulation substantially advance a legitimate state interest? If not, the regulation may result in a "taking". If "yes", no taking occurs *unless* the regulation nevertheless denies the owner all economically viable use of the property as a whole, in which event a compensable taking has probably occurred.

[c] Does the regulation, as applied, destroy a "vested" property right under state law?

V

Synopsis of U.S. Supreme Court Cases

SECTION 1:
INTRODUCTION

The U.S. Supreme Court cases presented in Section 2 have been selected because of their relevance to land use regulation. The summary of each case is divided into the following elements:

1. Type of regulation involved.
2. Land use issue(s).
3. Type of legal challenge.
4. Remedy sought.
5. Constitutional issue(s).
6. Facts.
7. Decision.
8. Opinion of the Court.
9. Dissenting or Concurring Opinion.

Matrix 2 and Matrix 3, which precede the case summaries, are designed to assist the reader in determining which of the Supreme Court cases have most relevance to a particular constitutional principle discussed in Part II or a planning problem solving area discussed in Part III. Matrix 2 shows which of the constitutional principles are at issue in each Supreme Court case and also identifies relevant problem solving areas. Matrix 3 shows which of the Supreme Court cases are relevant to particular planning problem solving areas, and also identifies applicable constitutional principles.

Matrix 2: Relationship of Supreme Court Cases to Constitutional Principles with Cross Reference to Planner Problem Solving Areas

Constitutional Principles

Legend

● Relationship exists

● III-2 Cross reference to applicable Planner Problem Solving Areas

U.S. Supreme Court Cases	Delegation of Power [II-1]	Void for Vagueness [II-2]	Procedural Due Process [II-3]	Substantive Due Process [II-4]	Equal Protection [II-5]	Just Compensation [II-6]	Ripeness [II-6]	Freedom of Speech [II-7]	Freedom of Religion [II-8]	Establishment Clause [II-8]	Free Exercise Clause [II-8]
Agins [V-2.01]						● III-1-4	● III-4				
Andrus v. Allard [V-2.02]						●					
Berman v. Parker [V-2.03]				●		●					
Block v. Hirsh [V-2.04]						●					
City of Cleburne [V-2.05]					● III-1-5 III-7-12						
City of Eastlake [V-2.06]				●							
City of Lafayette [V-2.07]											
City of Lakewood v. Plain Dealer [V-2.08]								● III-11			
City of New Orleans v. Dukes [V-2.09]					●						
City of Renton [V-2.10]								● III-7.01			
County Board of Arlington v. Richards [V-2.11]					●						
First English [V-2.12]						● III-1-4 III-6-12					
Fisher [V-2.13]					●	●					

Matrix 2 (con't.): Relationship of Supreme Court Cases to Constitutional Principles with Cross Reference to Planner Problem Solving Areas

Constitutional Principles

Legend

| Relationship exists | • |
| Cross reference to applicable Planner Problem Solving Areas | • III-2 |

U.S. Supreme Court Cases	Delegation of Power [II-1]	Void for Vagueness [II-2]	Procedural Due Process [II-3]	Substantive Due Process [II-4]	Equal Protection [II-5]	Just Compensation [II-6]	Ripeness [II-6]	Freedom of Speech [II-7]	Freedom of Religion [II-8]	Establishment Clause [II-8]	Free Exercise Clause [II-8]
Frisby v. Schultz [V-2.14]								•			
Goldblatt [V-2.15]				•		•					
Gorieb v. Fox [V-2.16]				•	•	•					
Hadacheck [V-2.17]				•	•	•					
Hawaii Housing Authority v. Midkiff [V-2.18]						•					
Hodel [V-2.19]				•		•					
Kaiser Aetna [V-2.20]						•					
Keystone [V-2.21]				• III-10		• III-10					
Larkin v. Grendel's Den [V-2.22]				•	•				• III-7.03	•	
Loretto [V-2.23]				•		•					
MacDonald [V-2.24]				•		•	• III-4				
Members of City Council of Los Angeles v. Vincent [V-2.25]				• III-11				• III-11			
Metromedia, Inc. [V-2.26]				• III-11				• III-11			

Matrix 2 (con't.): Relationship of Supreme Court Cases to Constitutional Principles with Cross Reference to Planner Problem Solving Areas

Constitutional Principles

Legend

■ • Relationship exists

■ (III-2) Cross reference to applicable Planner Problem Solving Areas

U.S. Supreme Court Cases

U.S. Supreme Court Cases	Delegation of Power [II-1]	Void for Vagueness [II-2]	Procedural Due Process [II-3]	Substantive Due Process [II-4]	Equal Protection [II-5]	Just Compensation [II-6]	Ripeness [II-6]	Freedom of Speech [II-7]	Freedom of Religion [II-8]	Establishment Clause [II-8]	Free Exercise Clause [II-8]
Miller v. Schoene [V-2.27]				•		•					
Monell [V-2.28]											
Moore [V-2.29]				•							
Mugler v. Kansas [V-2.30]				•		•					
Nectow v. City of Cambridge [V-2.31]				•		•					
Nollan [V-2.32]				• III-1-12		• III-1-4 III-6-12					
Owen [V-2.33]			•	•							
Penn Central [V-2.34]				•		•					
Pennell [V-2.35]				•	•	•	• III-4				
Pennsylvania Coal v. Mahon [V-2.36]				•		•					
Phillips [V-2.37]				•		•					
Pruneyard Shopping Center [V-2.38]				•		•		•			
Ruckelshaus [V-2.39]						•					
San Diego Gas and Electric [V-2.40]				•		•	• III-4				
Schad [V-2.41]				•				• III-7.01			

Matrix 2 (con't.): Relationship of Supreme Court Cases to Constitutional Principles with Cross Reference to Planner Problem Solving Areas

Constitutional Principles

Legend

■ • Relationship exists

■ • (III-2) Cross reference to applicable Planner Problem Solving Areas

U.S. Supreme Court Cases	Delegation of Power [II-1]	Void for Vagueness [II-2]	Procedural Due Process [II-3]	Substantive Due Process [II-4]	Equal Protection [II-5]	Just Compensation [II-6]	Ripeness [II-6]	Freedom of Speech [II-7]	Freedom of Religion [II-8]	Establishment Clause [II-8]	Free Exercise Clause [II-8]
Town of Hallie [V-2.24]											
United States v. Causby [V-2.43]						•					
United States v. Locke [V-2.44]			•			•					
United States v. Cherokee Nation [V-2.45]						•					
United States v. Riverside Bayview [V-2.46]						•					
Village of Arlington Heights [V-2.47]					• III-7.07						
Village of Belle Terre v. Boraas [V-2.48]					• III-7.05						
Village of Euclid v. Ambler Realty [V-2.49]				• III-1 III-2	• III-1-5 III-8-9	•					
Webb's Fabulous Pharmacies [V-2.50]				•		•					
Welch v. Swasey [V-2.51]				•	•	•					
Williamson County v. Hamilton Bank [V-2.52]				•		•	• III-4				
Young v. American Mini Theatres [V-2.53]				• III-7.01	III-7.01			• III-7.01			

SYMPOSIUM DISCUSSION

Topical Index

Matrix 3: Relationship of Supreme Court Cases to Planner Problem Solving Areas with Cross Reference to Constitutional Principles

Planner Problem Solving Areas

Legend

▪ Relationship exists

▪ II-2 Cross reference to applicable Constitutional Principles

U.S. Supreme Court Cases

Case	Discretionary Permitting [III-1]	Downzoning [III-2]	Specific Parcel Rezoning [III-3]	Special Exception [III-4]	Negotiated (Rezoning) Approvals [III-5]	Development Exactions [III-6]	Prohibition of Use(s) [III-7]	Growth Phasing [III-8]	Interim Land Use Controls [III-9]	Resource Protection [III-10]	Regulation for Aesthetic Purposes [III-11]	Amortization of Nonconforming Use(s) [III-12]
Agins [V-2.01]	● II-6	● II-6	● II-6	● II-6								
Andrus v. Allard [V-2.02]												
Berman v. Parker [V-2.03]												
Block v. Hirsh [V-2.04]												
City of Cleburne [V-2.05]	● II-5	● II-5	● II-5	● II-5	● II-5		● II-5					
City of Eastlake [V-2.06]												
City of Lafayette [V-2.07]												
City of Lakewood v. Plain Dealer [V-2.08]											● II-7	
City of New Orleans v. Dukes [V-2.09]	● II-5											
City of Renton [V-2.10]							● II-7					
County Board of Arlington v. Richards [V-2.11]				● II-5								
First English [V-2.12]	● II-6	● II-6	● II-6	● II-6		● II-6	● II-6	● II-6	● II-6	● II-6	● II-6	● II-6
Fisher [V-2.13]												

Matrix 3 (con't.): Relationship of Supreme Court Cases to Planner Problem Solving Areas with Cross Reference to Constitutional Principles

Planner Problem Solving Areas

Legend

● Relationship exists

● II-2 Cross reference to applicable Constitutional Principles

U.S. Supreme Court Cases

	Discretionary Permitting [III-1]	Downzoning [III-2]	Specific Parcel Rezoning [III-3]	Special Exception [III-4]	Negotiated (Rezoning) Approvals [III-5]	Development Exactions [III-6]	Prohibition of Use(s) [III-7]	Growth Phasing [III-8]	Interim Land Use Controls [III-9]	Resource Protection [III-10]	Regulation for Aesthetic Purposes [III-11]	Amortization of Nonconforming Use(s) [III-12]
Frisby v. Schultz [V-2.14]												
Goldblatt [V-2.15]												
Gorieb v. Fox [V-2.16]												
Hadacheck [V-2.17]												
Hawaii Housing Authority v. Midkiff [V-2.18]												
Hodel [V-2.19]												
Kaiser Aetna [V-2.20]												
Keystone [V-2.21]										● II-4 II-6		
Larkin v. Grendel's Den [V-2.22]							● II-8					
Loretto [V-2.23]												
MacDonald [V-2.24]				● II-6								
Members of City Council of Los Angeles v. Vincent [V-2.25]											● II-4 II-7	
Metromedia, Inc. [V-2.26]											● II-4 II-7	

Matrix 3 (con't.): Relationship of Supreme Court Cases to Planner Problem Solving Areas with Cross Reference to Constitutional Principles

Planner Problem Solving Areas

Legend

- ▪ Relationship exists
- ▪ II-2 Cross reference to applicable Constitutional Principles

U.S. Supreme Court Cases	Discretionary Permitting [III-1]	Downzoning [III-2]	Specific Parcel Rezoning [III-3]	Special Exception [III-4]	Negotiated (Rezoning) Approvals [III-5]	Development Exactions [III-6]	Prohibition of Use(s) [III-7]	Growth Phasing [III-8]	Interim Land Use Controls [III-9]	Resource Protection [III-10]	Regulation for Aesthetic Purposes [III-11]	Amortization of Nonconforming Use(s) [III-12]
Miller v. Schoene [V-2.27]												
Monell [V-2.28]												
Moore [V-2.29]												
Mugler v. Kansas [V-2.30]												
Nectow v. City of Cambridge [V-2.31]												
Nollan [V-2.32]	● II-4 II-6	● II-4 II-6	● II-4 II-6	● II-4 II-6	● II-4	● II-4 II-6	● II-4 II-6	● II-4 II-6	● II-4 II-6	● II-4 II-6	● II-4 II-6	● II-4 II-6
Owen [V-2.33]												
Penn Central [V-2.34]												
Pennell [V-2.35]												
Pennsylvania Coal v. Mahon [V-2.36]												
Phillips [V-2.37]												
Pruneyard Shopping Center [V-2.38]												
Ruckelshaus [V-2.39]												
San Diego Gas and Electric [V-2.40]				● II-6								
Schad [V-2.41]							● II-7					

Matrix 3 (con't.): Relationship of Supreme Court Cases to Planner Problem Solving Areas with Cross Reference to Constitutional Principles

Planner Problem Solving Areas

Legend

- ● Relationship exists
- ▣ III-2 Cross reference to applicable Constitutional Principles

U.S. Supreme Court Cases	Discretionary Permitting [III-1]	Downzoning [III-2]	Specific Parcel Rezoning [III-3]	Special Exception [III-4]	Negotiated (Rezoning) Approvals [III-5]	Development Exactions [III-6]	Prohibition of Use(s) [III-7]	Growth Phasing [III-8]	Interim Land Use Controls [III-9]	Resource Protection [III-10]	Regulation for Aesthetic Purposes [III-11]	Amortization of Nonconforming Use(s) [III-12]
Town of Hallie [V-2.24]												
United States v. Causby [V-2.43]												
United States v. Locke [V-2.44]												
United States v. Cherokee Nation [V-2.45]												
United States v. Riverside Bayview [V-2.46]												
Village of Arlington Heights [V-2.47]							● II-5					
Village of Belle Terre v. Boraas [V-2.48]							● II-5					
Village of Euclid v. Ambler Realty [V-2.49]	● II-5 II-4	● II-5 II-4	● II-5	● II-5	● II-5				● II-5	● II-5		
Webb's Fabulous Pharmacies [V-2.50]												
Welch v. Swasey [V-2.51]												
Williamson County v. Hamilton Bank [V-2.52]			● II-6									
Young v. American Mini Theatres [V-2.53]							● 11-4 II-5 II-7					

SYMPOSIUM DISCUSSION

Topical Index

SECTION 2:
SUPREME COURT CASES

Editors' Note

As explained more fully in Part II, Sections 4 and 6, the United States Constitution contains two limitations on the power of government to interfere with property rights. The first is the just compensation clause of the Fifth Amendment: "[N]or shall private property be taken for public use, without just compensation." The second is the due process clause of the Fourteenth Amendment: "[N]or shall any State deprive any person of life, liberty, or property without due process of law . . . " It is important to note that the language in these two guarantees of property rights is not identical. The Fourteenth Amendment prohibits states from taking property without providing due process of law, but does not contain the just compensation requirement.

The Fifth Amendment, along with the other nine amendments to the Constitution known as the Bill of Rights, was adopted in 1791 and initially was applicable only to the actions of the federal government. Over the past 60 years, however, the Supreme Court has incorporated most, but not all, of the constitutional guarantees found in the Bill of Rights into the Fourteenth Amendment, thus making them applicable to the actions of states and municipalities as well as the actions of the federal government.

Although some scholars dispute whether the Fifth Amendment's just compensation clause has ever been formally incorporated into the Fourteenth Amendment, the Supreme Court ruled that the Fourteenth Amendment's due process clause itself requires that government pay just compensation when it takes property for a public use [*Webb's Fabulous Pharmacies, Inc. v. Beckwith*, 449 U.S. 155 (1980); *Chicago B. & Q.R.R. Co. v. City of Chicago*, 166 U.S. 226 (1897)]. Thus, despite the different language of the Fifth and Fourteenth Amendments, and regardless of whether the just compensation clause of the Fifth Amendment has been incorporated into the Fourteenth Amendment, the substantive standard in a governmental takings of property is now identical under each.

In reading the summaries of U.S. Supreme Court cases involving takings claims in this section, it should be noted that the "Constitutional Issue" is stated in one of three different ways: (1) a claim under the Fourteenth Amendment, (2) a claim under the Fifth Amendment, and (3) a claim under the Fifth Amendment "as applied to the states" through the Fourteenth Amendment. Taking cases decided directly under the Fifth

Amendment involve a taking claim against the federal government. Cases decided under the Fourteenth Amendment or under the Fifth Amendment "as applied" through the Fourteenth Amendment involve taking claims against a state or local government. In general, the U.S. Supreme Court's older taking cases involving claims against state or local governments were decided solely under the due process clause of the Fourteenth Amendment, while its more recent decisions have tended to rely also on the just compensation clause of the Fifth Amendment as applied through the Fourteenth Amendment.

2.01 Agins v. City of Tiburon,   447 U.S. 255, 100 S.Ct. 2138 (1980).

1. *Type of Regulation:*   Zoning ordinance.

2. *Land Use Issue:*   Whether the adoption of two ordinances that restricted development of valuable residential land to between one and five dwelling units substantially deprived the owners of all reasonable use of their property.

3. *Type of Legal Challenge:*   Facial.

4. *Remedy Sought:*   Damages for inverse condemnation and a declaration that the ordinances were facially unconstitutional.

5. *Constitutional Issue:*   Taking of property without just compensation (Fifth Amendment as applied to the states through the Fourteenth Amendment).

6. *Facts:*   After the Agins acquired five acres of undeveloped land in the city of Tiburon, California, for residential development, the city, in response to state-mandated planning requirements, adopted two ordinances that modified existing zoning requirements. The ordinances placed the Agins' five acres in "RPD-1," a residential planned development and open space zone, which permitted the development of from one to five single-family residences on the property. The Agins did not submit a development plan to the city, but instead sued the city, seeking damages for inverse condemnation and a declaration that the ordinances were facially unconstitutional.

The California Supreme Court found that the city's zoning ordinances, on their face, did not constitute a taking of the Agins' property because the ordinance by its terms permitted construction of one- to five-acre residences on the five-acre tract and therefore did not prevent all use of their property. The court also ruled that inverse condemnation was not an available remedy in cases where a party alleges a regulatory taking; the exclusive remedies are injunctive and declaratory relief. The Agins sought review from the U.S. Supreme Court.

7. *Decision:* Zoning ordinances upheld as not constituting a taking of property.

8. *Opinion of the Court:* The ends sought to be achieved by enactment of the ordinances discouraging the premature and unnecessary conversion of open-space land to urban uses are legitimate state interests under the constitution. The means selected to achieve those goals—restricting the number of dwelling units—substantially advances those legitimate interests. Moreover, the zoning ordinance benefited the Agins as well as the public by serving the city's interest in assuring careful and orderly development of residential property with provision for open-space areas. As a result, the ordinances' provisions on their face did not constitute a taking under the Fifth and Fourteenth Amendments because the public interest in achieving those goals outweighs the landowners' interest in developing the land in the most profitable way possible. Because the court did not find a taking in this case, it declined to address the question of whether damages for inverse condemnation are a required remedy in regulatory takings cases.

2.02 Andrus v. Allard,   444 U.S. 51, 100 S.Ct. 318 (1979).

1. *Type of Regulation:* Trade regulation.

2. *Land Use Issue:* None. The issue in this case was whether federal regulations prohibiting commercial transactions involving artifacts deprived the artifacts' owners of their Fifth Amendment property rights.

3. *Type of Legal Challenge:* As applied.

4. *Remedy Sought:*

  a. Declaration that the Eagle Protection Act and Migratory Bird Treaty Act do not forbid the sale of artifacts and, if they do, that they violate the just compensation clause of the Fifth Amendment.

  b. An injunction to prevent application of both acts to the artifacts.

5. *Constitutional Issue:* Taking of property without just compensation in violation of Fifth Amendment.

6. *Facts:* The Migratory Bird Treaty Act and Eagle Protection Act make it unlawful to sell or otherwise conduct transactions involving certain species of birds and any parts, nests, or eggs of such birds. Regulations promulgated by the Secretary of the Interior pursuant to these statutes provide that migratory birds lawfully acquired alive or dead, or their parts, nests, or eggs lawfully acquired before the effective date of the statutes may be owned or transported without a federal permit but may not be imported, exported, purchased, sold, traded, bartered, or offered for purchase, sale, trade, or barter. The plaintiffs, who were engaged in the sale of artifacts containing bald eagle feathers acquired lawfully before the statutory protections became effective, had previously been prosecuted for violating both acts. The plaintiffs sued in federal district court, arguing that the statutes did not forbid the sale of the artifacts because the constituent bird parts were obtained prior to the effective dates of the statutes, and seeking declaratory and injunctive relief. Additionally, the plaintiffs alleged that if the acts and regulations did apply to the artifacts, the prohibitions constituted a taking of property under the Fifth Amendment.

7. *Decision:*   Acts upheld as not violating Fifth Amendment property rights.

8. *Opinion of the Court:*   By definition, government regulation involves the adjustment of rights for the public good. Although the prohibition on the sale of the artifacts prevents the plaintiffs from making the most profitable use of the artifacts, the regulations did not compel relinquishment of the artifacts nor impose any physical restriction against the property. The plaintiffs were still able to derive some economic benefit from the artifacts; for example, by displaying the pieces for an admission fee. A loss of future profits, without any physical restrictions on the property, is too speculative. The interest in anticipated gains has traditionally been viewed as a less compelling reason for finding a taking than other property-related interests.

2.03 Berman v. Parker,   348 U.S. 26, 75 S.Ct. 98 (1954).

1. *Type of Regulation:*   Legislation for urban redevelopment that authorizes condemnation (District of Columbia Redevelopment Act of 1945).

2. *Land Use Issue:*   Whether property condemned and compensated for by government action must actually be intended for a public use, or may condemnation achieve more general public purposes.

3. *Type of Legal Challenge:*   Both facial and as applied.

4. *Remedy Sought:*   Injunction to prevent condemnation and declaratory judgment that the legislation was unconstitutional.

5. *Constitutional Issues:*

  a. Use of eminent domain under the Fifth Amendment.

  b. Due process limitations (Fourteenth Amendment) on the police power.

  c. Role of legislative bodies and courts.

6. *Facts:* Congress, acting as the local governing and legislative body of the District of Columbia, adopted a plan for the redevelopment and beautification of the national capital area pursuant to the District of Columbia Redevelopment Act. The plan called for the District of Columbia Redevelopment Land Agency to acquire property by eminent domain and then to transfer that property to public agencies and private developers, who would carry out the redevelopment plan. The government planned to design development for the project to prevent blighting influences and improve the area aesthetically. The owners of a department store that was in sound condition objected to the appropriation of their property for redevelopment, contending that it was an unconstitutional exercise of the power of eminent domain, since their property would be redeveloped by private parties for private, not public use. They also contended that the purpose of the exercise of eminent domain under the act was to rid the area of slums, not to condemn property to develop a better balanced, more attractive community.

7. *Decision:* Redevelopment act upheld as constitutional exercise of the power of eminent domain.

8. *Opinion of the Court:* The use of the power of condemnation and the police power of government is a matter primarily for determination by legislative bodies, not the courts. The concept of the public welfare is broad and inclusive. The values it represents are spiritual as well as physical, aesthetic as well as monetary. When a legislative body determines that the public interest will be served by certain purposes, such determinations are "well-nigh conclusive." The role of the judiciary in determining whether eminent domain is being exercised for a public purpose is narrow. "The rights of these property owners are satisfied when they receive that just compensation which the Fifth Amendment exacts as the price of the taking." The legislative body may determine where, when, how much, and why the power of eminent domain will be used.

Here, Congress decided that the redevelopment plan should include aesthetic considerations as well as considerations of health. Such a determination—"that the community should be beautiful as well as healthy, spacious as well as clean, well-balanced as well as carefully patrolled"—is within the power of the legislature. Further, since the means for accomplishing a public purpose are for Congress alone to choose, Congress may conclude that the end of achieving a redevelopment plan is better served by using private developers than public agencies. Similarly, the choice of the size and scope of the plan, and the decision to redevelop the area as a whole—including existing sound structures—rather than to adopt a piecemeal approach targeted at blighted structures, is to be made by Congress. "Once the question of public purpose has been decided, the amount and character of land to be taken for the project and the need for a particular tract to complete the integrated plan rests in the discretion of the legislative branch."

2.04 Block v. Hirsh, 256 U.S. 135, 41 S.Ct. 458 (1921).

1. *Type of Regulation:* Rent control.

2. *Land Use Issue:* Reasonableness of legislative imposition of emergency two-year rent-control statute which allowed tenants to hold over but also provided a mechanism for rent adjustment.

3. *Type of Legal Challenge:* Facial.

4. *Remedy Sought:* Recovery of possession of the housing unit by the owner of the building.

5. *Constitutional Issue:* Substantive due process (a taking of property without just compensation under the Fourteenth Amendment).

6. *Facts:* A housing emergency caused by this country's entry into World War I resulted in the rent law of 1919 in Washington, D.C. The act provided that a tenant could continue to occupy rental property, despite the expiration of his lease, so long as that tenant continued to pay his rent and performed whatever other conditions were set out in the lease. The same law provided a mechanism for rent adjustment and allowed the owner to oust the tenant, after 30 days' notice, and have possession for himself and for his family. Mr. Hirsh wanted the apartment that he had rented to Mr. Block for his own use, but he did not comply with the 30 days' notice requirement. He challenged the law's validity, contending that such rent control inhibited his right to free-market enterprise.

7. *Decision:* Rent control statute upheld as valid temporary measure.

8. *Opinion of the Court:* The emergency declared by the statute is assumed to exist since legislative findings are entitled to a considerable degree of judicial deference. Because housing is a necessity of life, and because the public interest in the availability of housing during the state of emergency justifies some degree of public control, the statute is a valid temporary measure to achieve the goal of public health and welfare. This was so, despite the inevitable deprivation of a profit on high rent that the owners of apartments in Washington would otherwise have made. The

emergency, the two-year (or less) duration of the act, and the rent adjustment feature make the act reasonable under the circumstances.

2.05   City of Cleburne, Texas v. Cleburne Living Center,   473 U.S. 432, 105 S.Ct. 3249 (1985).

1. *Type of Regulation:*   Zoning ordinance.
2. *Land Use Issue:*   Whether requiring a special use permit for a proposed group home for mentally retarded persons was rationally related to a legitimate state interest.
3. *Type of Legal Challenge:*   Facial and as applied.
4. *Remedy Sought:*   Declaratory and injunctive relief to prevent the special use permit requirement from applying to the proposed home.
5. *Constitutional Issue:*   Equal protection (Fourteenth Amendment).
6. *Facts:*   Plaintiff purchased a building in the city of Cleburne, Texas, with plans to lease it to the Cleburne Living Center, which would operate the building as a group home for the mentally retarded. The building was located in an area zoned as an apartment house district, which included, among other uses: fraternity houses, hospitals, sanitariums and nursing homes; however, the ordinance specifically excluded uses for the care of the feeble minded. The city classified the proposed home as a hospital for the feeble minded and informed the center that a special use permit would be required. The city based its requirement of a special use permit upon factors such as the negative attitudes and fears of neighborhood residents, the location of the proposed home across from a junior high school whose students might harass the occupants, its location near a 500-year floodplain, and the number of people who would occupy the home. The application for the special use permit was subsequently denied by the city council.
7. *Decision:*   Special use permit requirement invalid as applied to group home.
8. *Opinion of the Court:*   The ordinance is invalid as applied because it violates the center's right to equal protection of the law. Although the mentally retarded are not a suspect class, such as racial or religious minorities, and thus the zoning ordinance is not subject to the strict scrutiny standard, the ordinance cannot survive even the normal rational relationship test under equal protection analysis. The record does not reveal any rational basis to believe that the group home would pose a special threat to the city's legitimate interests different from other uses permitted under the

zoning district; the special use permit requirement appears to rest solely on an irrational prejudice against mentally retarded persons.

2.06 City of Eastlake v. Forest City Enterprises, Inc.   426 U.S. 668, 96 S.Ct. 2358 (1976).

1. *Type of Regulation:*   Zoning change referendum.

2. *Land Use Issue:*   Legality of a city charter provision that requires zoning changes approved by the city council to be ratified in a referendum by 55 percent of the voters.

3. *Type of Legal Challenge:*   Facial.

4. *Remedy Sought:*   Declaratory judgment to invalidate the referendum as an unauthorized delegation of legislative authority.

5. *Constitutional Issue:*   Due process (Fourteenth Amendment).

6. *Facts:*   A developer's request for a zoning change was approved by the plan commission and the city council, but was not ratified by a favorable vote of the citizens at the referendum required by the city charter. The developer then sought to have the charter provision requiring the referendum declared unconstitutional. The primary contention was that the provision constituted an unauthorized delegation of legislative authority and that the provision had no standards to guide the decisions of the voters. The Ohio Constitution specifically reserves the referendum power to the people, and it has been frequently exercised in matters of local government within the history of the state.

7. *Decision:*   Zoning referendum charter provision upheld as constitutional.

8. *Opinion of the Court:*   A referendum cannot be characterized as a delegation of legislative power. The referendum power is, in fact, reserved by the people to deal directly with matters that they might otherwise assign to the legislature, and such direct legislation by the people is subject to the same constitutional standards of substantive due process as are regular legislative decisions. Since legislators are not required to have standards to guide their decisions, the same is true when the people exercise their reserved legislative power through a referendum.

2.07 City of Lafayette, Louisiana v. Louisiana Power & Light Co.   435 U.S. 389, 98 S.Ct. 1123 (1978).

1. *Type of Regulation:*   Federal antitrust laws.

2. *Land Use Issue:*   None. The question in this case was whether Congress intended local governments to be presumptively immune from the

federal antitrust laws under the state action doctrine when the government is defending a suit for using anticompetitive restraints which prevent local property owners from participating in the utility market.

3. *Type of Legal Challenge:* Not applicable.

4. *Remedy Sought:* Monetary damages and injunctive relief.

5. *Constitutional Issue:* Sovereign immunity (Eleventh Amendment).

6. *Facts:* The city of Lafayette owns and operates electric utility stations which provide electricity to Lafayette and surrounding cities. The state of Louisiana grants Lafayette and other cities power to engage in utility service. The city sued Louisiana Power and Light, a private electric utility service, alleging that the company violated the federal antitrust laws causing injury to the city's utility service. Louisiana Power & Light (LP&L) counterclaimed against the city, alleging antitrust violations, including a conspiracy to begin sham litigation against LP&L to eliminate them from the utility business. LP&L sought injunctive and monetary relief. The city moved to have the counterclaim dismissed on the grounds that it was immune from the antitrust laws under the state-action doctrine.

7. *Decision:* Local governments held not absolutely exempt from potential antitrust liability under the federal antitrust laws.

8. *Opinion of the Court:* Congress did not intend to prevent local governmental units from being subject to liability under the antitrust laws in the absence of some overriding policy which negates a presumption of applicability of the laws to all persons. Cities act as would a private corporation even though they may be engaged in business affairs designed to benefit the entire community. Citizens need to be afforded the opportunity to challenge these business practices of their cities even though they may, however unlikely, resort to the political process to express their pleasure or displeasure with the functioning of the city. Furthermore, cities are not sovereign entities as are states, but instead are subject to the protections guaranteed citizens under the antitrust laws. Therefore, cities are protected from antitrust liability only when engaged in those activities that are part of the state's policy to displace competition with regulation or monopoly service. This occurs when it can be shown that the state legislature intended the local governments to operate in a particular area of public service.

9. *Dissenting Opinion:* The antitrust laws were directed at preventing large concentrations of economic power in private bodies. Because municipalities are instrumentalities of the state and have only those powers explicitly delegated to them by the state legislature, they only act in con-

formity with the state's sovereign power. The city of Lafayette was not acting in a private capacity but pursuant to a state delegation of power. Hence, to follow the plurality's opinion will result in undue intrusions into state regulations, previously impermissible, in order to determine whether a state legislature has provided the explicit grant of power needed to escape liability under the plurality's formula.

2.08 City of Lakewood v. Plain Dealer Publishing Co., _____ U.S. _____, 108 S.Ct. 2138 (1988).

1. *Type of Regulation:*   Municipal permit ordinance.

2. *Land Use Issue:*   Placement of newsracks on public property.

3. *Type of Legal Challenge:*   Facial.

4. *Remedy Sought:*   Judgment that the ordinance is unconstitutional and injunction against its enforcement.

5. *Constitutional Issues:*

   a. Whether the newspaper could bring a facial challenge to the ordinance under the First Amendment without first applying for, and being denied, a permit.

   b. Whether the standards for granting or denying a permit are sufficiently definite to avoid constituting a prior restraint on freedom of expression.

   c. Whether the ordinance violates the First Amendment because it places financial requirements on the owners of newsracks located on public property that are not placed on the owners of other structures on public property.

6. *Facts:*   Prior to 1983, the city of Lakewood, Ohio prohibited the placement of any privately owned structure on public property. After the Plain Dealer successfully challenged this prohibition in federal court, the city adopted an ordinance that allowed newsracks to be located on public property in commercial districts, while still banning them in residential districts. The ordinance gave the mayor the authority to approve or deny applications for annual newsrack permits. If the mayor denied an application, he was required to "state the reasons for such denial." If the mayor granted an application, the city issued an annual permit subject to several terms and conditions, including: approval of the newsrack's design by the city's architectural review board; an agreement by the newsrack owner to indemnify the city against any liability arising from the newsrack, guaran-

teed by a $100,000 insurance policy; and any "other terms and conditions deemed necessary and reasonable by the mayor."

The Plain Dealer elected to challenge the ordinance rather than seek a permit. The federal district court declared the ordinance constitutional in its entirety. The U.S. Court of Appeals for the Sixth Circuit reversed, finding that the ordinance was unconstitutional for three reasons. First, it gave the mayor unbounded discretion to grant or deny a permit application and to place unlimited additional terms and conditions on any permit. Second, the architectural review board had unbridled discretion to deny applications. Third, the indemnity and insurance requirements violated the First Amendment because no similar requirements were placed on owners of other structures on public property. However, the court of appeals did decide that the absolute ban on newsracks in residential districts was constitutional and that this portion of the ordinance was severable from the portions regulating placement of newsracks in commercial districts.

7. *Decision:* Portions of the ordinance invalidated as constituting prior restraint on expression, in violation of First Amendment.

8. *Opinion of the Court:* Where First Amendment guarantees are involved, a licensing statute that allegedly gives a government official unbridled discretion over whether to permit or deny any expressive activity may be challenged facially by one who is subject to the law, without the necessity of first applying for and being denied a permit. This recognizes that such unbridled discretion can constitute a prior restraint on expression and may result in censorship. The prior restraint problem is particularly acute under this ordinance because it is directed specifically at expressive conduct: the circulation of newspapers. Those portions of the ordinance that give the mayor unbridled discretion to deny a permit application and unbridled authority to condition the permit on any additional terms he deems necessary and reasonable are unconstitutional. Since the ordinance contains no real constraints on the mayor's discretion, his licensing decisions cannot be measured against any constitutionally sufficient standard to determine the boundaries of that discretion, and thus the ordinance would render the First Amendment's guaranty against censorship little more than a high-sounding ideal.

2.09 City of New Orleans v. Dukes,   427 U.S. 297, 96 S.Ct. 2513 (1976).

1. *Type of Regulation:* Pushcart vendor permit ordinance.

2. *Land Use Issue:* Whether an ordinance prohibiting pushcart vending, but excepting vendors who had continuously operated in the area for

eight or more years, denied equal protection of the laws to all pushcart vendors.

3. *Type of Legal Challenge:* As applied.

4. *Remedy Sought:* Declaration that the ordinance was invalid and an injunction against its enforcement.

5. *Constitutional Issue:* Equal protection (Fourteenth Amendment).

6. *Facts:* In order to preserve the charm and character of the French Quarter, the city of New Orleans passed an ordinance prohibiting push-cart vending in that area. However, the ordinance made an exception for pushcart vendors who had continuously operated eight years or longer in the French Quarter. This provision permitted two vendors to maintain their operations. A pushcart vendor who had been in business for two years was barred from vending by the ordinance and brought suit to have the ordinance declared invalid for failing to provide equal protection of the laws to all pushcart vendors.

7. *Decision:* Ordinance upheld under Fourteenth Amendment (equal protection).

8. *Opinion of the Court:* Regulating vendors is merely regulating economic activity. When government regulates economic activity, its enactments need only be rationally related to a legitimate state purpose. Preserving the charm and character of the French Quarter is a legitimate government purpose, and prohibiting street vendors rationally furthers that purpose, since vendors tend to disrupt the charm of a historic area. As for the exception for vendors who had worked in the area for eight years, the government can rationally determine to eliminate vendors gradually and can even rationally decide that vendors who had been in the French Quarter for over eight years have become a part of the charm of the area. Therefore, the regulation does not violate equal protection of the law.

2.10 City of Renton v. Playtime Theatres, Inc., 475 U.S. 41, 106 S.Ct. 925 (1986).

1. *Type of Regulation:* Zoning ordinance.

2. *Land Use Issue:* Whether an ordinance that has the effect of concentrating all theaters in a 400-acre area in one corner of the city serves a substantial governmental interest and is thereby constitutional, and whether it is constitutionally permissible for one city to rely on the experience and studies done in other cities to support enacting an ordinance that regulates adult theaters.

3. *Type of Legal Challenge:* As applied.

4. *Remedy Sought:* Declaratory judgment and injunctive relief to prevent enforcement of ordinance.

5. *Constitutional Issue:* Freedom of speech (First Amendment).

6. *Facts:* Playtime Theatres, Inc. purchased two theaters in downtown Renton, Washington, to exhibit adult films. At about the same time, Playtime filed suit against the city of Renton on First Amendment grounds to invalidate the city's ordinance that restricted theaters that exhibit adult films to a 400-acre area on the edge of the city.

7. *Decision:* Ordinance upheld under First Amendment.

8. *Opinion of the Court.* The ordinance serves a substantial governmental interest in protecting the quality of urban life by preventing the serious secondary effects of adult theaters on the surrounding community. Renton could reasonably rely on the experience and studies produced by other cities to find that it was also likely to experience these secondary effects. The First Amendment does not require a city to conduct new studies or to produce its own independent evidence before enacting such an ordinance. Since this ordinance did not ban adult theaters altogether, it was characterized as a content neutral, time, place, and manner regulation. And, although the ordinance had the effect of concentrating adult theaters in an area of about 400 acres in one corner of the city, the ordinance was found to allow reasonable access to adult theaters.

2.11 County Bd. of Arlington County, Virginia v. Richards, 434 U.S. 5, 98 S.Ct. 24 (1977).

1. *Type of Regulation:* Parking permit ordinance.

2. *Land Use Issue:* Reasonableness of a residential zoning ordinance which denied parking permits to nonresidents of a community in order to stem traffic flow from commercial and industrial areas into residential neighborhoods.

3. *Type of Legal Challenge:* Facial.

4. *Remedy Sought:* Injunction to prevent enforcement of the ordinance.

5. *Constitutional Issue:* Equal protection (Fourteenth Amendment).

6. *Facts:* Arlington County, Virginia passed an ordinance directing the county manager to designate those residential areas which were crowded with nonresidential vehicles. The stated purposes of the ordinance included minimizing social and environmental concerns of the residents and encouraging reliance on alternative means of transportation to the industrial and commercial complex. The manager issued residents, persons doing business with residents, and some guests weekday parking permits, while denying permits to all others. Commuters working in the large commercial and office complex next to the designated area sued to enjoin enforcement of the ordinance on the grounds that the ordinance was facially unconstitutional.

7. *Decision:* Ordinance upheld under Fourteenth Amendment (equal protection).

8. *Opinion of the Court:* Because the social and environmental goals sought to be achieved by the ordinance are not prohibited under the Constitution, the county may select any rational means to meet them as long as the distinction made is not invidious. The distinction made between residents and nonresidents is not presumed to be invidious under the Constitution, and the means selected rationally promotes the regulation's objectives.

2.12 First English Evangelical Lutheran Church of Glendale v. County of Los Angeles, 482 U.S. 304, 107 S.Ct. 2378 (1987).

1. *Type of Regulation:* Interim flood protection ordinance.

2. *Land Use Issue:* Whether a landowner who was denied all reasonable use of its property by a public safety regulation can recover compensation for the loss of use prior to the time that a court determined that the ordinance constituted a regulatory taking.

3. *Type of Legal Challenge:* As applied.

4. *Remedy Sought:* Compensation for loss of land value between the time the regulation went into effect and the time the court determined that the ordinance was a regulatory taking.

5. *Constitutional Issue:* Taking without just compensation (Fifth Amendment as applied to the states through the Fourteenth Amendment).

6. *Facts:* First English Evangelical Lutheran Church owned and operated Lutherglen, a campground for handicapped children, located in a canyon along the banks of the middle fork of Mill Creek in the Angeles National Forest. The middle fork is the natural drainage channel for a watershed area. In 1977, a forest fire denuded the hills upstream of Lutherglen. Seven months later, in February 1978, a rain storm caused Mill Creek to overflow, flooding Lutherglen and destroying its buildings. In January 1979, Los Angeles County passed an ordinance prohibiting construction in the interim flood protection area for health and safety reasons. The church claimed that the regulation denied it all reasonable use of its property and a month later sued the county in inverse condemnation. Interpreting California caselaw as precluding a monetary remedy for a regulatory taking, the California state court granted a motion to strike the plea for monetary compensation.

7. Decision: Monetary compensation held proper remedy where government regulation has prevented all reasonable use of private property, regardless of whether such a regulatory taking was permanent or temporary.

8. Opinion of the Court: [*Editor's note:* The U.S. Supreme Court reviewed the remedy question only. The Court accepted as true the claim in the church's pleadings that it had been denied all reasonable use of its property and thus that a taking had occurred.] Where government regulation works a taking of property, as in this case, the just compensation clause of the Fifth Amendment is self-executing and requires that compensation be paid to the property owner for the period of time that the regulation denied all reasonable use of the property. This holding is limited to the facts of the case and does not address "the quite different questions that arise in the case of normal delays in obtaining building permits, changes in zoning ordinances, variances and the like." The case is remanded to the state court for a determination on the merits of the taking claim. If the state court on remand determines that this interim flood protection ordinance effected a regulatory taking, the county is free to amend the regulation, acquire the land by eminent domain, or abandon its regulation altogether. However, if a taking is found to have occurred, even if the county abandons the regulation, there has been a temporary taking of property rights between the time the regulation went into effect and the time the regulation was declared to be a regulatory taking. Consistent with this holding, the county would be liable for the value of the use of the land during this temporary period. A temporary taking of the landowner's property is not different in kind from a permanent taking of the property; both clearly require compensation under the self-executing, express terms of the Constitution.

9. Dissenting Opinion: There is a fundamental distinction between physical invasions—which are easily identifiable without making any economic analyses and may constitute a taking requiring compensation—and regulatory programs which affect property values in many ways and amount to a taking only when they are extreme. The majority fails to recognize that regulatory restrictions on property have a significant temporal element and that the duration of the challenged restriction is a critical factor in determining whether a taking has occurred. Just because a landowner can prove that a regulation would constitute a taking if left in effect does not mean that he can prove that a temporary application of the regulation also constitutes a taking.

2.13 Fisher v. City of Berkeley, California, 475 U.S. 260, 106 S.Ct. 1045 (1986).

1. *Type of Regulation:*   Rent control ordinance.
2. *Land Use Issue:*   None. The issue in this case was whether rent control ordinances adopted by a municipality and administered under the control of a rent stabilization board are unconstitutional because they are preempted by the Sherman Act.
3. *Type of Legal Challenge:*   Facial and as applied.
4. *Remedy Sought:*   Declaratory and injunctive relief barring enforcement of the ordinance against landlords owning rental property.
5. *Constitutional Issues:*
   a. Preemption by the Sherman Act (Supremacy Clause).
   b. Substantive due process (Fourteenth Amendment).
   c. Equal protection (Fourteenth Amendment).
6. *Facts:*   A Berkeley, California, ordinance, enacted pursuant to an initiative, imposed rent ceilings on residential property within the city under the control of a rent stabilization board. Landlords brought suit, challenging the constitutionality of the ordinance, first on Fourteenth Amendment grounds and later on the claim that the Sherman Act preempts such an enactment. The ordinance was upheld and declared constitutional on its face by the California Supreme Court. The U.S. Supreme Court noted probable jurisdiction limited to the Sherman Act antitrust preemption question.
7. *Decision:*   Ordinance upheld as not being preempted by the Sherman Act.
8. *Opinion of the Court:*   The ordinance is not preempted by the Sherman Act because it lacked the element of concerted action needed to be a *per se* violation of that act. The rent ceilings were unilaterally imposed by the city on landlords to the exclusion of private control. Just because a restraint imposed unilaterally by the government has a coercive effect on parties who must obey the law does not create a concerted action within the meaning of the Sherman Act.

2.14 Frisby v. Schultz, _____ U.S. _____, 108 S.Ct. 2495 (1988).

1. *Type of Regulation:*   Ordinance banning certain types of picketing.

2. *Land Use Issue:* Whether a ban on picketing individual residences violates the First Amendment.

3. *Type of Legal Challenge:* Facial.

4. *Remedy Sought:* Declaratory and injunctive relief finding the ordinance unconstitutional and barring its enforcement.

5. *Constitutional Issue:* Whether the ordinance was facially invalid under the First Amendment as a prior restraint on freedom of speech.

6. *Facts:* In 1985, persons opposed to abortion began to picket the residence of a doctor who performs abortions at clinics in neighboring towns. Although the picketing was peaceful and orderly, it generated substantial controversy and numerous complaints. In response, the town board enacted a total ban on all picketing before or about private residences. The ordinance stated that its primary purpose was to protect and preserve the tranquility and privacy persons enjoy in their own homes. The board believed a ban was necessary because such residential picketing causes emotional distress and is, in fact, intended to harass the occupants of the residence being picketed.

7. *Decision:* Ordinance upheld under First Amendment as not constituting prior restraint on freedom of speech.

8. *Opinion of the Court:* The ban on picketing must be judged against the stringent standards used for restrictions on speech in a traditional public forum because public streets and sidewalks, even in residential areas, have traditionally been used for public assembly and debate. Viewing the ban as a content-neutral time, place, and manner regulation, the Court's inquiry focused on whether the ordinance was narrowly tailored to serve a significant governmental interest and whether it leaves open ample alternative channels of communication.

Addressing the last question first, the ordinance may be interpreted narrowly as prohibiting picketing only when it is focused on and taking place in front of a particular residence. Under this narrow construction, it becomes apparent that alternative channels of communication are available, including marches in residential areas, door-to-door visits to distribute literature and discuss the abortion question, and mail or telephone contact.

The state's interest in protecting the privacy and tranquility of the home is significant, given the unique nature of one's home as a "last citadel" for escape from the tribulations of life. The ordinance is narrowly tailored to serve that privacy interest because it targets picketing only when it focuses on, and thus tries to disrupt the privacy and enjoyment of, an individual residence.

2.15 Goldblatt v. Town of Hempstead, New York, 369 U.S. 590, 82 S.Ct. 987 (1962).

1. *Type of Regulation:* Safety ordinance.

2. *Land Use Issue:* Whether a police power regulation may effectively terminate the operation of a previously existing sand and gravel mine for safety reasons.

3. *Type of Challenge:* As applied.

4. *Remedy Sought:* Injunction to prevent continued mining in violation of the ordinance.

5. *Constitutional Issue:* Taking without just compensation (Fourteenth Amendment).

6. *Facts:* Goldblatt had conducted a sand and gravel mining operation on a 38-acre tract of land since 1927. The excavations had reached the water table and had filled with water to a depth of 25 feet, creating a 20-acre lake. Recent population growth had brought 2,200 homes and four public schools with 4,500 pupils within a radius of 3,500 feet of the lake. After unsuccessful attempts to guarantee public safety through zoning, fencing and berm requirements, the town enacted an ordinance prohibiting any new excavation below the water table and requiring the refilling of the existing excavations below the water table. The ordinance completely prohibited the use of the property as a sand and gravel mine. Goldblatt contended that the ordinance confiscated his property without compensation, since the remaining acreage was used in connection with the mine.

7. *Decision:* Ordinance upheld under the Fourteenth Amendment as a reasonable exercise of the police power.

8. *Opinion of the Court:* There is no set formula to determine where valid regulation ends and a regulatory taking begins. An exercise of the police power which deprives an owner of its most beneficial use does not render such an ordinance unconstitutional. Although a comparison of values before and after is relevant, it is by no means conclusive. Since such ordinances are presumed to be constitutional and there is no evidence in the record as to reduction in value or that indicated unreasonableness, the ordinance is upheld.

2.16 Gorieb v. Fox, 274 U.S. 603, 47 S.Ct. 675 (1927).

1. *Type of Regulation:* Ordinance establishing minimum setbacks from street.

2. *Land Use Issue:*   Constitutionality of setback ordinances or similar provisions within a zoning ordinance.

3. *Type of Legal Challenge:*   Facial.

4. *Remedy Sought:*   Order to compel the issuance by the council of a permit to allow Mr. Gorieb to build up to the street line.

5. *Constitutional Issues:*

   a. Substantive due process (alleging vagueness and a taking under the Fourteenth Amendment).

   b. Equal protection (Fourteenth Amendment).

6. *Facts:*   Mr. Gorieb owned several lots in the residential district of Roanoke, Virginia. He applied to the city council for a permit to erect a brick store building on one of the lots. The council, in rendering its decision, took into account a 1924 ordinance which stated that the setback line for new buildings in the city had to be at least as far back from the street as that occupied by 60 percent of existing houses in the block. In accord with the ordinance, the council gave him permission to erect a brick store 34-2/3 feet back from the street line. Gorieb then sought an order in state court to compel the council to issue a permit allowing him to build up to the street line, stating that those owners who had been permitted to build closer to the street were afforded greater protection of the laws than he was, and that the portion of the lot not allowed to be built on was in effect taken.

7. *Decision:*   Ordinance upheld under the Fourteenth Amendment as reasonable exercise of police power.

8. *Opinion of the Court:*   Although the ordinance compels Mr. Gorieb to set his building back from the street line of his lot, it serves as a valid means of providing for the safety, comfort, and welfare of populations in an urban community, and therefore did not constitute a taking under the due process clause of the Fourteenth Amendment. Because it is impossible to anticipate in advance what setback is appropriate in given blocks, the reservation of authority by the council to fashion setbacks by looking at existing patterns of development and to deal in a special manner with exceptional cases is valid under the equal protection clause of the Fourteenth Amendment.

2.17 Hadacheck v. Sebastian,   239 U.S. 394, 36 S.Ct. 143 (1915).

1. *Type of Regulation:*   Ordinance prohibiting industrial brickmaking within city limits.

2. *Land Use Issue:* Reasonableness of the prohibition given the unique character of plaintiff's land.

3. *Type of Legal Challenge:* As applied.

4. *Remedy Sought:* Judgment declaring the municipal ordinance invalid.

5. *Constitutional Issues:*

    a. Substantive due process (taking of property without just compensation under the Fourteenth Amendment).

    b. Equal protection (Fourteenth Amendment).

6. *Facts:* Hadacheck challenged the validity of a Los Angeles ordinance which made it unlawful to operate a brickyard or brick kiln within certain areas of the city. He contended that the ordinance violated his Fourteenth Amendment rights because he had purchased and developed the land, containing valuable deposits of clay material suitable for brickmaking, for its only commercially feasible use—as a brickyard. The evidence indicated that Hadacheck's land, which he had purchased and developed before the ordinance was passed, was worth about $800,000 as a brickyard and about $60,000 when used for any other purpose. At the time of purchase, the property was outside the city limits and at some distance from dwellings and other developments. The brickyard was not a nuisance per se or in fact.

7. *Decision:* Ordinance upheld under the Fourteenth Amendment as a reasonable exercise of the police power.

8. *Opinion of the Court:* A municipality may, under its police power, prohibit particular land uses if such prohibition in good faith promotes the health, safety, and general welfare of the public. This police power was validly exercised in that the Los Angeles ordinance promoted these goals, although the prohibition adversely effected the value of Hadacheck's land. The fact that the city has chosen to deal with this area first, leaving other areas for later treatment, does not violate equal protection.

2.18 Hawaii Housing Authority v. Midkiff, 467 U.S. 229, 104 S.Ct. 2321 (1984).

1. *Type of Regulation:* Eminent domain.

2. *Land Use Issue:* Whether a land condemnation program that transfers title to property from lessors to lessees to reduce the concentration of land ownership in the state serves a proper public purpose.

3. *Type of Legal Challenge:* As applied.

4. *Remedy Sought:* Declaratory and injunctive relief.

5. *Constitutional Issue:* Public use requirement in the exercise of the power of eminent domain (Fifth Amendment as applied to the states through the Fourteenth Amendment).

6. *Facts:*   The Hawaii legislature enacted the Land Reform Act (1967), creating a land condemnation scheme in which title to real property is taken from lessors and transferred to lessees in order to reduce the concentration of landownership. The legislature found there was a need for this statute because concentrated landownership in Hawaii, a vestige of an earlier feudal land tenure system, was skewing the state's residential fee simple market, inflating land prices and injuring the public welfare. Under this act, lessees living on single-family residential lots within tracts of at least five acres are entitled to ask the Hawaii Housing Authority (HHA) to condemn the property on which they live. Following a public hearing to determine whether acquisition of the tract will "effectuate the public purposes" of the act, HHA is authorized to designate some or all of the lots for acquisition. HHA then acquires title to the lots, at prices set either by negotiation or by a judicial proceeding, and may then sell the land title to the lessees.

After negotiations for purchase of title to Midkiff's land failed, Midkiff refused to comply further with the procedures of the act and filed suit in federal district court, asking that the act be found unconstitutional and its enforcement enjoined. The district court found certain of the act's procedures unconstitutional, but upheld the rest of the act as being in conformance with the public use clause of the Fifth Amendment. The U.S. Court of Appeals for the Ninth Circuit reversed, holding that the Act violated the public use requirement of the Fifth Amendment.

7. *Decision:*   Act upheld as satisfying the public use requirement of the Fifth Amendment in the exercise of eminent domain.

8. *Opinion of the Court:*   The public use requirement of the Fifth Amendment is co-terminous with the scope of a state's police power, and thus is extremely broad, while the role of the courts in reviewing a legislature's judgment on what constitutes a public use is extremely narrow. The Court cannot substitute its judgment for a legislature's judgment as to what constitutes a public use unless the use is "palpably without reasonable foundation." In this instance, a rational basis for the condemnation scheme can be found in the state's effort to attack the perceived social and economic evils of concentrated property ownership in Hawaii.

2.19 Hodel v. Irving,   481 U.S. 704, 107 S.Ct. 2076 (1987).

1. *Type of Regulation:*   Indian Land Consolidation Act.

2. *Land Use Issues:* Whether a law abolishing the passing of an undivided fractional interest in Indian land by intestacy or devise and providing for the property to escheat to the tribe when the percentage interest is small and has provided little income is a taking of property without just compensation.

3. *Type of Legal Challenge:* Facial.

4. *Remedy Sought:* Declaratory relief.

5. *Constitutional Issue:* Taking without just compensation (Fifth Amendment as applied to the states through the Fourteenth Amendment).

6. *Facts:* In the late 1800s, Congress divided the Sioux Reservation into tracts and allotted specific tracts to individual Indians. To protect the Indians from improvident disposition of their land to white settlers, Congress provided for the land to be held in trust by the United States. Since land could be passed to the owner's heirs, the parcels splintered into multiple undivided interests, with some parcels having hundreds of owners. To remedy this situation, Congress passed a law providing that whenever an Indian landowner attempted to pass an undivided fractional interest in land representing 2 percent or less of the total acreage and earning its owner less than $100 in the preceding year, such interest should instead transfer to the tribe. Sioux Indians whose potential interest in land had transferred to the tribe under this law brought suit, claiming that the law was invalid for taking property without just compensation.

7. *Decision:* Act held unconstitutional under the Fifth Amendment for authorizing a taking of property without just compensation.

8. *Opinion of the Court:* Encouraging the consolidation of Indian lands is a valid and important government purpose. Nevertheless, the statute totally abrogated "an essential stick in the property bundle"— the right to pass these small property interests to one's heirs. The abrogation of this important right is not necessary to the legislative purpose. The fact that an Indian can still pass his property interest before death, and that other property will escheat to his tribe, does not obviate the need to have the right to transfer property at death. In addition, the loss of value to an affected Indian is not necessarily so minimal as to be unimportant. The values of the property interests in this case are as high as $2,700 and $1,816. Therefore, the law is a taking of private property without just compensation.

2.20 Kaiser Aetna v. United States, 444 U.S. 164, 100 S.Ct. 383 (1979).

1. *Type of Regulation:* Not applicable.

2. *Land Use Issue:*   Whether the federal government must provide compensation to the private owner of a navigable marina, made navigable by private means, in order to require the landowner to allow the public access to the waters.

3. *Type of Legal Challenge:*   Not applicable.

4. *Remedy Sought:*   Injunction to prohibit landowners from denying public access to the marina the public and requiring notice to the public of their navigation rights in the marina.

5. *Constitutional Issues:*

    a. Navigational servitude (Article I Commerce Clause).

    b. Taking without just compensation (Fifth Amendment).

6. *Facts:*   Owners of a private pond in Hawaii, with the permission of the Army Corps of Engineers, improved and dredged their land to make a marina. The marina connected the pond to a bay. The landowners denied the public access to the pond and marina and charged a fee for its use. The United States sued the landowners to determine whether the owners must obtain permission from the corps prior to making any further improvements to the marina and to enjoin the landowners from denying the public access to the marina.

7. *Decision:*   Owners of private marina that had become a navigable water of the United States through the owners' improvements could not be required to open marina to public access without payment of compensation.

8. *Opinion of the Court:*   The fact that water may be navigable and, therefore, subject to federal regulation does not mean that at the time it becomes navigable, the owners of that land do not have a property interest protected by the Fifth Amendment. Here, the owner of a private pond improved the land in such a way as to make it include navigable waters. The owner's investment in the land includes a reasonable expectation to profit from the improvement itself. The United States, by seeking to physically invade the land by requiring water accessibility for the public, must pay for that invasion.

2.21 Keystone Bituminous Coal Association v. DeBenedictis,   480 U.S. 470, 107 S.Ct. 1232 (1987).

1. *Type of Regulation:*   Subsidence regulations.

2. *Land Use Issue:*   Whether a state can prohibit mining that causes subsidence damage to preexisting public buildings, dwellings, and cemeteries.

3. *Type of Legal Challenge:* Facial.

4. *Remedy Sought:* Injunction against enforcement of the statute.

5. *Constitutional Issues:*

a. Taking without just compensation (Fifth Amendment as applied to the states through the Fourteenth Amendment).

b. Impairment of contract in violation of the express Constitutional prohibition of state impairment of contract (Article I, Section 10).

6. *Facts:* Pennsylvania passed a statute prohibiting mining that caused subsidence damage to preexisting public buildings, dwellings, and cemeteries. Regulations under the statute required 50 percent of the coal beneath such structures to be left in place to provide surface support. An association of coal miners sought an injunction against enforcement of the statute. The association claimed that the state was effectively taking without compensation approximately 27 million tons of coal and separately recognized "support estates" which the companies owned. The association also claimed that the statute impaired contracts the mining companies had entered into with surface landowners, waiving any damages that might be caused by subsidence.

7. *Decision:* Statute upheld under the Fifth Amendment as regulation enacted to prevent public harm and which did not deny mining companies economically viable use of their properties.

8. *Opinion of the Court:* A state can regulate land use without it being a taking of property that requires compensation if the regulation furthers a legitimate state interest and does not deny the owner an economically viable use of his land. This statute does advance a legitimate state interest since the statute was not enacted for the private benefit of the surface owners, but was enacted to prevent harm to the public from nuisancelike activity, to enhance the value of the lands for taxation, and to preserve water drainage and public water supplies. Nor does this statute deny the mining companies an economically viable use of their properties, since the 27 million tons of coal that have to be left unmined constituted less than 2 percent of the total coal and the mines could still be operated profitably. Although the statute does impair contracts by not allowing the mining companies to hold the surface owners to their waiver of damages, under the prior interpretations of the Court the state is justified in doing so in light of its strong public interest in preventing environmental harm.

9. *Dissenting Opinion:* The regulations have completely extinguished the coal companies' interests, in particular coal deposits which, under state law, are identifiable and separate property interests. Since, for all practical purposes, "the right to coal consists in the right to mine it," the regulations have destroyed the companies' interests as effectively as an actual physical appropriation and amount to a taking.

2.22 Larkin v. Grendel's Den, Inc., 459 U.S. 941, 103 S.Ct. 505 (1982).

1. *Type of Regulation:* Licensing.

2. *Land Use Issue:* Whether a Massachusetts statute which grants churches and schools the power to veto liquor license applications for premises located within a 500-foot radius of the church or school violates the establishment clause of the First Amendment or the due process clause of the Fourteenth Amendment.

3. *Type of Legal Challenge:* Facial and as applied.

4. *Remedy Sought:* Invalidation of the statute.

5. *Constitutional Issues:*

   a. Establishment clause (First Amendment).

   b. Equal protection and substantive due process (Fourteenth Amendment).

6. *Facts:* Appellee's application for a liquor license was denied because of the objection of an adjacent church acting pursuant to a Massachusetts statute which enabled a church or school to object to a liquor license application for a premises located within 500 feet of the church or school.

7. *Decision:* Statute held invalid under the First Amendment as violative of the establishment clause.

8. *Opinion of the Court:* The statute is not entitled to the deference normally due legislative zoning because it entrusts a private, nongovernmental entity with power ordinarily vested in governmental agencies. Arming churches with such a veto power violates the nonentanglement principle of the establishment clause. Further, while the statute has a secular goal, its primary effect is to advance religion, and it may be used for explicitly religious goals.

2.23 Loretto v. Teleprompter Manhattan CATV Corp., 458 U.S. 419, 102 S.Ct. 3164 (1982).

1. *Type of Regulation:* State statute that prohibited interference with installation of cable television lines.

2. *Land Use Issue:* Validity of statute requiring a landlord to permit a cable television company to install its cable facilities upon his property.

3. *Type of Legal Challenge:* Facial.

4. *Remedy Sought:* Injunction to prevent enforcement of statute and damages for the physical invasion of the landlord's property.

5. *Constitutional Issues:*

  a. Substantive due process (Fourteenth Amendment).

  b. Taking without just compensation (Fifth Amendment as applied to the states through the Fourteenth Amendment).

6. *Facts:* Jean Loretto purchased a five-story apartment building in 1971. The previous owner had granted Teleprompter permission to install a cable on the building. Teleprompter also installed two large boxes along the roof cables. Two years after Loretto purchased the building, Teleprompter connected a cable serving a tenant in her building. The state statute limited the compensation paid to building owners by cable companies for use of their property to a one time payment of $1. Loretto did not discover the presence of the cable until after the purchase. She then brought a class action suit, alleging that the cable company's installation was a trespass, and that the statute constituted a taking without just compensation.

7. *Decision:* Statute invalid under Fifth Amendment as authorizing a taking of property without just compensation.

8. *Opinion of the Court:* A permanent physical occupation authorized by government is a taking without regard to the public interests that it may serve. Constitutional protection for the rights of private property cannot be made to depend on the size of the area permanently occupied. Any physical invasion of property, regardless of the extent of the occupation, gives rise to a taking. Because the installation of plates, boxes, wires, bolts, and screws resulted in a direct physical occupation, the regulation works a taking of property.

2.24 MacDonald, Sommer & Frates v. Yolo County, 477 U.S. 340, 106 S.Ct. 2561 (1986).

1. *Type of Regulation:* Subdivision regulation.

2. *Land Use Issue:* Whether a denial of subdivision approval that is alleged to be a taking can be the basis of a claim for compensation when the developer has not attempted to obtain permission for other types of development.

3. *Type of Challenge:* As applied.

4. *Remedy Sought:* Declaratory judgment and compensation for inverse condemnation.

5. *Constitutional Issue:* Taking without just compensation (Fifth Amendment as applied to the states through the Fourteenth Amendment).

6. *Facts:* Approval of the tentative subdivision plat was rejected for inadequate street access, no public sewer services, inadequate police protection for the area and no provision of water service. The property owner accused Yolo County and the city of Davis of restricting the property to use for a "public, open space buffer" and did not seek approval of any other use for the property permitted under the zoning ordinances before instituting suit.

7. *Decision:* Case dismissed for lack of ripeness.

8. *Opinion of the Court:* The issue of compensation for a regulatory taking cannot be reached because it is impossible to determine if there has been a taking at all since the developer, after being denied approval for the subdivision, declined to present other proposals for review by the zoning authorities. In order to make a determination of fact on the taking question, there must be a final and authoritative decision establishing what development is permitted and what is prohibited; such a decision has not been made in this case because the developer refused to submit any further proposals for zoning approval. Therefore, the case was not ripe for consideration on the merits.

2.25 Members of The City Council of The City of Los Angeles v. Taxpayers for Vincent,   466 U.S. 789, 104 S.Ct. 2118 (1984).

1. *Type of Regulation:* Municipal sign ordinance.

2. *Land Use Issues:* Whether a city's advancement of aesthetic values is an interest sufficiently substantial to justify a city's ordinance forbidding the posting of all signs on public property, and whether utility poles are a traditional public forum for First Amendment purposes.

3. *Type of Legal Challenge:* As applied.

4. *Remedy Sought:* Injunction against enforcement of the ordinance to prohibit plaintiffs' political campaigning efforts, and for compensatory and punitive damages.

5. *Constitutional Issue:*
    a. Freedom of speech/expression (First Amendment).
    b. Substantive due process (Fourteenth Amendment).

6. *Facts:* A candidate support organization entered into a contract with a political sign service to make and post signs bearing candidate's name. City employees removed the signs attached to public property.

7. *Decision:* Ordinance upheld under First Amendment as not violative of freedom of speech.

8. *Opinion of the Court:* The plaintiffs' freedom of speech was not unconstitutionally violated. The ordinance is neutral concerning any speaker's point of view, and the state's interest in advancing aesthetic values is sufficiently substantial to justify the effect of the ordinance on plaintiffs' freedom of expression because the effect is no greater than necessary to accomplish the city's purpose. Utility poles are not a "traditional public forum," and their use may be restricted by the city to their primary purpose.

2.26 Metromedia, Inc. v. City of San Diego,   453 U.S. 490, 101 S.Ct. 2882 (1981).

1. *Type of Regulation:* Sign and billboard ordinance.

2. *Land Use Issue:* Whether San Diego's ordinance prohibiting most types of signs could withstand a constitutional challenge in light of the restrictions it placed on the petitioner's right to freedom of expression under the First Amendment.

3. *Type of Challenge:* Facial.

4. *Remedy Sought:* An injunction banning enforcement of the ordinance.

5. *Constitutional Issue:*
  a. Freedom of expression (First Amendment).
  b. Substantive due process (Fourteenth Amendment).

6. *Facts:* In 1972, San Diego enacted a comprehensive zoning scheme which prohibited a substantial number of signs and billboards throughout the city. The ordinance created two categories of exceptions to the general prohibition. First, it permitted certain onsite advertising—those "signs designating the name of the owner or occupant of the premises upon which such signs are placed or identifying such premises; or signs advertising goods manufactured or produced or services rendered on the premises upon which such signs are placed." Second, the ordinance permitted all signs which fell into 12 express exemptions, including, for example: governmental regulations, historical plaques, religious symbols, for sale/rent signs, and temporary political signs. The purpose of the ordinance was to eliminate hazards to pedestrians and motorists brought about by distracting sign displays and to preserve and improve the appearance of the city.

Outdoor advertising companies challenged the ordinance on its face, alleging that it destroyed their outdoor advertising businesses. They grounded their claim in the First Amendment's freedom of expression. The trial court held the ordinance unconstitutional on two grounds. First, San Diego had exceeded its police power, and second, the ordinance was an abridgment of the companies' First Amendment rights. The California Court of Appeal affirmed solely on the first ground. The California Supreme Court reversed, holding that the ordinance was within the city's police power because the city's interests in enacting the ordinance were legitimate.

7. Decision: Ordinance held invalid on its face under First Amendment because it afforded more protection to commercial speech than noncommercial speech.

8. Plurality Opinion of the Court: [*Editors' note:* A sharply divided Court rendered five separate opinions, with Justice White writing the plurality opinion, Justice Brennan (joined by Justice Blackmun) writing a concurring opinion, and Justices Stevens and Rehnquist and Chief Justice Burger each writing separate dissenting opinions.]

The ordinance affects two type of speech—commercial and noncommercial speech. Commercial speech is protected by the First Amendment if (1) it concerns lawful activity and (2) it is not false or misleading. Government regulation of such protected commercial speech is evaluated under a test enunciated in the *Central Hudson* decision. Under that decision, regulation of commercial speech is constitutional if it: (1) serves a substantial governmental interest; (2) directly advances the interest; and (3) reaches no further than necessary to accomplish the given objective. The city's safety and aesthetic goals are substantially legitimate, and the ordinance reaches no further than necessary because certain types of commercial signs are permitted. Also, the ordinance directly advances this substantial governmental interest, which is based on the accumulated common-sense judgments of local lawmakers. The distinction between permissible on-site advertising and prohibited off-site advertising is justifiable because the municipality could reasonably conclude that there is a stronger interest in identifying business locations and the products or services available there, than in allowing off-site advertising.

However, the ordinance is unconstitutional in its treatment of noncommercial speech because it provides more protection for commercial than noncommercial speech. The ordinance unconstitutionally restrains the more highly protected speech by allowing on-site commercial signs while prohibiting on-site noncommercial signs. For example, a store could have a sign advertising items for sale, but was barred from exhibiting a sign that contained a political message. The ordinance is not a valid time, place, and manner restriction because it unconstitutionally suppresses noncommercial speech, and it prohibits all off-site advertising.

9. *Concurring Opinion:* The entire ordinance is unconstitutional on its face because the practical effect of the ordinance is a virtual total ban on all billboards.

10. *Dissenting Opinions:* Justice Stevens: The issue is whether the entire billboard medium can be eliminated. This medium can be eliminated, and thus the ordinance is constitutional because: (1) the legitimate city interests are substantial; (2) the regulation is impartial and thereby does not favor one viewpoint over another; and (3) there are other ample modes or channels of advertising to the public.

Chief Justice Burger: The plurality's decision leaves the municipality "between two unsatisfactory options: (a) allowing all 'noncommercial' signs, no matter how many, how dangerous, or how damaging to the environment or (b) forbidding signs altogether." The distinction between different types of speech is constitutional because "[t]he means chosen to effectuate legitimate governmental interests are not for the court to select." Therefore, a governmental entity can ban a given medium so long as the legislature's approach is content neutral—it does not favor one type of speech over another—and does not suppress a protected form of expression by foreclosing adequate channels of communication.

2.27 Miller v. Schoene, 276 U.S. 272, 48 S.Ct. 246 (1928).

1. *Type of Regulation:* An act authorizing the destruction of infectious red cedar trees to prevent communication of plant diseases to other valuable species.

2. *Land Use Issue:* Reasonableness of an uncompensated destruction of one type of property to benefit another type of property.

3. *Type of Legal Challenge:* Facial.

4. *Remedy Sought:* Compensation for the value of standing cedar trees and for the decrease in the market value of the realty caused by their destruction.

5. *Constitutional Issue:* Substantive due process (taking without just compensation under the Fourteenth Amendment).

6. *Facts:* The Virginia Cedar Rust Act (1924) provided for the destruction of cedar trees to prevent communication of plant disease to nearby apple orchards. In passing the act, the legislature determined that the apple orchards were of significantly greater value to the public than the cedar trees. Pursuant to the act, the defendant state entomologist ordered Ms. Miller and some of her neighbors to cut down a number of ornamental red cedar trees on their property. Ms. Miller and her neighbors were allowed $100 to cover the expanse of removal of the cedars, as well as the privilege of using the trees (presumably for firewood) when felled. The statute did not provide compensation for the value of the standing cedars, nor for the decrease in the market value of the plaintiffs' property. Plaintiffs argued this was an unconstitutional taking of their property under the Fourteenth Amendment.

7. *Decision:* Act upheld under Fourteenth Amendment as reasonable exercise of the police power.

8. *Opinion of the Court:* Although the plaintiffs' property values were diminished by the destruction of the cedars, where a major agriculture interest (though private) was threatened, the statute validly protects public health, safety, and general welfare. The legislative balancing of competing interests and its preference of one interest over another is at the heart of every exercise of police power. If reasonable, as in this case, it will be sustained. Therefore, the plaintiffs are not entitled to compensation for their loss.

2.28 Monell v. New York City Dept. of Social Services, 436 U.S. 658, 98 S.Ct. 2018 (1978).

1. *Type of Regulation:* Not applicable.

2. *Land Use Issue:* None. The issue in this case was whether local governments could be considered persons within the meaning of 42 U.S.C. §1983 when equitable relief is sought for officially adopted policy.

3. *Type of Legal Challenge:* Not applicable.

4. *Remedy Sought:* Injunction to prevent maternity leave policy from being applied to them and monetary relief.

5. *Constitutional Issues:*

    a. Tenth Amendment.

    b. Eleventh Amendment.

6. *Facts:* Female employees of a city agency sued governmental officials in their official capacity for enforcing a maternity leave policy compelling pregnant employees to take unpaid leave of absences prior to the time when the leave was necessary for medical purposes. The employees brought suit under 42 U.S.C. §1983, alleging the practice to be unconstitutionally discriminatory and seeking injunctive and monetary relief for back pay.

7. *Decision:* Local governments are persons for purposes of suit under 42 U.S.C. §1983.

8. *Opinion of the Court:* Congressional debates of the Civil Rights Act of 1871 indicate that the reasons for not incorporating the Sherman amendment, which would have brought local government within the definition of people for purposes of the act, were not to prevent local governments from being sued. Instead, the amendment was defeated because the federal government did not want to require local and state governments to enforce federal laws. Therefore, Congress did intend local governments to be subject to Section 1983 when the action alleged to be unconstitutional executes or puts into use official policy of that government.

2.29 Moore v. City of East Cleveland, Ohio, 431 U.S. 494, 97 S.Ct. 1932 (1977).

1. *Type of Regulation:* Housing code.

2. *Land Use Issue:* Whether an ordinance limiting occupancy of a dwelling unit to members of a single family, but recognizing as a family only a few categories of related individuals, rationally promoted any legitimate government purpose.

3. *Type of Legal Challenge:* As applied.

4. *Remedy Sought:* Reversal of conviction under ordinance and a declaration that the ordinance was invalid.

5. *Constitutional Issue:* Substantive due process (Fourteenth Amendment).

6. *Facts:* Mrs. Moore lived with her son and two grandsons who were cousins rather than brothers. An East Cleveland housing ordinance limited occupancy of a dwelling unit to members of a single family. Because the ordinance defined family in a narrow way, Mrs. Moore violated the ordinance by having grandsons living with her who were not brothers. Mrs. Moore was convicted and sentenced to five days in jail and a $25 fine. She sought to have the ordinance declared invalid for failing to rationally further a legitimate government purpose.

7. *Decision:* Ordinance invalid under Fourteenth Amendment as violative of substantive due process.

8. *Opinion of the Court:* East Cleveland's stated purpose in limiting occupancy to a single family is to prevent overcrowding, traffic conges-

tion, and a financial burden on the school system. While this is a legitimate goal, the ordinance only marginally serves the goal. Large families which fit within the ordinance's definition of family can live together, but smaller numbers of related individuals who do not meet the definition of family cannot live together even if they cause less overcrowding and traffic than the large traditional families. The family receives special protection under the Constitution, and the city's failure to show why only allowing such a limited range of related people to live together will further its legitimate purposes renders the ordinance invalid.

2.30 Mugler v. Kansas,   123 U.S. 623, 8 S.Ct. 273 (1887).

  1. *Type of Regulation:*   Prohibition on brewing of beer.
  2. *Land Use Issue:*   Reasonableness of state legislation prohibiting the use of an existing brewery to manufacture beer to be sold for other than medicinal purposes.
  3. *Type of Legal Challenge:*   As applied.
  4. *Remedy Sought:*   Compensation for the application of state regulatory legislation to the plaintiff's brewery.
  5. *Constitutional Issues:*
     a. Substantive due process (Fourteenth Amendment).
     b. Privileges and immunities clause.
     c. An implicit taking argument.
  6. *Facts:*   Peter Mugler erected and furnished a brewery in Salina, Kansas, in 1877, which he operated for the manufacture of malt liquor. On May 1, 1881, the Kansas legislature enacted a state constitutional article, which stated that the manufacture and sale of intoxicating liquors would be prohibited, except those sold for medicinal, scientific, and mechanical purposes. Mr. Mugler's property, worth $10,000 as a brewery, was worth no more than $2,500 when used for any other purpose. Mr. Mugler continued to manufacture and sell beer after legislation implementing the constitutional provision was enacted and was indicted for offenses against the statute. He then sued the state, claiming a violation of due process, stating that the amendment violated the privileges and immunities clause and that he had to be compensated for the diminution in the value of his property.
  7. *Decision:*   State legislation upheld under Fourteenth Amendment and privileges and immunities clause.
  8. *Opinion of the Court:*   Because the legislative prohibition on the manufacture and sale of liquor for general public consumption may be

considered to be fairly adopted to the end of protecting the public's health, welfare, and morals, such state legislation violated neither the privileges and immunities clause nor the (substantive) due process clause of the constitution; nor does it effectuate a taking of property. The owner has full control of the property and can use it for any lawful purpose. Therefore, the act may be enforced against persons who, at the time, happen to own property whose chief value consists in its fitness for manufacturing alcohol, without compensating them for the diminution in the value of the property resulting from the legislation. "If the public safety or the public morals require the discontinuance of any manufacture or traffic, the hand of the legislature cannot be stayed from providing for its discontinuance by any incidental inconvenience which individuals or corporations may suffer."

2.31 Nectow v. City of Cambridge, 277 U.S. 183, 48 S.Ct. 447 (1928).

1. *Type of Regulation:* Zoning ordinance.

2. *Land Use Issue:* Reasonableness of residential zoning classification applied to a portion of plaintiff's property when the whole of the property is located in close proximity to land zoned for, and actually being used for business, industrial, and railroad purposes.

3. *Type of Legal Challenge:* As applied.

4. *Remedy Sought:* Injunction to prevent the application of the zoning district restrictions to plaintiff's property.

5. *Constitutional Issue:* Substantive due process (taking without just compensation under the Fourteenth Amendment).

6. *Facts:* Saul Nectow owned a 140,000 square foot parcel of land in Cambridge, Massachusetts. The city of Cambridge adopted a zoning ordinance dividing the city into three districts: residential, business, and unrestricted. Prior to the passage of the ordinance, Mr. Nectow had entered into a contract for the sale of most of the parcel. The ordinance placed most of his parcel in the unrestricted zone, while classifying a 100-foot strip on the west side of his property in the restricted residential district. The property to the south of the strip was devoted to industrial use. Immediately to the east were railroad tracks. Because of the new zoning restrictions, the contract purchaser refused to complete the transaction. Mr. Nectow then sued the city, challenging the reasonableness of the zoning classification as applied to his property.

7. *Decision:* Ordinance invalid under Fourteenth Amendment as applied.

8. *Opinion of the Court:*   The facts in this case prove that no practical use can be made of the property in question for residential purposes because of its proximity to land zoned for industrial and railroad uses. Judges should not lightly set aside the determinations of zoning officials. Here, however, the zoning classification has no foundation in reason and is a mere arbitrary or irrational exercise of power having no substantial relation to the public welfare. Therefore, the necessary basis for an exercise of the zoning power is lacking. A zoning classification, or any other action of a zoning authority, will be found to violate the due process clause of the Fourteenth Amendment if it does not bear a substantial relation to the public health, safety, and welfare.

2.32 Nollan v. California Coastal Commission,   483 U.S. 825, 107 S.Ct. 3141 (1987).

1. *Type of Regulation:*   Beach access condition on approval of building permit.

2. *Land Use Issue:*   Whether the grant of a building permit can be conditioned on the owner's granting an easement to the public without receiving compensation.

3. *Type of Legal Challenge:*   As applied.

4. *Remedy Sought:*   Invalidation of the requirement that the receipt of a building permit is conditioned on granting an easement to the public.

5. *Constitutional Issue:*

   a. Taking without just compensation (Fifth Amendment as applied to the states through the Fourteenth Amendment).

   b. Substantive due process (Fourteenth Amendment).

6. *Facts:*   The Nollans leased a bungalow on a beachfront lot in Ventura, California, with an option to purchase conditioned on their promise to demolish the bungalow and replace it. Public beaches are located, respectively, a quarter of a mile north and 1,800 feet south of the lot. The beach portion of the property is separated from the rest of the lot by a concrete seawall approximately eight feet high. The historic mean high tide line determines the lot's oceanside boundary. The Nollans submitted a permit application to the California Coastal Commission to demolish the existing structure and to replace it with a three-bedroom house. The commission approved the permit conditioned on the Nollans granting an easement across a portion of their property bounded by the mean high tide line on one side, and their seawall on the other side, to make it easier for the public to get to the public beaches located north and south of the Nollans' property.

The Nollans filed an action in the California Superior Court to invalidate the access condition and the court remanded the case to the Coastal Commission for a public hearing. At the hearing the commission reaffirmed its imposition of the condition, finding that the new house would increase blockage of the view of the ocean, thus adding to "a 'wall' of residential structures" that would prevent the public "'psychologically . . . from realizing a stretch of coastline exists nearby that they have every right to visit; that the new home would increase private use of the shorefront; that these effects of the new house when constructed would cumulatively 'burden the public's ability to traverse to and along the shorefront.'"

The Nollans again sought administrative review in the California Superior Court, which concluded that the administrative record did not adequately support the commission's conclusion that the replacement of the bungalow would create a direct or cumulative burden on public access to the sea. The court ordered the permit condition be struck. The commission appealed, and while the appeal was pending, the Nollans, without notifying the commission, tore down the bungalow, built the new house, and bought the property. The California Court of Appeal reversed the Superior Court, holding that the permit condition was sufficiently related to the burdens created by the new house and did not constitute a taking because it did not deprive the Nollans of all reasonable use of their property. The Nollans appealed the taking question to the U.S. Supreme Court.

7. *Decision:* Public access condition on permit approval invalidated under the Fifth Amendment as a taking without just compensation.

8. *Opinion of the Court:* The right to exclude others is one of the essential sticks in the bundle of rights commonly characterized as property. Where government action results in a permanent physical occupation, the Court's prior decisions have found a taking to the extent of the occupation, regardless of whether the action achieves an important public benefit or has only minimal economic impact on the owner. Where, as here, the commission required that, as a condition of permit approval, the landowners grant an easement that gives the public a permanent and continuous right to pass across their property, a permanent physical occupation has occurred. Had the commission simply required the conveyance of an easement for public access to the beach outright, without making the requirement a condition of permit approval, the result would have been a taking of a property interest.

The outcome is no different when the conveyance of the easement is made a condition of permit approval. Contrary to the dissenting opinion, the requirement of such an access easement is not a mere restriction on the use of the property. The Court has previously recognized that "a use restriction may constitute a taking if not reasonably necessary to the effectuation of a substantial government purpose." The standards applied to a takings claim are not the same as those applied to due process or equal protection claims. In assessing the latter claims, the Court has required that "the State could rationally have decided the measure adopted might achieve the State's objective." In assessing a taking claim, the Court requires that the regulation *"substantially* advance" the "legitimate state interest" sought to be achieved. Even though prior cases have not elaborated on the standards for determining what constitutes a "legitimate state interest" or what type of connection (nexus) between the regulation and the state interest satisfies the requirement that the regulation "substantially advance" the legitimate state interest, they have indicated that a broad range of governmental purposes and regulations satisfies these requirements.

Even assuming that the state has legitimate interests in the public's being able to see the beach so as to avoid psychological barriers to its access and in preventing congestion on the beaches, this easement does not substantially advance those interests. Being able to walk across the Nollan's property would not reduce the obstacle to seeing the beach created by the new house. Nor would being able to walk across the property lower psychological barriers to use of the public beaches or remedy congestion caused by the Nollans' activity. Since the condition does not remedy the problems caused by the new house, it fails to substantially advance a legitimate state interest and thus the condition was a regulatory taking, requiring the payment of just compensation.

9. *Dissenting Opinion:*   The majority's demand for a precise fit between development restrictions and the public program to be advanced by those restrictions creates an overly narrow conception of rationality for governmental exactions. Such a narrow conception of rationality is an unwarranted judicial usurpation of legislative authority.

2.33 Owen v. City of Independence,   445 U.S. 622, 100 S.Ct. 1398 (1980).

1. *Type of Regulation:*   Not applicable.

2. *Land Use Issue:* None. The issue in this case is whether a municipality is liable for damages under 42 U.S.C. §1983 for dismissing an employee without notice of charges and an opportunity to be heard.

3. *Type of Legal Challenge:* Not applicable.

4. *Remedy Sought:* Declaratory and injunctive relief, including a hearing on petitioner's discharge, back pay, and attorney's fees.

5. *Constitutional Issues:*

    a. Substantive due process (Fourteenth Amendment).

    b. Procedural due process (Fourteenth Amendment).

6. *Facts:* The city council charged petitioner, George Owen, with misappropriating police department property and other violations. The council released a report to the media on the misfeasance and the following day petitioner was discharged without being given a reason. Petitioner's request for notice of the charges and a public hearing with a reasonable opportunity to respond to the charges was ignored. Petitioner then brought suit, alleging that he was discharged without reason and without a hearing in violation of his constitutional rights. Petitioner contended that the city officials violated his due process rights entitling him to damages under Section 1983 for the unconstitutional deprivation.

7. *Decision:* A municipality can be held liable for damages under 42 U.S.C. §1983.

8. *Opinion of the Court:* Because the aim of the Civil Rights Act was to provide protection to persons wronged by the misuse of power by those clothed with authority of state law, a municipality may not assert the good faith of its officers or agents as a defense to liability under Section 1983. The broad language of the statute is absolute and unqualified and does not leave room for the assertion of a governmental immunity based on the good faith of municipal officers. Further, the policy behind Section 1983 of preventing abuses of governmental authority and deterring future constitutional violations militates against a finding of a good faith immunity.

2.34 Penn Central Transportation Company v. City of New York, 438 U.S. 104, 98 S.Ct. 2646 (1978).

1. *Type of Regulation:* Historic landmarks zoning regulation.

2. *Land Use Issue:* Whether the application of a landmark preservation law to property located in a valuable development area constitutes a taking of that property when the regulation prevents development of the property in the most lucrative manner possible and imposes an affirmative duty on the owner to keep the property in good repair.

   3. *Type of Legal Challenge:*   As applied.

   4. *Remedy Sought:*   Declaratory and injunctive relief to prevent application of the law to owner's land, and damages for the temporary taking that occurred between imposition of the regulation to the land and time when such application would be lifted.

   5. *Constitutional Issues:*
   a. Substantive due process (Fourteenth Amendment).
   b. Taking without just compensation (Fifth Amendment as applied to the states through the Fourteenth Amendment).

   6. *Facts:*   The city of New York passed the Landmark Preservation Law as part of a comprehensive measure to preserve existing historic buildings. The law places an affirmative duty on owners of those buildings designated landmarks under the law to keep the buildings in good repair. The owners of Grand Central Terminal in Manhattan sought to build a multistory office building over the terminal. The building plan was denied by the Landmark Preservation Commission on grounds that such a building would destroy the historic and aesthetic features of the building. The terminal's owners sued the city, alleging that the law, as applied to their property, constituted an unconstitutional taking without just compensation and deprived them of their property without due process of law.

   7. *Decision:*   Ordinance upheld as not violative of Fifth and Fourteenth Amendments.

   8. *Opinion of the Court:*   Although the landmarks law effectively prevents the owners from exploiting the valuable air rights above the terminal, the right to develop land is only one property right held by the owners. The character of the regulation is not a singling out of certain property owners for restrictive treatment, but rather is part of a comprehensive plan which affects others in positions similar to that of the terminal's owners. Other owners of buildings designated as landmarks are similarly burdened and benefited by the ordinance and, therefore, the law is not discriminatory, nor is it arbitrarily applied to the terminal. Finally, the owners of the property are not restricted from carrying on their already prosperous business in the terminal, but instead may receive a reasonable economic return from their investment.

   9. *Dissenting Opinion:*   The regulation applied to the terminal uniquely burdens the owners because they receive no reciprocity of advantage from similarly situated owners in their vicinity. Land use regulations may be used to prevent a harm, not confer a benefit as the landmark law has done. Therefore, New York City should pay the terminal's owners compensation for the restrictions place on their right to exploit the air space overhead. The ability of the owners to transfer their development rights does not afford them just compensation because the relief is not a perfect equivalent of the property taken: other land does not have the same attributes as the Terminal.

2.35 Pennell v. City of San Jose , ____ U.S. ____, 108 S.Ct. 849 (1988).

1. *Type of Regulation:*   Rent control.

2. *Land Use Issue:*   Whether a provision in a rent control ordinance that a hearing officer may consider the hardship of the tenant in fixing a reasonable rent renders the ordinance facially invalid.

3. *Type of Legal Challenge:*   Facial.

4. *Remedy Sought:*   Declaration that the provision of the rent control ordinance allowing the hearing officer to consider the hardship of the tenant was facially invalid.

5. *Constitutional Issues:*

   a. Due process (Fourteenth Amendment).

   b. Equal protection (Fourteenth Amendment).

   c. Taking without just compensation (Fifth Amendment as applied to the states through the Fourteenth Amendment).

6. *Facts:*   The city of San Jose passed a rent control ordinance that allowed a landlord to raise the rent of a tenant in possession by as much as 8 percent. If the landlord wished to raise the rent by more than 8 percent in a given year and the tenant objected, a hearing officer would determine whether the increase was reasonable. The ordinance set forth six objective factors for determining reasonableness, such as the landlord's actual costs and the condition of the rental market. The hardship which would be caused to the tenant was the only subjective factor. A landlord association sought to have the tenant hardship provision declared invalid insofar as it forced landlords to subsidize apartments below objectively reasonable rates.

7. *Decision:*   Ordinance upheld under Fourteenth Amendment as not violative of substantive due process and equal protection.

8. *Opinion of the Court:*   Because the ordinance has not yet been used to reduce rent on the basis of tenant hardship, and the ordinance only re-

quired that hardship be considered, not that it be determinative, the taking claim is premature.

With respect to the due process and equal protection challenges, price control is unconstitutional only if arbitrary, discriminatory, or irrelevant to a legitimate government purpose. Under the deferential due process standard for reviewing economic regulation, rent control may reasonably be said to promote the government purpose of "protecting consumer welfare." Furthermore, it is not irrational to treat landlords differently based on whether they have hardship tenants, since this ensures that only legitimate hardship cases are redressed. Since the classification neither implicates a suspect classification like race nor a fundamental right, the court must defer to the legislature on the reasonableness of the distinctions made in the legislation.

9. *Dissenting Opinion:* The ordinance is facially a taking because the subjective hardship factor placed a burden on an individual landlord, which should be borne by the public generally through the tax system. The key to avoiding a taking challenge is to show a "cause-and-effect relationship between the property use restricted by the regulation and the social evil that the regulation seeks to remedy."

2.36 Pennsylvania Coal Company v. Mahon, 260 U.S. 393, 43 S.Ct. 158 (1922).

1. *Type of Regulation:* Statute limiting the exercise of mineral rights.

2. *Land Use Issue:* Validity of Pennsylvania's Kohler Act, which prohibited coal mining in such a way as to cause the subsidence of houses, industrial structures, streets, or public facilities.

3. *Type of Legal Challenge:* Facial.

4. *Remedy Sought:* Declaration of invalidity of the Kohler Act so that the Pennsylvania Coal Company could exercise its mining rights without the constraints imposed.

5. *Constitutional Issue:* Substantive due process (taking without just compensation under the Fourteenth Amendment).

6. *Facts:* In 1878 the Pennsylvania Coal Company transferred property to Mr. Mahon, reserving in the deed the right to mine coal on the property. Mr. Mahon waived all of his rights to object to or be paid for any possible resulting damages. In 1921, the Pennsylvania legislature passed the Kohler Act, which forbade the mining of coal in such a way as to cause the subsidence of any human habitation, industrial structures, streets, and public facilities. When the Pennsylvania Coal Company decided to mine coal under his property, Mahon sought an injunction under the Kohler Act to prevent mining that would cause the subsidence of his home. The Pennsylvania Coal Company argued that the Kohler Act's requirement (that pillars of coal be left in place to provide support) violated the Fourteenth Amendment to the Constitution in that it took their property (unmined coal) from them without due process of law.

7. *Decision:* Act held invalid under Fourteenth Amendment as authorizing taking of property without due process.

8. *Opinion of the Court:* Although the value of private property may be diminished by valid governmental regulations, a regulation may be so extensive as to constitute a regulatory taking. The public interest (promotion of health, safety, and welfare) in protecting surface rights does not justify the significant destruction of mineral rights which the Pennsylvania Coal Company had reserved in the deed to Mr. Mahon. The act is also violative of preexisting contract rights between the coal company and Mahon.

2.37 Phillips Petroleum Company and Cinque Bambini Partnership v. Mississippi and Saga Petroleum U.S. Inc., _____ U.S. _____, 108 S.Ct. 791 (1988)

1. *Type of Regulation:* Not applicable.

2. *Land Use Issue:* Whether the state of Mississippi has title to lands under waters that are influenced by tides but are not navigable.

3. *Type of Legal Challenge:* Quiet title suit.

4. *Remedy Sought:* Clearing of title in private owners.

5. *Constitutional Issues:*

    a. Taking without just compensation (Fifth Amendment as applied to the states by the Fourteenth Amendment).

    b. Commerce Clause, Article I., Sec. 8. navigability, tidal lands, public trust property.

6. *Facts:* Record title to the land involved is in the private parties who trace their claims to prestatehood Spanish land grants. The state of Mississippi claims title in public trust of all land lying under any waters influenced by the tide, whether navigable or not. Both parties wish to reap the benefits of oil production on the lands in question. Private parties have paid taxes on the property from statehood to 1970s. It is disputed whether land held as public trust property must be under navigable water. The state claims that by virtue of the *equal footing doctrine,* it became the owner in fee simple of all such land at statehood—thus extinguishing Spanish claims without the necessity of compensation as required by the Fifth Amendment.

7. *Decision:* The state acquired fee simple title to all lands naturally subject to tidal influence by virtue of statehood and no compensation to private owners is required under the Fifth Amendment.

8. *Opinion of the Court:* By virtue of becoming a state, Mississippi acquired fee simple title to all lands naturally subject to tidal influence, inland to today's mean high water mark. Therefore, there was no taking and no compensation is required. It has been long established that the individual states have the authority to define the limits of land held in public trust and to recognize reasonable private rights in such lands as they see fit; the states' interests are not limited to lands under navigable water. State public trust interests include lands under freshwater lakes and rivers, but are subject to the federal navigation easements and the power to regulate commerce. As to the private parties claim that their reasonable property expectations were taken by the state, the expectation was unreasonable. That Mississippi's ownership could not be lost due to adverse possession, laches, or any other equitable doctrine has been established by state law; the law of real property should be left to the individual states to develop and administer.

2.38 Pruneyard Shopping Center v. Robins, 447 U.S. 74, 100 S.Ct. 2035 (1980).

1. *Type of Regulation:* Not applicable.

2. *Land Use Issue:* Whether California state constitutional provisions permitting individuals to exercise free speech rights on private property on which the public is invited violate the property owner's right to exclude others from his property under the Fifth and Fourteenth Amendments or his free speech rights under the First and Fourteenth Amendments.

3. *Type of Legal Challenge:* As applied.

4. *Remedy Sought:* Injunctive relief to prevent owner of property from denying individuals access to his property for the purpose of exercising their free speech rights.

5. *Constitutional Issues:*

    a. Free speech (First and Fourteenth Amendments).

    b. Taking without just compensation (Fifth Amendment as applied to the states through the Fourteenth Amendment).

6. *Facts:* High school students entered the Pruneyard shopping center and set up a booth to solicit support for their opposition to a UN resolution. The students' activities included handing out literature and soliciting signatures of visitors to the shopping center. The students were asked to leave the premises because they were in violation of a Pruneyard policy that prohibited solicitation activities on its premises. Subsequently, the students filed suit, seeking to enjoin Pruneyard from denying them access to the shopping center for solicitation purposes.

7. *Decision:* Solicitation in a private shopping center held not violative of property owner's Fifth, Fourteenth, and First Amendment rights under the California state constitution.

8. *Opinion of the Court:* Pursuant to its police power, a state has the power to adopt guarantees of individual liberties more expansive than those permitted under the federal constitution. California has interpreted its constitution to permit citizens to exercise free petition and expression rights in a private shopping center open to the public. Although this interpretation of the California constitution essentially destroys Pruneyard's right to exclude persons from its property, the destruction of that right does not unreasonably impair the value or use of Pruneyard's land as a shopping center. Therefore, there is no taking of Pruneyard's property; Pruneyard may still regulate the time, place, and manner of such exercises of rights to minimize their interference with its commercial functions. Furthermore, Pruneyard has not adequately shown that the demands made by the California constitution—permitting access to citizens for solicitation purposes—are unreasonable.

2.39 Ruckelshaus v. Monsanto Co., 467 U.S. 986, 104 S.Ct. 2862 (1984).

1. *Type of Regulation:* Federal Insecticide, Fungicide, and Rodenticide Act (FIFRA) data disclosure provisions.

2. *Land Use Issue:* None. The issues in this case were whether FIFRA's disclosure provisions effected a taking because they interfered with reasonable investment-backed expectation of property and whether they effected a taking for a private rather than a public purpose; whether equitable relief is available to enjoin an alleged taking of property; and whether the Tucker Act is applicable to an individual claiming that the United States has taken his property without just compensation.

3. *Type of Legal Challenge:* As applied.

4. *Remedy Sought:* Injunctive and declaratory relief to prevent the EPA from using and disclosing of trade secrets plaintiff voluntarily submitted to the EPA pursuant to FIFRA.

5. *Constitutional Issue:* Taking of property without just compensation (Fifth Amendment).

6. *Facts:* Monsanto, a major producer of chemicals and fibers, is one of a small number of companies that invents and develops ingredients for pesticides. Monsanto and other applicants, in order to register pesticides with the EPA, must present research and test data supporting the applications. FIFRA authorizes the EPA to use this data submitted by an applicant in evaluating the applications of subsequent applicants and to disclose publicly some of this submitted data to avoid research duplication and to expedite review.

7. *Decision:* Data disclosure provisions of FIFRA upheld under Fifth Amendment as not a taking and equitable relief not available to enjoin the alleged taking of private property for a public use, duly authorized by law, when a suit for compensation can be brought against the government subsequent to the taking.

8. *Opinion of the Court:* Trade secrets are property rights but with respect to any data Monsanto submitted after the effective date of the 1978 FIFRA amendments, or prior to the 1972 amendments, it had no reasonable investment-backed expectation that such data would not be disclosed to some extent by EPA. Monsanto's voluntary submission of data in exchange for the economic advantages of regulation is not a taking. Absent an express promise, there is no reasonable investment-backed expectation of confidentiality in an industry whose activities raise public interest concerns. However, EPA's consideration or disclosure of data Monsanto-submitted between 1972 and 1978, if the data were designated a trade secret as provided by the statute in effect at that time, would constitute a taking. The Tucker Act is still available to Monsanto as a remedy for any uncompensated taking it may suffer as a result of these challenged FIFRA provisions, but equitable relief is not.

2.40 San Diego Gas and Electric Co. v. City of San Diego, 450 U.S. 621, 101 S.Ct. 1287 (1981).

1. *Type of Regulation:* Downzoning; open space zoning.

2. *Land Use Issue:* Whether the U.S. Supreme Court can determine that a taking has occurred before the petitioner obtains a final judgment in the state courts, and whether monetary damages are available for inverse condemnation.

3. *Type of Legal Challenge:* As applied.

4. *Remedy Sought:* Damages for taking of private property without just compensation and injunctive and declaratory relief.

5. *Issues:*

a. Taking without just compensation (Fifth Amendment as applied to the states through the Fourteenth Amendment).

b. Substantive due process (Fourteenth Amendment).

c. Ripeness.

6. *Facts:* In 1966, San Diego Gas & Electric (SDG&E) acquired 412 acres in northwest San Diego with the intent of constructing a nuclear power plant in the 1980s. In 1967, the city of San Diego adopted its master plan under which the parcel was zoned industrial. In 1973, part of this property was downzoned to agricultural use with a minimum lot size of one to ten acres. At the same time, pursuant to a state mandate, the city established an open space plan which included SDG&E's parcel. Subsequently, the voters rejected a bond proposition that would have provided funds to purchase the SDG&E parcel, and the city made no further attempt to acquire the property, leaving SDG&E's parcel in an open space zone with little or no potential use.

Rather than attempting to seek approval for any kind of development plan, SDG&E filed suit in superior court alleging that the zoning scheme deprived it of its entire beneficial and economic use, thereby violating the Fifth and Fourteenth Amendments by taking the property without just compensation. SDG&E asserted that the parcel's only beneficial use was as an industrial park, which was prohibited by the zoning scheme. SDG&E sought damages, mandamus, and declaratory relief as a result of the alleged taking.

The superior court found that a taking had occurred as a result of the zoning scheme because SDG&E was deprived of all beneficial and economic viable uses. Further, the submission of any development plan would be futile because of the open space zone. The court of appeal affirmed, holding that SDG&E's failure to seek approval of a development plan did not preclude an award of damages. On appeal, the California Supreme Court vacated the damage award when the city's petition for a hearing was granted, then transferred the case back to the court of appeals for reconsideration in light of its decision in *Agins* v. *Tiburon*, 598 P.2d 25 (1979), *aff'd.* 447 U.S. 255 (1980), which held that a plaintiff's only remedy for inverse condemnation is invalidation of the regulation.

On reconsideration, the court of appeal reversed, although it did not invalidate the regulation. Rather, the court avoided the takings issue, because factual disputes precluded monetary relief on the existing record. It stated further that plaintiff's exclusive remedy was mandamus and declaratory relief. The California Supreme Court denied review, and SDG&E's appeal to the U.S. Supreme Court was granted.

7. *Decision:*   Appeal dismissed for lack of ripeness.

8. *Opinion of the Court:*   The appeal must be dismissed because the California courts had not rendered a final judgment. The judgment of the California Supreme Court to vacate SDG&E's damages award was not final, because it did not address the taking issue; rather, it dealt only with mandamus and declaratory relief. Thus, the Supreme Court lacked jurisdiction because there was no final judgment or decree rendered by the highest court of the state in which a decision could be rendered.

9. *Dissenting Opinion:*   Since the taking issue was addressed in the superior court, the judgment was final and therefore ripe for consideration on the merits, even though it was reconsidered after *Agins* and was then reversed on the issue of proper remedy. Inverse condemnation is equivalent to eminent domain because "[p]olice power regulations such as zoning ordinances and other land-use restrictions can destroy the use and enjoyment of property in order to promote the public good just as effectively as formal condemnation or physical invasion of property."

There is nothing within the just compensation clause of the Fifth Amendment that prohibits the granting of temporary damages. Once private property has been taken for public use, whether by eminent domain or inverse condemnation, just compensation is required for the period commencing on the date the regulation first affected the property and ending on the date the government entity chooses to rescind or otherwise amend the regulation. Invalidation of the offending regulation is not the appropriate remedy for two reasons. First, invalidation does not compensate the aggrieved party for injuries sustained as a result of the taking. Second, invalidation merely tells legislators to enact a new regulation without the fear of having to pay damages for taking the property by inverse condemnation. Thus, the imposition of temporary damages puts legislators on notice to be much more cautious when implementing land use regulations in order to prevent infringing the rights of the landowner.

2.41 Schad v. Borough of Mt. Ephraim,   452 U.S. 61, 101 S.Ct. 2176 (1981).

1. *Type of Regulation:*   Commercial use zoning.

2. *Land Use Issue:*   Whether a commercial zoning ordinance construed to prohibit all live entertainment, including nonobscene nude dancing, violated the rights of free expression guaranteed by the First and Fourteenth Amendments.

3. *Type of Legal Challenge:* As applied.

4. *Remedy Sought:* Reversal of criminal conviction resulting from conduct held violative of the Borough Ordinance.

5. *Constitutional Issues:*

  a. Right of free expression (First Amendment).

  b. Substantive due process (Fourteenth Amendment).

6. *Facts:* Appellants operated an adult bookstore in a commercial zone which sold adult books, magazines, and films. Subsequently, a permit was obtained permitting the installation of coin-operated adult film viewing booths. Thereafter, the store introduced a coin-operated device which enabled a customer to view a live, usually nude, dancer perform behind a glass panel. Appellant's conduct was found violative of a use ordinance which, while not explicitly prohibiting live nude dancing, excluded all uses not expressly permitted by the ordinance. Appellants claimed the ordinance, as applied, violated their rights of free expression guaranteed by the First and Fourteenth Amendments.

7. *Decision:* Ordinance held invalid under First and Fourteenth Amendments.

8. *Opinion of the Court:* The ordinance, as applied, effectively bans all live entertainment, thus prohibiting a wide range of expression long held within the protections of the First and Fourteenth Amendments. Where protected First Amendment interests are at stake, zoning regulations do not receive minimal scrutiny under the rational relationship test, but can be upheld only if shown to be narrowly drawn and in furtherance of a sufficiently substantial government interest. The town failed to satisfy these tests. The argument that the ordinance was reasonable because nude dancing was permitted in nearby communities is without validity because freedom of expression cannot be limited merely because it may be available in another nearby community. *Young* v. *American Mini-Theatres*, 427 U.S. 50 (1976) is not controlling as that case upheld an ordinance which merely dispersed communicative activity, whereas the Mount Ephraim ordinance has resulted in a total ban of all live entertainment.

2.42 Town of Hallie v. City of Eau Claire, 471 U.S. 34, 105 S.Ct. 1713 (1985).

  1. *Type of Regulation:* Not applicable.

  2. *Land Use Issue:* Whether it is a violation of the federal antitrust laws for a city to refuse to provide sewage treatment services to neighboring towns, while offering to supply sewage treatment services to property owners in those towns only if a majority of the individuals in the area to be serviced agree in a referendum to be annexed by the city.

3. *Type of Legal Challenge:* Not applicable.

4. *Remedy Sought:* Injunctive relief.

5. *Constitutional Issue:* Exemption from federal anti-trust laws.

6. *Facts:* The city of Eau Claire, Wisconsin, operates the only sewage treatment plant that is available to four neighboring unincorporated towns, but the city refused to supply sewage treatment services to the towns. It does supply these services to individual landowners in areas of the towns if a majority of the individuals in the area vote in a referendum to have their homes annexed by the city. The towns, alleging that they are potential competitors of the city in the collection and transport of sewage, sued the city in federal district court, contending that the city used its monopoly over sewage treatment to gain a monopoly over the provision of sewage collection and transport services in violation of the Sherman Antitrust Act. Both the district court and the court of appeals ruled for the city on the ground that the city's allegedly anticompetitive conduct fell within the state action exemption to the federal antitrust laws.

7. *Decision:* Affirmed lower federal courts' ruling that the city's anticompetitive activity fell within the state action exemption.

8. *Opinion of the Court:* The Court's prior decisions have established that to escape the reach of the antitrust laws, municipalities must demonstrate that their anticompetitive activities were authorized by the state "pursuant to state policy to displace competition with regulation or monopoly public service." However, the Court has never decided how clearly a state policy must be articulated to allow a municipality to claim the exemption, and the question whether a municipality, like a private party, must satisfy the requirement that there be "active state supervision" of the anticompetitive behavior.

To pass the *clear articulation test,* the state legislature does not have to state expressly that it intends for the municipal action to have anticompetitive conduct, it is enough that the legislation authorizes conduct from which anticompetitive effects would logically result. Further, the clear articulation test does not require that the legislature compel the anticompetitive action by the municipality. Finally, active state supervision of anticompetitive conduct is not a prerequisite where municipalities are concerned. This is required of private parties to ensure that the anticompetitive conduct is undertaken pursuant to state policy, but this danger is remote where a municipality is already acting pursuant to a clearly articulated state policy.

2.43 U.S. v. Causby,   328 U.S. 256, 66 S.Ct. 1062 (1946).

1. *Type of Regulation:*   Government regulations permitting overflight of airspace above private property.

2. *Land Use Issue:*   Whether frequent and low-level overflight of the airspace over private property constitutes a taking of that property interest.

3. *Type of Legal Challenge:*   As applied.

4. *Remedy Sought:*   Compensation for diminution in value of land and lost profits caused by low-level overflights.

5. *Constitutional Issue:*   Taking without just compensation under the Fifth Amendment.

6. *Facts:*   The Causbys lived and raised chickens on land adjacent to a municipal airport leased by the United States for military purposes. The glide path to the airport's runway passed directly over the Causby's land, at what the government asserted was a safe height and at a Civil Aeronautics Authority-approved angle. The military airplanes made considerable noise and, coupled with the glare from the planes' lights, disturbed the Causbys enjoyment of their property and caused about 150 chickens to kill themselves. The property's usefulness as a chicken farm was destroyed and the value of the land for residential purposes was diminished. The Causbys sued the United States government for their lost profits and to recover the reduction in value of their property.

7. *Decision:*   Flights over private land by U.S. aircraft that are so low and so frequent as to be a direct interference with the use and enjoyment of the land were tantamount to a taking, little different from a physical occupation of the land.

8. *Opinion of the Court:*   The government's actions have, in effect, taken an easement interest. The frequency and low-level character of flights in this case was clearly established at the trial level, as was the depreciation of the Causby's land and the loss of their chickens. The government was required to compensate them for the damage. Because the record is not clear as to whether the injury (or the easement interest acquired) and thus the measure of damages was more or less permanent or only temporary in nature, the case must be remanded to the Court of Claims to make the necessary findings regarding the amount of damages.

2.44 U.S. v. Locke, 471 U.S. 84, 105 S.Ct. 1785 (1985).

1. *Type of Regulation:* Federal Land Policy and Management Act (1976)(FLPMA) establishes annual filing requirements for mining claims.

2. *Land Use Issues:*

a. Whether declaring a mining claim to be abandoned and extinguished when a claimant is one day late filing his statutorily rquired papers to hold the claim is an unconstitutional taking.

b. Whether the automatic forfeiture provision of the statute is a reasonable restriction designed to further a legitimate legislative objective.

3. *Type of Legal Challenge:* As applied.

4. *Remedy Sought:* Declaratory and injunctive relief to prevent the forfeiture of plaintiff's mining claims.

5. *Constitutional Issues:*

a. Taking without just compensation (Fifth Amendment).

b. Procedural due process (Fifth Amendment).

6. *Facts:* Locke and four others purchased ten unpatented mining claims on public lands prior to the enactment of the FLPMA, which took effect on October 21, 1976. The two-part recording scheme imposed by the act applied to claims located before its enactment. Plaintiffs met the initial filing requirement by filing their claims with the Bureau of Land Management (BLM) within three years of FLPMA's enactment. Plaintiffs, however, failed to meet the second requirement, wherein all claimants must file prior to December 31 in the year of initial recording and all subsequent years a notice of intention to hold the claim, an affidavit of assessment of work performed on the claim, or a detailed reporting form. In 1980, plaintiffs did not file this information until December 31. BLM then informed the plaintiffs that their claims had been declared abandoned and void. Plaintiffs then filed an action, alleging that the agency's action constituted an unconstitutional taking without just compensation and denied them due process.

7. *Decision:* Application of forfeiture provision of act upheld under Fifth Amendment as not constituting a taking.

8. *Opinion of the Court:* The plain language of the act read in conjunction with the FLPMA regulations makes it clear that annual filing must be made on or before December 30. This deadline cannot be complied with substantially or otherwise by filing late. A specific intent to abandon is not required by the act. The automatic forfeiture provision of the act is not unconstitutional. Congress has the power to condition the continued retention of vested property rights on the performance of certain affirmative duties so long as the duty imposed is a reasonable restriction designed to further a legitimate objective. Ridding federal lands of state mining claims and the provision of up-to-date information on existing claims is a legitimate governmental objective. The act provides all the process constitutionally due. Adequate process merely requires the enactment of a statute, publishing it, and providing those within its reach a reasonable opportunity to familiarize themselves with the general requirements imposed and to comply with those requirements.

2.45 U.S. v. Cherokee Nation of Oklahoma, 480 U.S. 700, 107 S.Ct. 1487 (1987).

1. *Type of Regulation:* Not applicable.

2. *Land Use Issue:* Whether compensation was due the Cherokee Nation for damage to sand and gravel deposits in riverbed property interests caused by navigational improvements of the Arkansas River.

3. *Type of Legal Challenge:* As applied.

4. *Remedy Sought:* Compensation for taking of private property for public purpose.

5. *Constitutional Issues:*

    a. Taking without just compensation (Fifth Amendment).

    b. Commerce Clause, Article I. Sec. 8. (navigational rights).

6. *Facts:* The Cherokee Nation brought suit in federal court claiming that under the general intent of its treaties with the United States, its ownership of the riverbeds is unique in scope and extends beyond fee simple title. This argument was based on a prior decision of the Supreme Court in *Choctaw Nation v. Oklahoma* 397 U.S. 620, 90 S. Ct. 1328 (1970), which the Cherokees contended makes the rivers private streams, thus not subject to federal control under the commerce clause. The improvement of the Arkansas River for barge shipping involved dredging and constructing locks and dams on the Arkansas and the Verdigris Rivers to reach the new port of Catoosa. The riverbed lands that have not been sold are owned in fee simple by the Cherokees and include the mineral rights. The government claims that the commerce clause gives it a unique legal position with regard to navigable waters of the United States in the form of a dominant servitude, which is a superior right of a navigational easement over any private property rights.

7. *Decision:* Indian nation's fee simple title to riverbeds pursuant to treaties with federal government not exempt from government's

navigational servitude and the government's exercise of that servitude did not require compensation under the Fifth Amendment.

8. *Opinion of the Court:*   The proper exercise of the government's navigational easement authorized by the commerce clause is not a taking in violation of the Fifth Amendment; therefore, no compensation is due. Private property interests in the riverbed are subordinate to the right of the government to exercise its authority under the commerce clause. The court of appeals' balancing test, which considered the private property interests as adversely affected by the government's use of its navigational easement, and which would have awarded damages for diminution of value is not appropriate in this case.

2.46 U.S. v. Riverside Bayview Homes, Inc.,   474 U.S. 121, 106 S.Ct. 455 (1985).

1. *Type of Regulation:*   Dredge and fill regulations under the federal Clean Water Act.

2. *Land Use Issue:*   Whether the imposition of this permit requirement or the denial of a permit for the waters in question is *ultra vires* and constituted a taking without just compensation.

3. *Type of Legal Challenge:*   As applied.

4. *Remedy Sought:*   Injunction to bar defendant from filling his property without a permit.

5. *Constitutional Issue:*   Taking without just compensation (Fifth Amendment).

6. *Facts:*   In 1976, the defendant began to place fill materials on his property in preparation for the construction of new homes. This land consisted of low-lying, marshy land near the shores of Lake St. Clair. The corps of engineers classified this property as a freshwater wetland. The source of the saturated soil condition on the defendant's property was groundwater. According to regulations promulgated by the corps, those wetlands qualify as a "waters of the United States." The defendant did not obtain a dredge and fill permit, and the corps than filed suit against defendant to enjoin him from filling his property.

7. *Decision:*   Dredge and fill regulations of federal Clean Water Act under Fifth Amendment as applied to wetlands as not constituting a taking.

8. *Opinion of the Court:*   Neither the imposition of the permit requirement itself nor the denial of a permit necessarily constitutes a taking. The United States had a legitimate governmental interest in passing the Clean

Water Act. The corps' inclusion of wetlands adjacent to, but not regularly flooded by, open bodies of navigable water as "waters of the United States" is a reasonable construction of the act. Requiring a person to obtain a permit before engaging in a certain use of his property does not "take" the property, unless the effect of the denial is to prevent economically viable use of the land. Equitable relief is not generally available to enjoin an alleged taking of private property for public use, duly authorized by law, when a suit for compensation can be brought subsequent to the taking. The Tucker Act is available to provide compensation that may result from the corps' exercise of jurisdiction over wetlands.

2.47 Village of Arlington Heights v. Metropolitan Housing Development Corporation, 429 U.S. 252, 97 S.Ct. 555 (1977).

1. *Type of Regulation:* Denial of rezoning.

2. *Land Use Issue:* Whether proof of a racially discriminatory intent or purpose is required to show a violation of the equal protection clause of the Fourteenth Amendment.

3. *Type of Legal Challenge:* As applied.

4. *Remedy Sought:* Injunctive and declaratory relief.

5. *Constitutional Issue:* Equal protection (Fourteenth Amendment).

6. *Facts:* Metropolitan Housing Development Corporation (MHDC) applied to the village for a rezoning of a 15-acre parcel from single-family to multifamily residential, to permit construction of 190 federally subsidized housing units for low- and moderate-income tenants. After the village denied the rezoning request, MHDC and other plaintiffs brought suit in federal district court, alleging that the denial was racially discriminatory and violated both the Fourteenth Amendment and the federal Fair Housing Act. The district court ruled for the village, but the court of appeals reversed, finding that the ultimate effect of the denial was racially discriminatory and thus in violation of the Fourteenth Amendment's equal protection clause.

7. *Decision:* Petitioners failed to prove racially discriminatory intent or purpose as required in challenging denial of rezoning as racially discriminatory under equal protection clause of the Fourteenth Amendment.

8. *Opinion of the Court:* Official action is not unconstitutional solely because it results in a racially disproportionate impact. To show a violation of the equal protection clause of the Fourteenth Amendment, it is necessary to prove that racially discriminatory intent or purpose was a motivating factor in the village's rezoning decision. Such a racially discriminatory

intent could be shown by evidence of a number of factors. Disproportionate impact, while not conclusive on its own, may be one of the factors; others include: the historical background of the challenged decision, particularly if it reveals "a series of official actions taken for invidious purposes;" departures from the normal procedural sequence or from substantive considerations normally considered important; and the legislative or administrative history, "especially where there are contemporary statements by members of the decisionmaking body." In this case, an examination of these factors fails to show that racial discrimination was a motivating factor in the denial of the rezoning. The case is remanded to the federal district court for a ruling on the Fair Housing Act claim.

2.48 Village of Belle Terre v. Boraas,   416 U.S. 1, 94 S.Ct. 1536 (1974).

1. *Type of Regulation:*   Zoning ordinance.
2. *Land Use Issue:*   Whether an ordinance restricting land use to single-family dwellings and defining *family* as any number of related people or not more than two unrelated people living together rationally promoted any legitimate government purpose.
3. *Type of Legal Challenge:*   Facial.
4. *Remedy Sought:*   Declaration that the ordinance was unconstitutional and an injunction against its enforcement.
5. *Constitutional Issues:*
   a. Equal protection (Fourteenth Amendment).
   b. Freedom of association (First Amendment).
   c. Privacy (the penumbras and emanations of the First, Third, Fourth, Fifth, and Ninth Amendments).
6. *Facts:*   Belle Terre restricted land use within the village to single-family dwellings. The ordinance defined *family* as any number of related individuals or not more than two unrelated individuals living together. The Dickmans owned a house in the village and leased it to six unrelated students at a local university. When the village ordered the Dickmans to remedy the violation, the Dickmans brought suit to have the ordinance declared unconstitutional.
7. *Decision:*   Ordinance upheld under Fourteenth Amendment as rationally furthering a legitimate governmental purpose.
8. *Opinion of the Court:*   Protecting a neighborhood's peace and quiet to help promote family values is a legitimate purpose in zoning. "A quiet place where yards are wide, people few, and motor vehicles restricted are legitimate guidelines in a land use project addressed to family needs." This

legitimate purpose is rationally served by prohibiting more than two unrelated persons from living together, since boarding houses, fraternity houses, and the like tend to increase urban problems such as proliferation of crowds and noise. Freedom to associate with people as one pleases and the right to privacy are not violated, since unmarried couples are not prohibited from living together and a family can still entertain guests. Since the ordinance rationally furthers a legitimate government purpose, it is held valid.

2.49 Village of Euclid, Ohio v. Ambler Realty Company, 274 U.S. 365, 47 S.Ct. 114 (1926).

1. *Type of Regulation:* Zoning ordinance.
2. *Land Use Issue:* Constitutional validity of zoning ordinances dividing a village into residential, commercial, and industrial areas.
3. *Type of Legal Challenge:* Facial.
4. *Remedy Sought:* Injunction to prevent enforcement of the ordinance.
5. *Constitutional Issues:*
   a. Substantive due process (taking without just compensation under the Fourteenth Amendment).
   b. Equal protection (Fourteenth Amendment).
6. *Facts:* Ambler Realty owned 68 acres of land in the village of Euclid. Euclid instituted zoning ordinances including restrictions on use, height, and area, which affected Ambler Realty's property. As a result of this zoning, the value of Ambler Realty's property declined from $10,000 per acre if used for industrial purposes to $2,500 per acre if restricted (as per the ordinance) to residential use. Ambler Realty then brought suit, seeking an injunction to prevent the village of Euclid from enforcing the ordinance. Ambler argued that the zoning regulations diminished the value of their property, which in their view constituted a taking of property without compensation or due process of law. After the lower court ruled in favor of Ambler Realty, the village appealed, contending that zoning was a valid means of promoting public health, safety, welfare, and morals.
7. *Decision:* Ordinance upheld under Fourteenth Amendment as having a rational relation to the public health, safety, morals, and general welfare.
8. *Opinion of the Court:* An ordinance is only unconstitutional when it is clearly arbitrary, where its provisions bear no rational relation to the public health, safety, morals, or general welfare. Property rights are not

absolute. Modern urban life necessitates the placing of new and increased restrictions on development to ensure the comfort and safety of urban dwellers. The desired end of public welfare and safety is sufficient to justify the ordinance as a valid exercise of police power. Therefore, Ambler Realty's request for an injunction is denied. [*Editor's note:* The Court also noted with approval the increased national use of zoning as a tool for dealing with a range of urban safety and quality of life problems.]

2.50 Webb's Fabulous Pharmacies v. Beckwith,   449 U.S. 155, 101 S.Ct. 446 (1980).

1. *Type of Regulation:*   Circuit court clerk's entitlement to interest accrued on interpleader accounts held by the court.

2. *Land Use Issue:*   Not applicable.

3. *Type of Legal Challenge:*   As applied.

4. *Remedy Sought:*   An injunction mandating the return of all interest accrued on the interpleader account or alternatively, just compensation.

5. *Constitutional Issues:*

a. Taking without just compensation (Fifth Amendment as applied to the states through the Fourteenth Amendment).

b. Substantive due process (Fourteenth Amendment).

6. *Facts:*   Eckard's of College Park, Inc. purchased substantially all of the assets of the financially troubled Webb's Fabulous Pharmacies, Inc. In order to protect its investment and assure fair distribution to all of Webb's creditors, Eckard's filed an interpleader complaint against Webb's and its creditors and tendered the purchase price to the clerk of the circuit court pursuant to Florida's Bulk Transfers Act. The clerk then deposited the sum into an interest-bearing account pursuant to the act.

During litigation, a receiver for this fund was appointed, and the court turned over the monies in the fund, minus the authorized statutory service charges and the accrued interest. The receiver then moved to compel the clerk to pay the accrued interest, charging that a refusal to do so was a taking of private property without just compensation under the takings clause of the Fifth Amendment as applied to the states through the Fourteenth Amendment.

The circuit court directed the clerk to pay the interest to the receiver, holding that the clerk was not entitled to the interest earned on the account established solely for the benefit of the creditors. The Florida Supreme Court reversed, holding that during the time the clerk administers the fund, it is considered public (not private) money. Appellants sought review to the Supreme Court.

7. *Decision:* County's taking of accrued interest on private funds under authority of statute was unconstitutional under Fifth and Fourteenth Amendments.

8. *Opinion of the Court:* The act is constitutional when applied to interest on funds clearly owned by the county but, when applied to accrued interest withheld on private funds, the act violates the takings clause. The fund, including the incidental earning of interest must be deemed private because it was established solely for the benefit of the claimants, Webb's creditors. The mere labeling of the principal as public money, while temporarily being held by the court, does not render the account public.

2.51 Welch v. Swasey, 214 U.S. 91, 29 S.Ct. 567 (1909).

1. *Type of Regulation:* Building regulation.

2. *Land Use Issue:* Reasonableness of building height regulations as applied in residential and commercial districts of Boston.

3. *Type of Legal Challenge:* As applied.

4. *Remedy Sought:* Order to compel the building commissioner to issue a building permit to the plaintiff to enable him to build above the height limit imposed on buildings in that district.

5. *Constitutional Issues:*

    a. Substantive due process (taking without just compensation under the Fourteenth Amendment).

    b. Equal protection (Fourteenth Amendment).

6. *Facts:* The Massachusetts legislature enacted a statute in 1904 which separated the city of Boston into "A" (business) districts and "B" (residential) districts, imposing 125-foot height restrictions on buildings in "A" districts and 80 to 100-foot restrictions on those in "B" districts. Francis Welch applied for, and was denied, a permit to erect a 124.5-foot building in a "B" district. He then sued the building commissioner, alleging that the regulations were only imposed for aesthetic reasons and that he was denied equal protection of the laws by the state's discrimination between "A" and "B" zones.

7. *Decision:* Regulations upheld under the Fourteenth Amendment as reasonable.

8. *Opinion of the Court:* The statutes passed by the Massachusetts legislature under an exercise of the state's police power have a real, substantial relation to the objectives of fire safety, comfort, and the convenience of the people of Boston. Although considerations of an aesthetic nature also entered into the legislative decisionmaking, they were not a primary motive and do not render the statutes invalid. The building limitations, while discriminatory, are not so unreasonable as to deprive Mr. Welch of the profitable use of his land without justification, and, therefore, do not deprive him of either due process (no taking) or the equal protection of the laws.

2.52 Williamson County Regional Planning Commission v. Hamilton Bank, 473 U.S. 172, 105 S.Ct. 3108 (1985).

1. *Type of Regulation:*   Subdivision regulation.
2. *Land Use Issues:*
   a. Whether damages are available for an alleged temporary taking of a landowner's property due to denial of subdivision approval;
   b. What constitutes a final administrative decision necessary to satisfy ripeness requirements for judicial review; and
   c. Whether a claimant may seek just compensation for an alleged taking in federal court without first utilizing the procedures available under state law to obtain such compensation.
3. *Type of Legal Challenge:*   As applied.
4. *Remedy Sought:*   Damages for a temporary taking and injunctive relief requiring approval of the subdivision.
5. *Constitutional Issues:*
   a. Taking of property without just compensation (Fifth Amendment as applied to the states through the Fourteenth Amendment).
   b. Ripeness.
6. *Facts:*   A developer received approval of a preliminary subdivision plat for a large clustered development in 1973, with the provision that it would seek reapproval as it phased in additional portions of the development. Although the zoning regulations required that land located on steep slopes not be included in calculating permissible density for the development, no such deduction was made.

Development continued for a number of years, during which the zoning ordinance was amended to reduce allowable densities; however, the commission continued to apply the 1973 ordinance to this development and regularly renewed its approval of the preliminary plat. In 1979, the commission reversed its position and began to evaluate the plans submitted for approval under the amended zoning ordinance, although still granting renewed approvals.

In 1980, the commission asked the developer to submit a revised preliminary plat before it sought final approval for the remaining sections of the subdivision. The commission found this request necessary in light of a number of changes that had occurred since the project was first approved and because of errors and omissions in the originally approved plat. The commission found several problems with the revised plat and declined to approve further development. The developer appealed the commission's decision to the county board of zoning appeals, which determined that the commission should apply the 1973 zoning ordinance and subdivision regulations in evaluating the plat.

The commission declined to follow the board's decision, stating that the board lacked jurisdiction to hear appeals from the commission. The commission disapproved a new plat submitted by Hamilton Bank, which had acquired the original developer's remaining interest in the property in a foreclosure proceeding. The bank then filed suit in federal district court, claiming that the commission had taken its property without just compensation. The jury awarded the bank $350,000 in damages for a temporary taking of its property, but this verdict was set aside by the judge on the ground that a temporary deprivation of a property right could not, as a matter of law, constitute a taking. The court also required the commission to evaluate the subdivision plat using the 1973 zoning ordinance and subdivision regulations. A federal court of appeals reinstated the jury's verdict, finding that there had been a temporary taking of the bank's property and that this required compensation.

7. *Decision:*   Case dismissed for lack of ripeness.

8. *Opinion of the Court:*   The basic question presented in this case is whether government must pay money damages to a landowner whose property allegedly has been taken by the application of government regulations. However, this question cannot be answered because the bank's claim is premature, that is, not ripe for judicial review.

A taking claim is not ripe until a government entity has reached a final decision regarding the application of its regulations to the property claimed to have been taken. In this case, the bank failed to seek variances that would have allowed it to meet several of the regulatory requirements imposed by the commission. The commission's decision cannot be considered final while the bank still had the right to request variances; without a final determination regarding the effect of the regulations on the bank's property, it would be impossible to determine whether a taking had occurred.

The fact that this claim was brought under 42 U.S.C. §1983 does not alter the requirement that the bank seek variances from the commission. While it is true that a plaintiff does not have to exhaust administrative remedies before bringing a Section 1983 action, exhaustion of administrative remedies is distinct from the requirement that an administrative action must be final before it is judicially reviewable. The exhaustion requirement refers to administrative and judicial procedures by which an injured party may seek review of an adverse decision and obtain a remedy for unlawful or otherwise improper decisions; finality requires that the administrative agency has arrived at a definite position on the property in question, and that the decision causes actual injury to the property owner.

The bank's failure to seek compensation through the inverse condemnation procedures provided by state law is a second reason why the claim was not ripe. A plaintiff cannot seek just compensation for an alleged taking under federal law unless it can show that it has sought and not obtained just compensation under the state's inverse condemnation procedure, or that the procedure is either unavailable or inadequate.

2.53 Young v. American Mini Theatres, Inc.,   427 U.S. 50, 96 S.Ct. 2440, (1976).

1. *Type of Regulation:*   Zoning ordinance.
2. *Land Use Issue:*   Whether zoning ordinance requiring adult theaters to be geographically dispersed is invalid for classifying on the basis of the content of communication protected as free speech.
3. *Type of Legal Challenge:*   As applied.
4. *Remedy Sought:*   Declaration that the ordinance was unconstitutional and an injunction against its enforcement.
5. *Constitutional Issues:*
    a. Due process (Fourteenth Amendment).
    b. Prior restraint on speech (First Amendment).
    c. Equal protection (Fourteenth Amendment).
6. *Facts:*   The Detroit Common Council determined that a concentration of adult theaters and adult bookstores in an area was injurious to the neighborhood and therefore adopted an ordinance prohibiting concentration of such establishments. Two operators of adult theaters were denied certificates of occupancy because they had located their theaters in violation of the zoning ordinance.

7. *Decision:*   Ordinance upheld under First Amendment as not regulating content or constituting prior restraint.

8. *Opinion of the Court:*   The ordinance neither places a total ban on adult theaters nor so limits the number of adult theaters as to deny the public access to adult films. The ordinance does not regulate the content of the films that can be shown but merely the location of adult theaters. Thus, the ordinance is not an impermissible prior restraint, under the First Amendment. The city has an important interest in protecting the character of its neighborhoods, and this interest is rationally furthered by requiring the dispersal of adult theaters.

Index